GASCONY, ENGLAND'S FIRST COLONY

Gascony, England's First Colony

1204–1453

Margaret Wade Labarge

HAMISH HAMILTON

First published in Great Britain 1980
by Hamish Hamilton Limited
Garden House, 57–59 Long Acre, London WC2E 9JZ
Copyright © 1980 by Margaret Wade Labarge

British Library Cataloguing in Publication Data

Labarge, Margaret Wade
 Gascony.
 1. Gascony – Politics and government
 I Title
 944'.77'02   DC611.G25

 ISBN 0-241-10309-6

Printed in Great Britain by
Ebenezer Baylis and Son Ltd., The Trinity Press, Worcester, and London

Contents

Contents

Acknowledgments

This effort to sketch summarily the complex history of English Gascony leans heavily on the work of many scholars to whom my debts, as acknowledged in the notes, are obvious. However, I am particularly grateful to those who generously helped me along the trail, pointed out relevant material and patiently answered questions: Dr. Pierre Chaplais, Prof. B. Guillemain, Dr. John Parsons, Dr. T. Runyan and Dr. M. G. A. Vale. M. Pierre Capra of the Université de Bordeaux not only gave me use of his *thèse doctorale* on the Gascon administration of the Black Prince, but also shared his infectious enthusiasm and extensive knowledge of medieval Gascony. For the errors that remain despite such help I am, of course, totally responsible.

I have received hospitality from many libraries: in England, the British Library and the Institute of Historical Research; in France, the Bibliothèque Municipale de Bordeaux and the history library of the Université de Bordeaux; in Canada, the National Library and those of the Pontifical Institute of Medieval Studies and of the Universities of Toronto, Queens, Ottawa and Carleton (where Frances Montgomery was unfailingly helpful). The text was read, in part or in whole, by Prof. N. E. S. Griffiths, Dr. J. Greatrex and Miss P. Blackstock, profiting greatly from their helpful criticisms. My conclusions on thirteenth-century Gascony and the work of Edward I were debated, most helpfully, by Prof. C. M. D. Crowder and his Queens seminar. The exploration of the geography of Gascony was aided and enhanced by Prof. Griffiths and Miss B. E. Nash. Mr. Henry Lawless, Canadian Consul General in Bordeaux, greatly facilitated my research there. I am grateful to A. D. Peters and Harvill Press Ltd. for permission to quote from Froissart's *Chronicles*, edited and translated by John Jolliffe. Finally, I owe a debt of affection and gratitude to my children and the devoted friends who have for several years listened patiently and intelligently to my harangues on medieval Gascony and have provided needed stimulus and support.

M. W. Labarge

Illustrations

5.a.) Richard II gives the duchy of Aquitaine to John
of Gaunt, from Froissart.
BL Harley 4380, f 21 © British Library

b.) Henry VI appoints John Talbot, earl of Shrewsbury, constable of France.
BL Royal 15 vi, 405 © British Library

6.a.) A nineteenth-century view of the castle of
Bénauges, fortress of the Graillys.
L. Drouyn, *La Guienne Militaire* (Bordeaux, 1865),
II, p. 114 © British Library

b.) A nineteenth-century view of the city-gate of
Bazas.
Drouyn, II, p. 107 © British Library

7.a.) View of the central square and *cornières* of the
bastide of Montpazier.
French Tourist Office

b.) Bordeaux: Pey Berland's Tower.
French Tourist Office

8.a.) Seal of John Streatley, constable of Bordeaux.
PRO E404/500/14

b.) A Gascon vineyard worker of the fourteenth
century.
PRO E36/275/f192

c.) Ceremony of surrendering a town, late fourteenth
century.
BL Royal ms 20. cvii, f 190 © British Library

Maps

A*

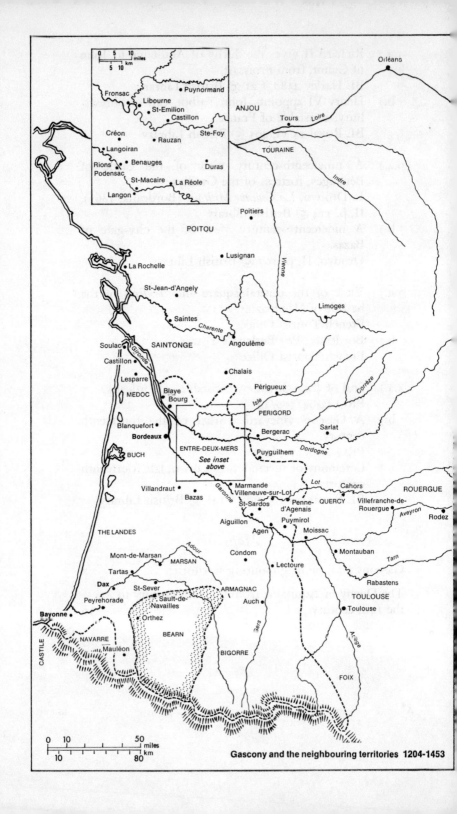

Gascony and the neighbouring territories 1204–1453

Prologue

In May and June of 1252 the peaceful refectory of Westminster Abbey rocked to the violent accusations of a delegation of Gascon nobles led by the fiery archbishop of Bordeaux. Simon de Montfort, earl of Leicester and brother-in-law of the king, responded with equal vigour to the complaints against his rule as the king's lieutenant in Gascony for the last three and a half years. King Henry III had been bombarded with Gascon protests about the vehemence and ferocity of Simon's government. After sending a commission of inquiry to the duchy the king agreed to provide safe-conducts to the Gascons so they could bring their cases before him. The earl was ordered back to England to meet their charges in a hearing before king and council which has been likened to the trial of Warren Hastings.[1] The dramatic insults, the specious pleadings, the behind-the-scenes manoeuvrings—all vividly reported by Matthew Paris and more soberly described by Simon's Franciscan friend Adam Marsh—have served to mask the underlying significance of the encounter. At issue was the very nature of the relationship of Gascony and the Gascons to the English king as duke of Aquitaine as well as the authority of his officials there.

The history of English rule in Gascony is frequently brushed aside as irrelevant to the mainstream of either English or French history. The relationship between the kingdom and its overseas duchy was bedevilled from the beginning by problems of distance, feudal definition and mutual incomprehension. It suffered from the inherent ambivalence of the Gascons themselves and the constantly fluctuating balance of power in the duchy caused by French aggression. Inevitably affairs in Gascony often exercised a major influence on the direction of English policy and the development of its diplomacy, while it absorbed a disproportionate amount of English time, energy and resources. Although it is no longer historically fashionable to make comparisons across the centuries Montagu Burrows, the Chichele professor of history at Oxford in the more self-confident 1880s, who was one of the first English scholars to become interested in Gascon history, was fascinated by the likenesses between English administration in medieval Aquitaine and nineteenth-century India. He drew attention to some of the comparable factors: 'the multifarious nature of the administration, the multitude of English families engaged in the process, the interchange of products, the action and reaction of the two countries upon one another in peace and war, and the extremely delicate nature of their mutual relations'. He saw a likeness between the work of Edward I in Aquitaine and that of the duke of Wellington in India, and emphasized a point worth remembering—that the Englishman was, and almost always remained, a foreigner in Aquitaine.[2] He might spend many years there in the service of the king-duke and use the local opportunities to lay a foundation for personal advancement and financial gain but, except in a small minority of cases, his home was elsewhere and he left Gascony when his duties were finished.

Thus, the history of the 250 years of direct rule by the English king of Gascony cannot be summed up merely in the long-drawn-out confrontation of French and English which ended in the Hundred Years War, final English defeat and French absorption of the duchy. It is both more subtle and more interesting than that. England experimented for the first time with the government of an overseas possession where it was essential to keep the loyalty and support of its inhabitants. Despite the inherent difficulties of the task it succeeded remarkably well until the last fifty years. The report of Simon de Montfort's trial personifies the importance the English kings placed on this overseas territory, the calibre of the magnates who wrestled with its problems, and the never-ending struggle to reconcile Gascon demands and English needs. Although these many factors help to make the history of English rule in Gascony interesting in itself, it is also enlivened by the careers of a number of colourful individuals. In addition, the very fact of the dual rule of the monarch as king of England and duke of Aquitaine, with its built-in stresses and contradictions, helps to explain medieval England's involvement in a wide range of continental interests. It also suggests the gains and losses in which the rule of Gascony involved England from the thirteenth to the fifteenth centuries.

CHAPTER I

The Duchy of Aquitaine: the Inheritance

The complexities of Gascon history start with the simple matter of terminology. Why is the English king referred to as the duke of Aquitaine while the usual description of the territory itself is Gascony? For those unfamiliar with the south-west of France the distinction is both confusing and inexplicable, but it has legitimate historical roots. From the earliest days the term Aquitaine has been used primarily to designate a territory which was an administrative unit, while Gascony was basically a land bound by a common language.

Aquitaine's history is the longer one. For Julius Caesar it described a conquered province in Gaul, bounded by the Atlantic Ocean, the Garonne River and the Pyrenees. Augustus extended his administration of the south-west north to the Loire River and east to the Massif Central. By the end of the fourth century this enormous expanse had been divided into three provinces: Aquitania Prima, with its capital at Bourges, covering the territory east of Limoges and Cahors; Aquitania Secunda, of which Bordeaux was the capital, and which ran from Poitiers in the north to Agen in the south; and Novempopulana, stretching from Bazas in the north to the Pyrenees as far east as St-Lizier. All of this district was profoundly influenced by Roman culture and civilization for over four centuries, and enjoyed a deceptive peace during the declining years of the Roman Empire. Bordeaux, favoured by its protected port on the Garonne and its strategic location at the axis of the known commercial routes, was further enhanced by its administrative importance and distinguished schools. Its prosperous, cultured life was embodied in two remarkable men of the fourth century, symbols of the old and the new. The charming versifier, Ausonius, was a native of Bordeaux, a teacher of rhetoric, a civil servant, and tutor to Gratian, the emperor's son, who rewarded him with the title of consul. A nominal Christian, his real concern was for his lands and vineyards in the area,* and for his wife and friends. From the evidence of his poetry, his deepest emotion was reserved for his young and brilliant pupil, Paulinus, who came from the same well-to-do level of society as his master. Paulinus had a brilliant career in the Roman administration which he abandoned for an active Christian life and a monastic career at Nola, where he corresponded with the great Christian lights of his time—St. Martin of Tours, St. Jerome, and St. Augustine—and wrote the pleasant poetry which is among the earliest Christian verse. Indeed, at that time the culture and learning of Aquitaine were considered so superior to that of the north that Gallus of Tours, a friend and disciple of St. Martin, could write humbly to a priest of Aquitaine:

> I tremble when I reflect that I, a poor Gaul, will be required to converse at length with two gentlemen of Aquitaine, for my rustic mode of speech will surely grate unpleasantly on your refined ears.[1]

Unfortunately the culture of these men was the final fruit of an era.

With the fifth century the comfortable life of this highly civilized outpost of the empire disappeared in the general break-down brought on by the invasion of the Visigoths from Spain. They swept through the passes of the Pyrenees up to the Loire, and made Aquitaine part of their kingdom. Their efforts to expand to the north were met by the counter-attacks of the Franks, who made sporadic attempts to control the distant lands of the south-west. In turn, the remote and ineffectual rule of the Franks was contested towards the end of the sixth century by the Vascones, a tribe of non-Latinized Iberians. They first established themselves in the valleys of the Pyrenees down to the River Adour, vigorously imposing their own language, Basque. Over the years they finally conquered the flat lands between the Adour and the Garonne, and in a mingling process with a larger population developed a new dialect, Gascon, close to that of Languedoc.

When Charlemagne became Holy Roman Emperor in the year 800 the idea of Gascony as a linguistic entity and of Aquitaine (or Guyenne, the French form) as an administrative division, both

---

* Château-Ausone is still a highly respected name among the vineyards of St-Emilion.

civil and religious, had already existed for some time. Aquitania Secunda and Novempopulana would form the more usual portions of the medieval duchy of Aquitaine, but on occasion most of Aquitania Prima would also be included, and the name Aquitaine stretched comfortably enough to cover the whole complex. Over the following three centuries there were sporadic efforts among Charlemagne's descendants to create a kingdom of Aquitaine, but their failure was accompanied by a long process of development of warring feudal lordships within this large territory. Gradually the talented family which held the dukedom of Aquitaine also acquired possession of the duchy of Gascony and the county of Poitou and enforced its lordship over a host of the quarrelsome barons of the south-west. By the beginning of the twelfth century the court of the duke of Aquitaine at Poitiers was rich and powerful, as well as renowned as the centre of the new culture of courtly love, of romance and poetry. Its lustre and resources far outshone both the court of the struggling French king at Paris, whose impressive title masked his scant actual power, and the remote court of Henry I, duke of Normandy and king of England by the conquest of his father William.

Duke William X of Aquitaine died on a pilgrimage to Compostella in April of 1137 and left as his heiress a daughter Eleanor, a girl of around sixteen.[2] She was a prize to be coveted by any prince in Christendom for the richness of her dowry and the extraordinary strength her widespread lands would add to any holding. Her personal qualities would leave their mark on the history of her century and would be amply demonstrated over the urse of a long life, for she remained indefatigable into her eighties in pursuing the best interests of her beloved Aquitaine. The French king, as feudal overlord of the duke of Aquitaine, had the valuable right of controlling her marriage, and acted quickly to make sure that the great prize did not escape. In the summer of 1137 Eleanor was married to Louis of France a few weeks before his father's death. The gains this marriage brought to the kingdom of France when he ascended the throne as Louis VII were enormous. They meant the administration of wide new lands as well as added riches and prestige. The marriage was not a successful one: Louis was pious, honest, and probably rather dull; Eleanor was headstrong and capricious, and produced only daughters. In one of the most momentous divorces of history, her marriage was dissolved after fifteen years by the

3

archbishop of Sens. Eleanor resumed her personal control of the lands of her duchy, but she was already planning her next marriage. Within two months, and quite unknown to Louis, who retained the right to approve his vassals' marriages, Eleanor married Henry Plantagenet. From the French king's point of view there could not have been a more unfortunate match. Henry had recently inherited his father's lands of Maine, Anjou and Touraine, added to the duchy of Normandy and the suzerainty of Brittany which he had received three years before. It was hard enough for the French king to lose direct rule over the great extent of Aquitaine; to find those rich lands in the hands of a vassal who thus controlled more of the kingdom of France than the king himself was a disaster. The dangers were further accentuated when, in 1154, Henry was recognized as Stephen's rightful heir and crowned Henry II of England. The marriage of Henry Plantagenet and Eleanor of Aquitaine and the joining of their extensive territories provoked three centuries of almost continuous struggle between England and France.

The Angevin empire, as it is frequently called, was an artificial creation, only possible because of the extraordinary energy and political skill of Henry II. For a brief time it united by the bond of personal fealty to a common overlord widely assorted territories with very different traditions. This bond was enforced by military means and by an administrative structure which attempted to provide a common framework of institutions. The newly acquired southern lands were very different from the northern ones. They were marked by a strong Roman influence on their law and on their customs, to which they clung tenaciously. The rural economy was less rich because of the nature of the land, the influence of the mountains and the enormous extent of the forests, while the cities and towns claimed, and exercised, a position of superiority enshrined in the Roman urban tradition. The feudal structure was fragile and the local lords warlike and quarrelsome. Their struggles were exacerbated by a tradition of equally divided inheritances while, lower in the social scale, the frequency of allods (i.e., lands held in absolute ownership as opposed to fiefs) meant a more individualistic, less cohesive approach to the problems of government. Perhaps the greatest gift of Henry II and Richard to the southern lands of Aquitaine was the beginnings of a better system of organization, copied from the more structured lands to the north, as well as the continuous

4

exchange of personnel and policies throughout their wide lands. It was a brief and strenuous period of glory but it was to break apart within fifty years.

Henry II's government and ambitions were made easier for much of his reign by the inability of Louis VII to exploit to his greatest advantage the turbulence and rebellions of Henry's four sons. When Philip Augustus came to the French throne in 1180—to rule for forty-three years—the balance shifted. Philip, with political cunning and determination, never lost sight of his main objective—to destroy the power of his over-mighty vassal in France, who was also king of England. He was successful in encouraging rebellion among Henry's sons who as they grew older resented their father's firm hold on the power and the profits, while their own titles were empty honours. He encouraged Queen Eleanor's struggles against her husband and in favour of her sons, especially her favourite Richard. Richard during his ten-year reign managed to retain his far-flung lands, despite his absence on crusade and his captivity in Germany. The intrigues of John were not able to withstand the whirlwind activity of his elder brother on his return, but the inherent weaknesses of this wide patchwork of territories were only too apparent. It required only the accession of the less competent John in 1199 to begin in earnest the rapid disintegration of the Angevin empire. Within twenty-five years all the English territories on the continent had been effectively lost except for a much truncated duchy of Aquitaine, reduced to even less than the Aquitania Secunda and Novempopulana of the Romans.

The history of Aquitaine or Gascony (and the chroniclers and many of the documents use the names interchangeably) as an overseas territory ruled directly by the English king as duke begins in John's reign. Eleanor of Aquitaine, despite her husband's title and Richard's installation as duke in a solemn ceremony at Poitiers in 1172, never really gave up her control over the duchy. Sometimes in opposition to her husband, sometimes in ardent support of her son, she continued to maintain both her personal position as duchess of Aquitaine in her own right and her close links with the turbulent southern barons. When John became king of England in 1199 Eleanor remained in charge of the duchy although she recognized John as her heir. The indomitable queen died at the abbey of Fontevrault in 1204. Although formally in retirement, she had emerged only two years before to help rescue her beloved county of Poitou from the attack of Arthur of Brittany. She had particularly resented this treachery since Arthur was her grandson as well as the pawn of Philip Augustus in his efforts to dismember the Plantagenet inheritance.

However, even before her death, the treaty of Le Goulet of May 1200[3] between John and Philip cast warning shadows on the future. Some of its terms were to have a continuing influence on the nature of the English lands in France and the relationship between the kings of England and France. The treaty was primarily designed to bring peace to Normandy, which Philip had been busily attacking, and to set a new frontier there. The arrangement was to be sealed by a marriage between the two houses: Blanche of Castile, Eleanor's granddaughter and John's niece, was to marry Philip's son. In this, as in other matters, the treaty anticipated the future. For the next two and a half centuries whenever optimistic negotiators tried to arrive at some settlement of the continual quarrels between the French and English kings they almost always included in the final settlement a marriage, or even two, between the royal families. It was piously felt this would insure a firm peace. It never did, for each sovereign continued to act with the interests of his own realm as his primary consideration, while the closeness of the relationship brought unexpected claims.

Other provisions of the treaty of Le Goulet also carried the seeds of further disputes. Philip recognized John as Richard's lawful heir, despite the claims of Arthur of Brittany, the son of John's older brother Geoffrey. John, in his turn, recognized Philip as his overlord for his continental fiefs and agreed that the counts of Boulogne and Flanders, who had been John's allies against Philip, were vassals of France, not England. Moreover the English king would not countenance any attack by them on their rightful lord. It was an unequal exchange, as Philip's court had already adjudged Anjou and Brittany to John and ordered that Arthur was only to hold Brittany as John's vassal, so Philip was bound to recognize John. Finally, John paid Philip 20,000 marks sterling as a relief for his lands and the recognition of his overlordship of Brittany. By these three clauses John accepted a far stricter interpretation of his feudal position as the French king's vassal; submission to the judgment of his lord's court, recognition of the duty of a vassal to support his suzerain, and the payment of specifically feudal dues which had never before been exacted or offered from those lands. The agreement immeasurably strengthened Philip's legal position among his contemporaries, and enabled the wily French king in 1202 to order the confiscation of John's French fiefs with the general consent of his barons. After all, John had refused to answer a summons to the king's court, and was thus a rebellious vassal against whom his overlord was privileged to act. The duchy of Aquitaine had not been specifically included in the treaty of Le Goulet, as Queen Eleanor was still alive, and the feudal provisions of the treaty became a dead letter when open war between Philip and John broke the feudal bond. However, these conditions remained an ideal and a goal for French kings and French diplomacy, to be resurrected when the next peace treaty was drawn up some fifty years later.

The stages of John's rapid loss of his northern French fiefs are not of particular concern here. The southern half of the duchy of Aquitaine was relatively sheltered from the power of Philip Augustus by its distance from Paris and by Philip's insistence on first making sure of Normandy, the keystone for the security of his kingdom. Although Poitou, northern Saintonge and the port of La Rochelle were finally captured by Louis VIII's expedition in 1224, the sentence of confiscation was unenforceable in the more southern lands. A shrunken duchy of Aquitaine, protected by the difficulty of access and its formidable river system, had time to strengthen its defences and consolidate its resources.

The truncated duchy soon became the essential, if fragmentary, remnant of King John's extensive continental inheritance. The lands of Poitou and the changeable lords of the Limousin and Périgord would occasionally for brief periods revert to their original allegiance, but they were slowly and inexorably being assimilated by French power and won to French interests. Poitevin lords became more ready to accept and even serve the French king. Occasional rebellions might bring them momentarily to the English side, but the balance had permanently shifted—England now had to attack Poitou, not defend it. As a counterweight to the loss of Poitou and its great port La Rochelle, Bordeaux rose to an importance and supremacy it had not enjoyed since Roman rule. It played a pre-eminent role in the life and loyalty of the duchy.

To understand the Gascon adhesion to the English connection

for the next two and a half centuries it is essential to appreciate the varied nature of its make up and the factors which helped to encourage its loyalty to its distant duke. English Gascony was profoundly influenced by its geography. A bird's eye view of the duchy would reveal an expanse of territory running from the river Charente to the Pyrenees, and from the Atlantic Ocean to a rough eastern boundary running up through Agen on the Garonne and along the frontier of Perigord. A closer look reveals how much the various sections, some of them relatively small, differed from each other. The pungent comments of Aymery Picaud, a twelfth-century Poitevin priest who wrote a practical guide for pilgrims detailing the various stages along the route to Compostella, provide a contemporary picture. Picaud hurried through English Saintonge, that rich and well-populated land stretching from the Charente to the Gironde, without commenting on the vines and grains which flourished along the northern bank of the river. The pilgrim was particularly anxious to get to Blaye, the most important of the estuary towns, since the great Roland was believed to be buried there in the church of St-Romain. The pilgrim, or any other traveller from the north, might have time for this visit while he waited for a boat with which to cross the Gironde and reach the flourishing city of Bordeaux, for during the middle ages no bridge crossed the Garonne further down-stream than Agen. Picaud, as a cultured Poitevin and a man of the *langue d'oil*, rather looked down on his southern neighbours and what he considered their barbarous speech. He admitted that in the Bordelais the wine was excellent and the fish abundant, but he added that the tongue was rude. He felt that the men of Saintonge already had a rustic accent, but that of the Bordelais was worse.[4]

Picaud made no mention of the Médoc, that region to the north-west of Bordeaux which is so well known today for its wines. In the middle ages there were some fields for grazing along the coast, only a few vines, and the abbey of Nôtre-Dame-de-la-fin-des-terres at Soulac, which acted as harbour and church for pilgrims using the sea route from England, Normandy or Brittany. Both the harbour and the abbey have been destroyed over the centuries by the encroaching sands, that enemy which was even more devastating in the Landes, or sandy moors, south and west of Bordeaux. The Poitevin guide could find no good word for what he called 'a desolate countryside where everything is lacking.

8

There is neither bread, nor wine, nor meat, nor fish, nor water nor springs'. He emphasized that it took three days of hard tramping to cross it, during which the unwary traveller might find himself up to his knees in drifting sand or pursued by a plague of horse-flies and wasps. There were few villages in this sandy waste, although the pilgrim might be interested in Belin where the tomb of Oliver and Charlemagne's other companions on that fatal expedition to Spain was proudly displayed to the credulous.[5] Once the Landes were passed the pilgrim found himself in Gascony proper, a much more hospitable land. Aymery Picaud drew attention to its woods and fields, its rivers and pure springs, a land where white bread and excellent red wine were abundant, although he disapproved of the Gascons themselves, finding them 'verbose, cynical, lecherous, drunkards, and badly clothed'. He admitted in their favour that they were trained for combat and remarkable for their hospitality to the poor.[6] As he approached the Pyrenees and the pass of Roncesvalles where the little kingdom of Navarre straddled the mountains the pilgrim came to the Basque country. Here too his guide was rather censorious, finding the wooded, mountainous country poor in bread and wine. He was appalled by the 'barbarous language', although admitting that there were apple orchards (and good cider) as well as milk, so obviously grazing was general.[7] Bayonne was the main town of the Basque country. Situated at the mouth of the Adour it was not only the natural export point for all the merchandise carried by the river, but also an important shipping centre for the Bay of Biscay, trading with Castile as well as Bordeaux and England.

The Compostella pilgrims were not as likely to cross the northern centre of the duchy which was divided and defined by its river valleys. Best known was Entre-deux-Mers, a title which perhaps inflates the importance of the Dordogne and Garonne rivers, although these are great waterways where the tides are felt upstream more than 100 miles from the ocean. These two rivers defined the nature of the land, its commerce and its pattern of habitation. The steep cliffs, which mark the northern bank of the Dordogne from the estuary at Blaye to the frontier of Péri-gord, constituted the indispensable line of defence for the duchy. Like much of the rest of Gascony, the centre of Entre-deux-Mers was occupied by a vast forest where the monks of the abbey of La-Sauve-Majeure encouraged the clearing of the land. Small

9

new towns, such as Créon, were planted in the developing open spaces. Further up the Garonne lay La Réole, whose frontier was the line between the dioceses of Bordeaux and Bazas. The country around La Réole was rich and prosperous, but open to attack from the Agenais, the territory of the next major town upriver. In the early thirteenth century it was under the control of the count of Toulouse, but was soon to pass to the brother of St. Louis. Since La Réole was jealous of Bordeaux's commercial supremacy, it used its exposed position to extract concessions from the English king in return for its uncertain loyalty.

La Réole is a reminder of how inadequate it is to speak of the duchy only in terms of its lands, for it was its towns which gave it its value, its strength, and the greater enthusiasm for the English connection. After the French conquered Poitiers and La Rochelle, Bordeaux once more became a provincial capital of importance. It had already established commercial links with England, which were enhanced when there was no longer any competition from La Rochelle for the wine trade. Despite spirited opposition from such upstream towns as La Réole, Bordeaux generally dominated the towns on the Garonne and, because it controlled the Gironde, influenced those on the Dordogne. It had the most to lose if the English connection was broken, since neither France nor Spain provided such an unchallenged and accessible market for its wines. Bayonne was also important. Besides its notable fleet and ship-building activities, it was also a frontier port. It provided the ships, and usually the sailors, for Bordeaux's commerce and the export of Gascon wines to England, so that it too had a vested interest in the continuation of English rule. On its own account it traded actively with Castile and Navarre, and controlled the commerce of the Adour.

Certainly in the first half of the thirteenth century the loyalty of Bordeaux, Bayonne, and the inland territory they dominated, was essential for the maintenance of English control, and this loyalty was actively encouraged by royal grants of privileges.[8] However, the peaceful government of the towns was undermined by the development of warring parties within them. These groups do not fit easily into a simple set of alternatives, although one faction was likely to be more pro-English than the other. Both normally came from the bourgeois aristocracy so that there is no question of the 'proletariat' versus the 'oligarchy', but rather a less clear division between those who profited more or less from trade with England. So much emphasis has been put on the very great extent of the wine trade that it has been easy to overlook the local trade between Gascony and Languedoc or Bayonne's interest in trading with Spain. These could on occasion exert considerable influence As well, in Bordeaux especially, the ranks of those enjoying the privileges of a citizen of Bordeaux included representatives of the lesser noble families, who thus had one foot in town as well as one in their country fiefs. The records show that there was some inter-marriage between well-to-do and powerful bourgeois and members of the lesser nobility, so that commercial considerations were at least familiar to the feudal class, unlike the situation in northern France. Smaller towns, like Saintes, Dax, and Bazas, were of less concern and importance though they served as political and administrative sub-centres.

Around the fringes of the duchy were a number of relatively independent lordships, whose loyalty the dukes tried to buy by concessions and pensions. Their lords were an opportunistic group and their constantly changing alliances made a consistent policy almost impossible. Béarn, Bigorre, and Armagnac were the most important and the king-duke's efforts to attach them to himself and thus protect his frontiers, especially on the east, represent a constant thread in English policy in Aquitaine. The problem of Aquitaine's frontiers was acute for there was no easily defensible agreed line, as the frontier consisted of a number of isolated fortresses in a kind of no-man's-land. Thus the capture of one castle could appear to have a disproportionate effect, but might not matter fundamentally since the basic strength of the duchy lay in the continued loyalty and support of the towns.

Until the time of King John the ties of Aquitaine with its duke had been reinforced by frequent personal contacts. Richard, as well as Queen Eleanor, had preferred to spend much time in the duchy, though in Poitiers rather than Bordeaux. After the continental disasters of the early years of his reign, John was needed in England to safeguard his throne or fought unsuccessfully in Flanders in a vain campaign against Philip Augustus. The immediate presence and prestige of the duke could no longer be counted on to guarantee order, to put down factions, or even to repel attacks. Henry III, for example, did not even enter the duchy until 1230, fourteen years after he had come to the throne; though his brother, Richard of Cornwall, had been sent to the aid of Gascony in 1225 when Count Hugh of La Marche was attempting to take it over while Louis VIII conquered Poitou.

With this new pattern of government by remote control, a very difficult matter in the middle ages, two elements became more important. One was the maintenance of adequate routes of communication; the other was the pattern of day-to-day administration and its financial support. There were routes by both land and sea from England to Aquitaine, but both had certain disadvantages. The most ordinary land route was London, Dover, Wissant (near Calais), Paris, Poitiers, Angoulême or Saint-Jean d'Angely, and thence to the duchy. This could be travelled at full speed in less than three weeks. For example, in 1305 John Benstede, returning from Bordeaux with urgent news for Edward I, made it to Wissant in sixteen days—an average journey of some forty miles per day.[9] A more leisurely pace was more frequent. Another possible itinerary called for crossing the Channel to Rennes or the Cotentin, and then proceeding by way of lower Poitou and Saintonge. The complete sea route from England to Bordeaux was a major voyage at the best of times. It might take as little as two weeks from Plymouth to Bordeaux when the weather was good and the winds favourable, but conditions were frequently bad and Plymouth was a long distance from London. The Black Prince and his entourage were held up in Plymouth for six weeks in 1355 waiting for a favourable wind, although the voyage itself only took eleven days.

Nevertheless the sea route was always a necessary, and often a dreaded, evil. The transport of military expeditions and heavy commerce were essentially maritime undertakings. The great wine fleets which left Bordeaux in October after the vintage often travelled together across the Bay of Biscay for mutual assistance against storms and marauding seafarers, for there was frequent piracy. The changeable weather of the Bay had its own terrors, particularly for those unused to the sea. A fourteenth-century chronicler tells the story of the pious and terrified clerks travelling to Gascony, who were so overcome by the dangers of the storm they encountered that they took refuge in prayer, singing the *Ave Maria Stella*, the hymn to Our Lady of the sea, and were rewarded with the protection of her veil until the storm had passed.[10] But, despite its delays and alarms, the passage was well known to a fair number of Englishmen and Gascons, since the land routes could easily be disrupted in times of war. The one through Brittany called for a good relationship with the count of Brittany, while the route through Paris and the French kingdom usually required safe-conducts, could be perilous in troubled times and impossible during war. Even the sea route was somewhat dependent on good relations with Brittany, since medieval sailors preferred to navigate in sight of land when possible, and landings for fresh water were often made. The flow of orders, supplies and personnel from England to Gascony was always possible, but frequently difficult and delayed.

Within the duchy men travelled over the network of Roman roads, in rather poor repair by the thirteenth century, and on the large number of navigable rivers. The old Roman roads linked Bordeaux with its most important neighbours: the Médoc, Saintonge, Périgord, Agen and Toulouse, along routes that normally ran parallel to the rivers. As well, there was a coastal road in the Landes, one to Dax and on to Bayonne, while it was possible to reach St-Sever by way of Bazas and Marsan. Many of these were rough tracks and there were few bridges to cross the frequent deep rivers. The unhappy traveller found himself at the mercy of greedy ferrymen whose boats, according to Aymery Picaud, were often small and made of a single tree trunk. Horses were also carried in these precarious craft but Picaud warned that for safety, as well as to avoid extortionate charges, it was wiser to hold your horses' bridle and let him swim behind the boat. Otherwise all might risk drowning when an overcrowded boat capsized.[11] Despite any possible dangers the river routes were vital. The Garonne has been described without exaggeration as 'the artery by which the life of the Bordelais circulated'.[12] Its smallest tributaries, as well as those of the Dordogne, and to a degree the Adour, were the natural freight routes of the duchy. They emphasized the importance of all the main river towns, as well as the essential superiority of Bordeaux because of its commanding location and its predominance in the rich export trade of wine.

The administration of the duchy in these early years was confided to a seneschal appointed by the king-duke, having no fixed term and recallable at the king's will. Nominally the seneschal had extensive powers, but these were exceedingly ill-defined, and his authority suffered from insufficient revenues and the absence of a permanent force with which to enforce obedience. All these weaknesses affected his prestige and made it almost impossible for him to control the restless and ambitious feudal lords for whom Gascony was noted. War was for many their principal occupation in the employment of either the king of France or the king of England or waged for the increase of their own lands and power. Thus the seneschal's task was formidable, and Geoffrey Neville, who filled the office on Henry III's accession, was only the first to complain of the difficulties of his position. He wrote plaintively to the young king's council that without help he could not defend Poitou and Gascony from the French king, or even from its own barons who devastated the ducal lands, and kidnapped and then ransomed the burgesses. He was too poor, he wrote, to be able to interfere and—crowning insult— was no more able to borrow money than a young boy, so low was the ducal credit. Help must be sent at once, or the situation was hopeless.[13] His agitated pleas were disregarded, partly because of pressures in England, and Poitou did in fact succumb to the French invasion in 1224.

The French, however, were not the only aggressors against the duchy. Alfonso VIII of Castile put forward a claim to Gascony as part of the dowry of his wife Eleanor, daughter of Eleanor of Aquitaine. Trying to take advantage of John's weakness, Alfonso made an alliance with Philip Augustus and invaded the duchy in 1205. He had already gained some support the previous year from such southern notables as the bishop of Bayonne, the count of Armagnac, and the viscount of Béarn, and expected an easy victory. Instead the city of Bayonne closed its gates against him, despite the sympathies of its bishop. In the northern part of the duchy opposition to the Castilian attempt had been organized by Elie de Malemort, archbishop of Bordeaux, who had gone personally to England in the summer of 1204 to seek help from John. With the subsidy he received he hired more troops, which he put under the command of his brother, and ensured the loyalty of La Réole and Bordeaux. The discouraged Alfonso withdrew, and his minor conquests were easily won back, but his invasion shows the Spanish interest in the lands beyond the Pyrenees.

Yves Renouard, the French historian who has added so much to our knowledge of medieval Bordeaux and Aquitaine, has argued that the lasting features of western Europe were defined in the first quarter of the thirteenth century, and were reinforced by three major battles which fundamentally changed twelfth-century alignments and ambitions.[14] The battle of Las Navas de

Tolosas in 1212 marked the crushing defeat of the Moors in Spain, the beginning of the Reconquest, and the growing importance of the Castilian kings in the Iberian peninsula, which demanded most of their attention. In the battle of Muret in 1213 Simon de Montfort the Elder and his army of northern Frenchmen defeated the Aragonese and the men of Toulouse. They not only ensured the triumph of orthodoxy over Albigensianism, but the end of the dream of a new Mediterranean federation uniting Aragon, Toulouse and Provence with their common culture and related tongues. The weight of the French monarchy, through the marriage of the heiress of the count of Toulouse to Alphonse, brother of Louis IX, was extended to Languedoc which ultimately became a loyal bastion of French power. The battle of Bouvines in 1214, in which Philip Augustus defeated King John and his northern allies, set an irrevocable seal on the breakdown of the Angevin empire and affected the government of the two countries. The victorious Philip Augustus laid the foundations of strong centralized royal power in France; John had to concede the liberties of Magna Carta in England.

The effects of all this on Aquitaine were important. Until this time the duchy had been subjected to considerable Spanish influence, since Aragon and Navarre both spanned the Pyrenees and Castile made frequent claims to Gascon lands. Now both Castile and Aragon became more involved in their struggle within the peninsula, while during the thirteenth century the kingdom of Navarre fell into the hands of the French house of Blois, and ultimately passed to the French king himself. Relations between Aquitaine and Toulouse had been marked by their mutual recognition of their essential differences from the northern Frenchmen, perceived as foreigners, and of the contrast between the *langue d'oc* and the *langue d'oil*. Now the county of Toulouse was to become still another centre of French power and influence, menacing the duchy on its relatively unprotected eastern frontier. John's defeat underlined the weakness of the English king and his inability to give adequate protection to his continental fiefs. Gascony, as his only remaining overseas territory, would find itself for over two centuries in a continuing struggle against French power and French influence. The advantage swayed to one side or another over the years, but France held the stronger cards. Much of the inherent fascination of the history of English Gascony in the middle ages lies in the remarkably long-lived and surprisingly successful struggle it waged against the forces of French domination, both legal and military. The following chapters attempt to trace the stages of that struggle and bring once more to the spotlight the individuals most intimately concerned.

CHAPTER II

The Restless Duchy: Simon de Montfort

Although France and England had been technically at war ever since the sentence of confiscation pronounced by Philip Augustus on King John in 1202 and John's subsequent withdrawal of his homage, there were relatively few periods of actual war during the first half of the thirteenth century. Louis VII's campaign in Poitou in 1224–25, and the concurrent threat against Gascony led by Hugh de Lusignan Count of La Marche, had ended in the total French conquest of Poitou, except for the island of Oléron, but had had only a superficial effect on Gascony. The Gascon expedition led by Richard of Cornwall in 1225 had immediately regained the lost strongholds and reaffirmed English interest and concern for the duchy. In 1230 Henry III made what might more properly be called a royal progress rather than a campaign through Brittany and Poitou to put forward his claims. There was no substance behind the shadow of force, although he was accompanied by the notorious Pierre Mauclerc, the count of Brittany. Despite promises and protestations of loyalty, the military display achieved absolutely no permanent result in returning Poitou to the English allegiance. A more serious attempt to recapture Poitou was made in 1242 when Henry launched a campaign there, encouraged by the promise of Poitevin help from the mercurial Hugh of La Marche, now his stepfather for he had married King John's widow. Henry's military incapacity was demonstrated by the withdrawal from Taillebourg and the disastrous defeat at Saintes, while his lack of political perspicacity was evidenced by his misplaced confidence in the unreliable Poitevin barons who, at the first defeat, promptly abandoned his cause and made their peace with Louis IX. The subsequent five-year truce left Louis in control of all his gains and underlined the fact that the English had lost all real control in Poitou and Saintonge except for Oléron.[1]

The situation in Gascony itself was unsettled. Henry had spent a year there after the inglorious setback at Saintes, and a daughter was born to the queen at Bordeaux. The king had made considerable efforts to conciliate the towns by granting them further privileges and to reconcile the nobles by providing them with money grants and pensions. It was an expensive policy and one that was difficult for a mere seneschal to carry on after the king left. The changeability of the Gascon nobles was a byword and the surrounding powers were more than willing to improve their own positions by stirring up revolt and disaffection among the local lords. The king of Navarre was happy to encourage the restless Gaston de Béarn; the king of Aragon joined the king of Castile in putting forward a claim to Gascony through their mutual ancestor, the daughter of Eleanor of Aquitaine who had married Alfonso VIII of Castile. Fortunately for England, Louis was preoccupied with his own preparations for the crusade and had no energy to spare for a local war of conquest. Such was the situation when Henry decided on stronger measures and in 1248 appointed his brother-in-law, Simon de Montfort, as his lieutenant in Gascony.

Simon de Montfort was one of the most fascinating characters of the thirteenth century and one around whom argument still swirls.[2] He was the third son of Simon de Montfort, leader of the crusade against the Albigensians, who had used this position to raise himself from a minor noble of the Ile-de-France to a man of enormous if transitory power. Simon as the third son had nothing to hope for from the family inheritance in France, but his mother had been the sister of the earl of Leicester who had died without male heirs and thus had a claim to the earldom. It was the pursuit of this claim which led Simon to England and which ended in his acceptance by Henry III as earl of Leicester and in his marriage to Eleanor, the king's widowed sister. He thus became one of the most important men of the realm and had won a reputation as a crusader and as a vigorous fighter in the campaign of 1242. Because of his family connections he could move easily between the courts of Paris and London, and had also links with Gascony through his brother Guy's marriage to the countess of Bigorre, that small county on its south-eastern frontier, whose homage was much debated. All these considerations may well have been in Henry's mind when he appointed his masterful brother-in-law as king's lieutenant in Gascony for the fixed term of seven years. The patent of his appointment shows how carefully Simon had enforced conditions for his acceptance of the post to give him some power to deal with its difficulties. The terms asserted that he was to have all the issues and rents owing to the king in the duchy, except those assigned to others in fee, the king was to aid him in the wars which he had to sustain, and Simon was to take custody of the castles as he thought necessary.[3] A series of references which follow in the summer of 1248 suggest the amount of money that was being committed to Simon to provide him with the necessary fighting force, to pay the wages of garrisons in the king's castles, and to fortify and equip the main castles of Gascony.[4] When the earl of Leicester set forth for Gascony in the autumn of 1248 he was furnished with more extensive powers than anyone had ever exercised in Gascony except the king himself. Could he succeed in this new task?

His first moves were to make sure of external peace. He went to Paris and arranged with Queen Blanche, regent while Louis was on crusade, for a renewal of the truce with France. Within a month he had travelled to the valleys of the Pyrenees to come to an agreement with King Thibault of Navarre, submitting all disputes between the two kings regarding Gascony to arbiters chosen from each side. Probably about the same time he reinforced the south-eastern frontier of the duchy by persuading the aged and much-married countess of Bigorre (his brother Guy had been her third husband of five) to give him the guardianship of the county of Bigorre in return for an annual rent. These diplomatic moves achieved, Earl Simon could turn his energies to the pacification of Gascony itself. The problem was not an easy one, for many of the nobles indulged in guerrilla warfare. In one of his letters to the king, Simon complained about the difficulty of putting down this kind of activity, even with a military force 'because they rob the earth, and burn and pillage . . . and ride by night in the manner of thieves'.[5] The most dangerous of all the rebellious nobles was Gaston de Béarn, the ambitious and changeable viscount of Béarn who ruled that county from 1229–90, and changed his allegiance with every breeze, or insubstantial promise of possible gain. A frontal attack seemed unwise but the neutralization of Navarre, the guardianship of Bigorre and the imprisonment of the viscount of Soule, Gaston's neighbour to the west, for non-appearance at court, encouraged the effectiveness of the truce which the earl arranged with Gaston.

Although Bordeaux was the principal city of the duchy, Gascony was not administered solely from there, for courts were held as well at Bazas, St-Sever and Dax. It was customary at these courts for the seneschal to swear to govern according to the laws and customs of the country, while the vassals of the area came to do homage, and feudal justice was enforced by the king's representative. Simon duly made the rounds of these centres but, backed by the military force which the king had provided, he treated the local barons harshly and irritated the easily aroused towns by refusing to observe their customary privileges. In addition, in order to assure peace, he seized such important castles as Fronsac and Gramont: both were of major strategic importance and both had a bad name. Fronsac, for example, had been a stronghold for several centuries since its superb natural position on a plateau overlooking the junction of the Dordogne and Isle rivers had inspired Charlemagne to build a castle there to survey his conquest of Aquitaine. It was a key location for controlling the traffic on both rivers and the most essential of the fortresses near Bordeaux. Gramont held an equally commanding position in the valley of the Adour. In times of upheaval such strongholds could, and often did, become centres for brigandage, while the larcenous nature of the castellans did not seem to change much over the centuries. Picaud, the pilgrim guide, was complaining in the twelfth century that the men of Gramont forcibly extorted unjust tolls from pilgrims and travellers, frequently double-charging merchants. Five centuries later the Bordelais dedicated flowery French and Latin poems to Louis XIII in gratitude for his razing of the castle of Fronsac, whose castellan had been harassing the countryside.[6] In order to ensure local peace, as well as provide necessary stronghold against outside attack, such castles needed to be in royal hands.

When Earl Simon first arrived in Bordeaux the two rival factions, one led by the Soler family and the other by the Colom, were at first quiet. However, in June 1249 a bloody riot broke out in the city which Simon put down most vigorously. To bring peace between the opposing parties in a civil war requires a Solomon and in this case the Soler felt that the earl had unfairly favoured the Colom and treated their own faction with unjustified severity. Certainly, Montfort appears to have been particularly complaisant to the Colom, and at least some of the Soler complaints were justified. His primary tactic when dealing with rebels was to confiscate their vineyards or cut their vines, which in that wine-growing country was the ultimate penalty. Such tactics and such harshness inevitably encouraged a stream of Gascon complaints to the king in England. Henry III found it almost impossible to pursue a consistent policy, nor could he resist the claims of kinship when Gaston de Béarn (his wife's cousin) came to seek the return of his lands. Gaston was reinstated, and Simon warned against excessive severity. Nevertheless revolt soon broke out again, the earl reacted with a heavy hand, and again Gascon complaints streamed in to Westminster.

In January 1252 the king decided to act. He appointed Henry of Wingham, a confidential clerk who later became chancellor and Bishop of London, and the Master of the Temple in England as a commission of enquiry. They were to go first to France to deal with the French queen about infringements of the truce and then go on to Gascony and report to him on the state of the duchy. Henry had had in mind for some years to give the duchy to Edward, once it had been wrestled into submission, but he deplored his constant involvement in its internal squabbles. His commissioners sent their first report at the beginning of March.[7] They had been joined by Henry's half-brother, Geoffrey de Lusignan, and had found Gascony 'in great perturbation'. A vigorous struggle was going on at La Réole between the townspeople and the defenders of the castle and it seemed that a truce was essential, but difficult to achieve. Gaston de Béarn, supported by the lords of Dax and the Bazadais, led the party against the castle, using two catapults and other machines, and could only produce 'weak and insufficient excuses' when given the king's letters demanding that a truce should be arrived at and that the complaining Gascons come to London to bring their accusations to the king's court. With persuasion by the archbishop of Bordeaux, the promise of comprehensive safe-conducts and of the presence of the earl in England to hear their complaints, the quarrelling Gascons finally agreed to the truce and the unprecedented voyage to England to the king's court.[8] The stage was set for the dramatic hearing before the king's council in the refectory of Westminster Abbey in May and June in 1252.

The confrontation was a violent one, since all the parties possessed to full measure the medieval passion for extreme and emotional language. As well, the archbishop of Bordeaux, leading the Gascons, and the earl of Leicester were bitter opponents. Géraud de Malemort, archbishop since 1227, was a vigorous and determined churchman, adamant in the pursuit of his rights. Once before, in 1236, he had led concerted action to complain of the behaviour of English officials in the duchy. On that occasion he had brought together the heads of all the religious institutions of the diocese to make a joint complaint against the exactions of the current royal officials. His initiative had sparked an inquiry ordered by Henry III and some temporary improvement. It is not surprising that he should clash with the equally determined earl and it would appear that Géraud was in fact responsible for some of the upheaval. Certainly the earl later complained at the Papal Curia that the archbishop had encouraged the barons, knights, burgesses and other people of Gascony to conspire against him, after having sworn fidelity and had also done him grave acts of injustice. As well, the archbishop excommunicated Simon at a time when he was protected by a papal indult from such a local sentence.[9]

Sixteen of the Gascon complaints brought forward at this trial have survived and they are detailed, if one-sided, statements of accusations against the earl.[10] They suggest an arbitrary highhandedness, a disregard for traditional forms, and a reliance on inadequate subordinates. In one case they suggest still another subconscious reason for the Gascon distrust of Earl Simon, for they 'had heard tell of the evil behaviour of the race of Montfort'.[11] We only have Simon's responses in one case, but their tenor, and his usual behaviour, make it impossible to accept without cynicism Adam Marsh's report to Bishop Grosseteste that throughout the whole difficult affair the earl had displayed towards both the king and his Gascon accusers 'the moderation of gentleness and the fullness of magnanimity'. Matthew Paris, in sharp contrast and probably with some exaggeration, describes a shouting match between King Henry and Simon in which wounding personal insults were exchanged.[12] The upshot of the hearing was a decision by the council in favour of the earl, urged by the barons who understood the difficulties of the situation, but this did not end the matter. Overnight the decision was repudiated by the king as he was influenced by those close to him who continued to press the case against Simon. The bitter dispute raged on and the king's final decision was an apparent compromise which satisfied no one. The truce between the earl and his Gascon opponents was to be continued until the following February when Henry and

22

Edward would go in person to the duchy to settle the various controversies. Meanwhile a conservator of the peace was to go to Gascony and make the immediate necessary decisions on the disputed castles of Bourg and Fronsac, but other quarrels and the earl's claims for money owed him were all put off till the king's arrival.[13] With the grudging permission of the king, Earl Simon returned to Gascony. The fighting immediately began again as he retaliated against his enemies who fought back with renewed enthusiasm despite the official truce. In England the Gascons remained to enjoy the king's hospitality and Edward was officially invested with the duchy. Henry's eldest son had just passed his thirteenth birthday and, in the euphoria of the occasion, marked by feasting, princely gift-giving and Gascon performance of homage, the Gascons boasted happily they would soon capture the earl or drive him out of Gascony. The problem of the legal transference of the government of the duchy was settled when a covenant between Edward and Simon finally solved the disputed question. In return for Simon's withdrawal from the remainder of his term and his turning over not only the castles which he held from the king, but also those he had acquired and improved during his stay, Edward was to pay the earl 7,000 marks of silver during 1253. An agreement was also made regarding the prisoners held.[14] With this settlement the earl withdrew from Gascony to France and the troubled duchy awaited the arrival of King Henry.

The experiment of sending a great magnate to Gascony as king's lieutenant had ended in at least partial failure. Some of the lack of success rested with Simon de Montfort himself, since he had been excessively high-handed and harsh, but it is reasonable to wonder whether anyone who exercised—or attempted to exercise—real power over the Gascons would have been better received, or how different the result might have been if the king had followed a constant policy towards the duchy. Certain problems were recurrent, especially the financial one. Despite the terms of his appointment and the application of other revenues to his support, the earl was always in financial difficulties. It was expensive work to pay men-at-arms, to fortify and equip the royal castles; occasionally to buy a strategically located stronghold such as Bourg from its owner; or to build from the beginning as at Cubzac. The apparatus of government and its officials had to be maintained. The revenues of Gascony, which had been assigned to Simon, were difficult, frequently impossible, to collect for a number of reasons. In the spring of 1250, for example, the earl wrote to the king that he had not had a penny from the royal rents in the duchy because they were all held by the king of France.[15]

The delays and the complex arrangements required for finding the necessary funds, the lack of trustworthy and adequately supervised administrative personnel, the extraordinarily varied and unfamiliar tissue of local customs and traditions, the Gascons' notorious changeability, and the continuing factional strife within the towns: all contributed to the exceedingly difficult task of controlling and pacifying Gascony. Simon, by his own admission, knew that he was disliked by the great men of Gascony, but claimed that this was because he upheld the king's rights and those of the poor man. In Simon's favour it must be said that he had been sent to Gascony at a time of much upheaval to put down the unrest among the Gascons; to tame the insubordinate vassals and especially their leader Gaston de Béarn, who claimed that he was bound by no ties to England; to make peace between the factions of the burgesses in the towns, so that their commercial life could flourish and bring economic advantage to England; and to gain control of those castles which commanded the most important strategic locations in the duchy. He had succeeded in much of this programme, though with little concern for those affected by his harsh actions, and he had legitimate suspicions of the Gascons' sudden conversion to devoted loyalty. Nevertheless he had failed to generate sufficiently widespread support to enable him to continue. Somehow a successful administrator of the duchy had to balance royal rights, the proud claims of the nobility, and the commercial interests of the towns who provided the major support and revenue for the king. Simon had tried and failed. Now it would be the turn of the king himself.

Henry's facile optimism that all would be quiet and peaceful in Gascony after the removal of the earl's heavy hand was soon proved false. While the trial at Westminster was under way a new king had acceded to the throne of Castile, Alfonso X, whom chroniclers have called the 'Wise'. He saw that the troubled state of Gascony left without a strong governor encouraged profitable interference. He once more put forward the old and vague Castilian claim to Gascony and encouraged the Gascon nobles to recognize him as overlord. The changeable Gaston de Béarn answered the invitation, as did several others, so that by the spring of 1253 there was a strong Castilian party in Gascony. Unfortunately, Henry III's intended departure had been delayed for six months and it was only in September 1253 that the king arrived in Bordeaux to find the duchy once more in ferment. Gaston de Béarn was in open revolt, and a fair number of the lesser lords with him. They had menaced Bordeaux itself and were firmly ensconced in La Réole, while rumours ran riot as to the dangerous plans of the king of Castile. Excitement ran so high that Henry wrote back in December to the regents in England not only asking for further help against Gaston, but also claiming that Alfonso was planning a major invasion of Gascony in the spring. The regents took prompt action to put together an armed force in the case of the invasion of Gascony and to raise the necessary funds. To encourage generosity on this occasion they suggested that the king should renew the charters of liberties once again and —for the first time—that two elected knights from each shire should be brought to Westminster to agree for their shires on a grant in aid. The actual situation was nowhere near as desperate as Henry had originally made it out, and by February the alarm was recognized as a false one, though the plans for an aid went ahead. Nevertheless, as one historian has cogently remarked, 'The gossip of the Pyrenees had made a contribution towards the development of the English constitution.'[16]

King Henry had already decided on an attempt to use a marriage alliance to solve his problem with Castile and was suggesting the marriage of Edward to Eleanor, Alfonso's half-sister. By February 1254 negotiations were well under way, with John Mansel, the king's most trusted confidential clerk, and the bishop of Hereford as negotiators. They were able to announce from Toledo as early as 1 April that they had arrived at an agreement. Alfonso had agreed to give up all claims to Gascony, while Henry promised to help Alfonso in his efforts against Navarre and to pay careful attention to the rights and claims of Gaston de Béarn. Before the end of April Alfonso wrote to Gaston and his other supporters that he had made an amicable agreement with King Henry regarding Gascony. He therefore ordered them to be obedient to the king and Edward as their liege lords and to return to Henry and his son any castles, towns or lands which were rightfully theirs.[17] Arrangements had been under way in England for some time for the queen's departure for Gascony with Edward, and by the end of May orders had gone out in Gascony that the hall and chamber of the archbishop of Bordeaux should have the necessary repairs made before the royal party arrived.[18] * Edward celebrated his fifteenth birthday a few days after his arrival in Bordeaux in June and, in the autumn, set out for Castile to meet his future bride. The ceremonies were suitably impressive. Alfonso knighted the young prince and Edward and Eleanor were married at Las Huelgas, the royal convent outside Burgos, towards the end of October. It proved to be one of the happiest of royal marriages. The young couple returned to Gascony, arriving at Bayonne on 21 November, at Dax on 26 November, and made a ceremonial entry to Bordeaux on 15 December. In their honour the whole city was decorated, and spices and incense were burned at its four corners.[19]

The costs connected with his son's knighting and marriage and the suitable welcome for the newly-married pair were high, but they were only one segment of Henry's multitude of financial problems on this Gascon expedition. There was the expensive matter of subduing Gaston de Béarn's revolt. The king had realized even before he left for Gascony that the skill and experience of Simon de Montfort would be of great assistance in the necessary fighting, but that the earl had good reason to refuse to serve. Henry's letter to Simon from Benauges on 3 October 1253 is most conciliatory in tone. The king asks Simon to come but assures him that he does not have to stay and can leave without incurring the king's ill will.[20] The earl obeyed the king's request and had arrived by 20 October, but he made profitable use of his acquiescence and the king's resultant goodwill. The Gascon Rolls and the Close Rolls for October and November show a flurry of gifts to the earl, including a preliminary grant on his arrival as he was not provided with sufficient money. Besides such special favours as £500 of silver from the profits of the coinage at Bordeaux and the profits of a ship loaded with wine free of customs, the earl made sure that the financial terms of his covenant with Edward would be carried out. The king had difficulty getting this sum paid at the proper times and, at one time, was writing anxiously to England that he had sworn on his soul that this money should be paid and that the Exchequer must see that this is done without delay to save him from perjury.[21] Before Earl

* The royal right to use the archbishop's palace when the king or his representative was in Bordeaux was invoked on many occasions, sometimes for long periods.

Simon left the king in February 1254 the matter seems to have been satisfactorily adjusted.

Other costs are suggested by the agreement with Géraud d'Armagnac in September 1254, which exemplifies the method by which Henry was attempting to ensure the loyalty of the Gascon nobles. Géraud recognized that he owed homage to the English king for Armagnac and Fezensac; in return for this Henry agreed to assume Géraud's debt to Esquivat de Chabanais, the count of Bigorre.[22] The settlement balanced English efforts to ensure the performance of homage by their most important Gascon subjects while recognizing the Armagnac interest in Bigorre. It is an interesting example of a continued tactic by all those involved in Gascon politics—the attempt to buy the loyalty of the Gascon nobles—and the generally successful Gascon efforts to sell themselves to the highest bidder. Through the centuries of English rule in Gascony English voices would frequently be raised to deplore 'the levity and inconstancy of these barons'.[23]

Even these occasional examples illustrate the extreme difficulty of the king in financing foreign excursions. As a practical measure the wardrobe had accompanied Henry to Gascony and acted almost as his exchequer. Its keeper, Peter Chaceporc, was faced with the problem of finding money to cover even the day-to-day needs of the royal household. The king was chronically without money and in need of loans. On one straitened occasion he could not even raise 20 marks without selling the horse of one of his clerks and putting off repayment until his treasure arrived. In June 1254 Simon Passelewe brought from England gold bars worth £1,088 as well as immense quantities of jewels, plate and assorted coins, yet even with further deliveries of over £4,500 the king still needed more money.[24] Somehow, in the manner of most medieval monarchs whose financing was always hand to mouth and who left behind them anxious queues of unsatisfied creditors, Henry managed to keep afloat.

The king finally left Gascony in November 1254 having achieved his main objectives. He had neutralized the Castilian danger by arranging an alliance with Alfonso. He had put down the revolt and Gaston de Béarn had lost the possibility of using Castile as a lever for his own ambitions. He had tried to attach as many of the Gascon nobles as possible to his allegiance and had provided special privileges for the towns which were the most reliable bulwark for the English connection, as well as encouraging the normal commerce between Toulouse and Gascony down the Garonne and the peaceful circulation of Toulouse merchants with their goods. It was a creditable balance sheet and the king could feel that he had left his son in charge of a duchy which was more closely linked to England, and its king-duke than it had been for years. No fundamental decisions had been made, no basic changes in patterns, but for the moment the best use was being made of the old rather makeshift arrangements.

Henry's trip north—to rebury his mother at Fontevrault and visit the shrine of Archbishop Edmund of Canterbury at Pontigny —led him homewards through France and an extraordinary family reunion. Henry's queen and the French queen were sisters, daughters of the count of Provence, as were also the wives of Richard of Cornwall and Charles of Anjou. Louis IX, recently returned from his crusade, was glad to welcome his brother-in-law to Paris and to show off the sights of that city, bursting with artistic and intellectual excitement. It appears it was at this meeting that the two kings talked between themselves of the advantage of concluding a real peace treaty, not merely the continually extended truces which had marked their relations for the last fifty years. The seeds of the Treaty of Paris were planted, though they would take five more years to bear fruit.

CHAPTER III

The Peace Treaty That Brought War

The garden of Louis IX's palace on the Ile-de-la-Cité in Paris was the scene of a brilliant gathering on 4 December 1259. The kings of France and England and their retinues had assembled to hear the archbishop of Rouen officially proclaim the peace treaty between the two kingdoms.[1] It was the final formal step in a long-drawn-out series of negotiations and marked English acceptance of their loss of legal title to those lands confiscated from John and confirmed in French possession by conquest. The treaty marked a crucial turning-point in the long history of intermittent conflicts between France and England over the English possessions in France.

The time was propitious for a settlement between the royal brothers-in-law. Although the point has been somewhat over-stressed, it is worth remembering that the courts of England and France were on extraordinarily good terms during the long reigns of Henry III and Louis IX. There was a very real family feeling in evidence, not only between the two sister-queens, but also between Louis and Henry. Henry seemed to exhibit towards Louis that mixture of unwilling admiration, respect and affection reminiscent of a younger brother's attitude to an impressive elder. Although Louis was actually the younger, he was undeniably superior in prestige, ability and the growing strength of his government and kingdom. Louis wanted a peace treaty—it would contribute to his goal of pacification around the borders of France—but he wanted it on his own terms. His desire to create a situation which would encourage a joint effort by Christian Europe to rescue the Holy Land was genuine, but did not require immediate action. On the other hand, Henry's desire for a treaty was due, not to his own initiative, but to the inexorable pressure of Pope Alexander IV. As Henry had accepted from the pope the title of king of Sicily for his younger son, Edmund—a papal manoeuvre which was designed to commit English funds and fighting men to the dubious and expensive effort to gain Sicily back from the Hohenstaufens—Alexander was particularly anxious to see Henry at peace elsewhere. This was a first essential if there were to be funds and men available for the 'crusade' against Sicily. The pressure of events, both at home and abroad, combined to force Henry down a path he might not otherwise have chosen.

The first of the English embassies to Louis IX, dispatched under papal pressure in 1257, came to nothing, as the English envoys appear to have insisted on the return of *all* the English overseas territories. Not surprisingly, this was laughed out of court by the French. In turn, Louis' suggestions for the basic terms of the peace were put forward at the mid-Lent Parlement of 1258 at which the abbot of Westminster represented the English negotiators. Although the details are unrecorded the general line seems to have embodied much of the later agreement. Henry was not happy with the French proposals, but his freedom of action was being progressively limited. The disastrous consequences of his financial agreement with the papacy over Sicily were becoming more evident in England with the growing weight of papal taxation. The English barons added their disapproval of Henry's mortgaging of English revenues for an unpopular foreign adventure to their dislike of the swarms of the king's foreign relatives who were rewarded with titles, marriages and lands. At the Parliament, which convened in London in the second week after Easter 1258, these two separate forces pushed the king towards further peace negotiations. Arlotus, the papal legate, and other papal envoys were present to put forward in person the papal demands for the English military and financial contribution, which would make settlement of the Sicilian business possible. They insisted that it was essential that a peace treaty be signed with France and suggested that perhaps the French king would be willing as one of its terms to pay for a certain number of knights who could then be used in Sicily. At the same Parliament the English barons refused categorically to provide any subsidy for the Sicilian affair. Henry, faced with the continuing pressure of the papal officials and the intransigence of his barons, realized that he had no choice and decided to negotiate on the basis of the proposals suggested by the French king.

The negotiators were appointed in the first week of May, and suggest a family settlement. They included two of the king's Poitevin half-brothers; his wife's uncle, Peter of Savoy; Simon de Montfort, his brother-in-law; as well as Hugh Bigod, brother of the earl marshal and at this time leader of the barons' party. They were given full powers to negotiate the treaty and swear the required oaths and appear to have departed at once for Paris and arrived there while the Whitsun Parlement was still sitting. There seems to have been little argument over the terms for within eight days the text of the articles of peace had been agreed on by the English envoys and their French counterparts. Since the papal envoys had also come to Paris to encourage and perhaps speed the process of negotiations, a copy of the articles was deposited in the Temple of Paris under the seals of the archbishop of Tarentaise, representing the pope, and the archbishop of Rouen. By 28 May 1258 the formal meeting had taken place in which Simon de Montfort, Peter of Savoy and Hugh Bigod swore on behalf of Henry III to keep the articles, and the French envoys did the same on behalf of Louis. If all this had been achieved by the end of May 1258 it is difficult to understand why the treaty was only finally proclaimed eighteen months later. The answer lies in the unresolved but immediate political problems hidden in the articles of peace.

A summary of the terms of the treaty is essential to any understanding of the dual nature of its relation to the English politics of its time and its determining effect on the English position in Gascony.

1. King Henry and his son were to renounce all rights in Normandy, Anjou, Maine, Touraine and Poitou—and to remove these titles from the English royal style. Henry must also obtain from his brother, Richard of Cornwall, and his sister, Eleanor de Montfort, a full and public renunciation of any claims they could make on these lands.
2. The king of France would give the king of England the sum of money necessary to support 500 knights for two years. They were to be employed for the service of God and the church, or to the profit of the kingdom of England.
3. Louis was to give all he held in fief or domain in the dioceses of Limoges, Cahors and Périgueux to Henry, saving the homages of his brothers and those fiefs indissolubly attached to the crown. He would also give Henry the territory of the

31

Agenais, if it should escheat to him from Jeanne of Toulouse, wife of Alphonse de Poitiers, and in the meantime would pay him a yearly sum equivalent to its value. The same would be done for Quercy, if it could be proved that it, like the Agenais, had formed part of the marriage portion given by Richard the Lionheart to his sister when she married the count of Toulouse. As well, after the death of the count of Poitiers, the English king was to have all the lands in Saintonge south of the Charente.

4. The vassals and towns of these lands were to take an oath to the king of France that they would not aid the king of England to break the treaty by counsel, subsidies or aids. If the English king broke the treaty those who had taken this path were bound to help the king of France against the king of England if the English king did not wish to make amends within three months of his being summoned by the king of France. This oath was to be renewed every ten years at the demand of the king of France.

5. The English king as duke of Aquitaine and peer of France was to do liege homage to the king of France for these lands, and also for the lands which he already held, including the islands. He was to do the appropriate services when an inquest had determined what the appropriate services were. The disputed matter of the homages of Bigorre, Armagnac and Fezensac was to be adjudged by law.

6. The two kings pardoned each other reciprocally for all damages due, whether caused by war or not, and with their sons bound themselves to guard and maintain the peace.[2]

Even at first glance it is easy to see why the Treaty of Paris was destined to cause trouble. One of its aims had been to reinforce and put in indisputable legal form the recognition by the English king of the French king's rights in the territories which he had first confiscated and then conquered from the English in the last fifty years. In other words, it was to serve as the final seal on the conquests of Philip Augustus and Louis VIII. In this aim it was the companion-piece to the other peace treaty which Louis was arranging at the same time—the Treaty of Corbeil with Aragon. In this treaty James of Aragon gave up his claims to lands in southern France which had been won for the French king by the northern successes in the Albigensian Crusade, while Louis surrendered his nebulous claims to Aragonese lands bordering the Pyrenees. The treaty was reinforced by the marriage of Louis' son to James' daughter, and no delay was encountered in the final ratification.

There were two distinct sets of problems involved in the Anglo-French settlement, the one immediate and the other long term. The immediate issue was the requirement that the necessary renunciation to the lands in France once held by the English king must be made, not only by Henry and his son, but also by his brother and one of his two sisters. Richard of Cornwall's renunciation did not present many difficulties, but that of Eleanor de Montfort, and therefore of her husband Simon, did for they obstinately insisted that her claims on Henry for the insufficient payment of her dower must be satisfied before they would provide the necessary renunciation. King Louis himself continued to urge that the treaty must include Eleanor's renunciation—and thus Henry's satisfaction of her grievances. Since Earl Simon was not only helping to negotiate the peace, but also taking a more and more important place in the councils of the barons, and in their attempts to control King Henry's wilful exercise of his royal powers, this dispute further poisoned the relations between them. Edward's opposition to the required renunciation was less immediately opportunistic, but he was almost equally reluctant, recognizing the fact that it undermined both his present and future position in Aquitaine and as heir to the throne. Nevertheless, the pressure exerted by the papal envoys, the lack of knowledge or concern about the far-away province among the barons and the immediate financial advantages of the treaty encouraged both the king and his barons to persevere in their efforts to bring the treaty to a final conclusion.

That ceremony in the garden of Louis' palace not only marked the legal end of the Angevin empire and the abandonment of its titles by the English king; it also opened a veritable Pandora's box of troubles for English rule in Gascony. These were implicit in the imprecise terms in which the treaty was written. Immediately after the archbishop of Rouen had proclaimed the treaty King Henry fulfilled his obligations, did liege homage to King Louis and was recognized as duke of Aquitaine and peer of France, but without any safeguards to ensure French fulfilment of their commitments under the treaty. There was considerable angry reaction in both England and France, for no one was really satisfied. The English chroniclers felt that their king was giving up his legal rights to lands without adequate compensation, while the French complained at the alienation of territories which they themselves now occupied. Joinville records that King Louis' insistence on the treaty was against the advice of his council, who reproached him for throwing away territory by ceding it to the king of England if he believed that the English had no right to it. Louis answered that he knew the king had no rights, but emphasized his desire to have peace between the two closely related families. Louis was more far-seeing than his council, for apart from pious hopes he reminded them of the treaty's great advantage for France: 'the king of England is now my vassal, which he was not before'.[3]

Here was truly the nub of the matter, for an unparalleled situation had been created. Until the Treaty of Paris Louis and Henry were brother monarchs, both anointed kings and equals. Henry by doing homage as duke of Aquitaine to the French king for all his territories in France became the latter's vassal, a subordinate, subject to all the galling reminders of his inferiority in this relationship. This change in status occurred at a time when the French king, conscious of his growing power, was transmuting the casual ties of an older feudalism, loosely carried and often inadequately enforced, into a precise code of obligations. Such legal codification detailed the vassal's duties and subordination and the developing royal power ensured that the old penalty of confiscation for failure or defiance of obligations could be promptly carried out. A vassal who owed liege homage was bound to do homage at each change in the succession of lord or vassal. Such a ceremony, symbolically insisting on the inferiority of the vassal to his overlord, was inevitably galling to the English king and a blow to his prestige, particularly if done in person. In fact, by this period the French king had already made it an axiom that he could never do homage to anyone, no matter what the lands he acquired might require. The vassal was also bound to provide men for service against the lord's enemies and to make no alliances against his lord or without his consent. A vassal also owed obedience in cases of sovereignty and *ressort*, which implied the acceptance within the duchy of Aquitaine of all general ordinances made for the kingdom of France and the right of the Gascons to appeal to the Parlement de Paris as the court of the king of France, their overlord. Such restrictions in the case of a two-headed personage like a king-duke were bound to interfere both with the freedom of action of the monarch and the administrative functions of the duke, as well as with his relations with his own vassals.

Ressort, or the right of the overlord to hear appeals from the courts of his vassals, was in this case the most important point of all. It was the prime issue which was to envenom Anglo-French relations until the outbreak of the Hundred Years War. Louis IX had always been extremely conscious of his obligations and his rights as the final resort of justice in the realm. One of the more attractive pictures of Louis, which has withstood seven centuries of repetition, is the scene described by his friend Joinville when the king in his short cloak and hat of white peacock feathers would dispense justice to all comers under the oaks of Vincennes or in his palace gardens.[4] But there was another and harsher side to that nostalgic picture which appears in Louis' treatment of his feudal barons. When any feudal lord, even his own brother, was accused of failing to give justice to the inhabitants of his lordship Louis was convinced that it was his right and duty as king and overlord to provide justice, to hear such appeals from their courts and to make and enforce his own decisions. It was undoubtedly an interest and a concern for justice and due legal process which encouraged King Louis to outlaw the old trial by battle and to substitute the use of inquests, but he was also alive to the political advantages of such moves. They helped to erode the power of the great feudal lords and to promote the rapid development of the Parlement de Paris as the final court of appeal in the kingdom. Although the right of appeal was technically circumscribed by certain legal requirements, French royal officials over the years became less and less scrupulous in their encouragement of appeals, whether they were legally justified or not. They correctly saw them as a means of extending both the royal prerogative and their own powers. The creation of these new mechanisms encouraged the centralizing tendencies inherent in strong government and led to a continued insistence on royal rights at the expense of feudal traditions. Although the subjection of the Gascon courts to the final decision of the Parlement de Paris often resulted in a judgment which overlooked or brushed aside the different customs and tradition of the various parts of the duchy and ultimately eroded Gascon rights, the constantly squabbling Gascons needed little urging to pursue any possible avenue of apparent advantage.

It is an accepted axiom that the later middle ages saw the transformation of the suzerain into the sovereign, and this process was already well under way in the thirteenth century. Louis IX himself served as a pivotal factor in this development. He had inherited the older feudal code and his piety and devotion to kingly duty won the admiration of many of his contemporaries. Nevertheless, his emphasis on good government and the king's duty of justice to all helped to encourage the newer centralizing tide. It inevitably entailed the strengthening of the king's courts, the growing importance of royal judges and jurists, and the proliferation of royal officials. In the middle ages the control of justice was power and its exercise meant valuable revenues. The feudal lords had gradually to surrender this power and these revenues to their overlord, the king. The newer pattern might lessen feudal anarchy, but it also gave unscrupulous monarchs with inadequately controlled officials great opportunities for royal oppression and local misuse of power.

Such consequences of the treaty might have been foreseen, but they do not seem to have been considered by either King Henry or his barons, who were perhaps blinded by the immediate difficulties facing them in England. Edward's reluctance appears to have been overcome by the pressure of events. What seems to have been completely overlooked by the English negotiators was the extraordinary imprecision of the terms by which the French king was to recompense the English king for his renunciation and act of homage. All the listed cessions were to depend on local inquests taken by French officials, and on the goodwill of the French king at the time of the death of Alphonse de Poitiers and his wife Jeanne. No mechanism for assuring enforcement was envisaged or included. Probably Louis would have been scrupulous in carrying through these obligations; his son and grandson certainly were not. The border territories assigned to the English were a confused mosaic of noble fiefs and ecclesiastical holdings, some with long-standing links to the French crown, of municipal privileges, assorted tenures and customary rights. Most of their inhabitants had no tradition of loyalty to the English duke and no desire to see their status change. The situation was made to order for legal delays, foot-dragging, and a fine exhibition of obstructive tactics ideal for French exploitation. As well, the extraordinary clause in the treaty which required an oath to the king of France from the magnates and towns of the territories newly given to the king of England was unprecedented and against all custom in the rest of France. In such a delicate situation it was bound to cause further disruption. The oath was not enforced at first because of the pressure of events in England, but Edward made real efforts when he came to power to see that it was taken. His efforts were opposed by the magnates and towns affected since they felt that taking the oath would leave them no recourse from either side. Within twenty years it had to be dropped as impractical.

The story of events, even in the first years after the treaty, shows a consistent pattern of arbitrary restriction and encroachment by French officials. Since these men farmed their offices, i.e., paid a fixed sum for their appointment against which they applied the revenues actually received, they literally could not afford to permit any lessening of their jurisdictions. They were naturally tempted to increase their resources by attracting the rightful subjects of the king-duke into the orbit of the French king. It was a French historian at the beginning of this century who first called attention to Louis' 'policy of political penetration' and to the French manipulation of the obscurities of the Treaty of Paris to make it serve 'as an instrument of conquest'.[5] A contemporary observer, Archbishop John Pecham, wrote to the pope in 1279 that it was the Treaty of Paris which had despoiled King Henry of a noble part of his hereditary right because he was deceived.[6] It is certainly true that its result was that the supposed gains for the duchy of Aquitaine were in most cases elusive, while the vassal status of its duke, and the overriding powers of the French king, were more and more firmly enforced.

Obviously King Louis' emphasis on the value of his having the king of England as a vassal was justified, but there was perhaps another much greater advantage for France in the treaty. Little contemporary attention was focused on the important point of whether Henry's performance of liege homage was merely a renewal of an old feudal tie between the duke of Aquitaine and the king of France, as it had been understood in the time of John and Philip Augustus, or whether it also included something quite new—homage for the county of Gascony, which up till then had remained free of feudal ties. Part of the confusion—for us, and probably for contemporaries too—arises from the extraordinary ambiguity of the term 'Aquitaine'. When, for example, Eleanor of

Aquitaine did homage to Philip Augustus for her duchy, was Gascony included in it, or was the homage rendered only for the northern half centring around the county of Poitou? The evidence is too vague to say, but the fact would make a considerable difference in the legal rights of the king of France. One contemporary French chronicler, Primat, specifically touches on this point and says flatly that until 1259 the land of Gascony, which in the mid-thirteenth century was territorially identical with the English duchy of Aquitaine, had not been held as a fief from the king or kingdom of France.[7] The previous independence of Gascony from feudal ties to France is a thesis which can be argued both for and against, and both sides have distinguished advocates, though both are handicapped by the sparsity of the sources.[8] If Louis achieved in this treaty the subordination of Gascony for the first time to the overlordship of France then he had certainly achieved a stunning diplomatic success. In the light of this his territorial concessions were minor gestures of appeasement and he had manoeuvred Henry into an alienation of his royal rights. If, on the other hand, the homage of 1259 merely renewed a feudal tie broken over fifty years before, the treaty could be seen in its immediate terms as rather generous to the English. The legal advantages for France which accrued over the years were a later development, not necessarily envisaged by Louis. Our decision on this controversy affects our judgment of Louis' own character and reputation for fair dealing, but does not change the situation in Gascony. Whatever its status before the Treaty of Paris, afterwards it was a fief of the king of France with all the unfortunate consequences for the duke of Aquitaine which followed therefrom.

The future possibilities of controversy and injustice which lurked beneath the surface of the Treaty of Paris were obviously not apparent to the shortsighted King Henry in December of 1259. The English king settled down happily to spend Christmas in Paris. He married his daughter Beatrice to John of Brittany, and joined the sad cortège to Saint-Denis and Royaumont when King Louis' eldest son died suddenly in January 1260. However, one cloud—the precursor of many future storms—had already appeared before Henry's return to England. This was the immediate recognition by the Gascons of the personal advantages they might gain through the now available process of appeal to the court of the king of France. In this first case the matter was one of a disputed inheritance. Elie Rudel III, lord of Bergerac and Gensac and a loyal vassal of the English king, had died in 1254 leaving his daughter Marguerite as his universal heir. She, in turn, had married Renaud de Pons, a vassal of the king of France. The situation had been made more difficult by the fact that Elie Rudel II, who had died in 1250, had asked King Henry to see that if his son Elie III should die without male heirs the lands should revert to his younger brother. King Henry was anxious to keep his promise to Elie II and was all the more anxious to aid the young Rudel in his claims since he was his vassal and these were valuable border lands. Gensac was willing to accept him, but Bergerac was not and a small war began which Henry and Edward had dealt with during their stay in the duchy in 1254-55. Each side had its own weapons: Henry used commercial sanctions; Renaud de Pons, upholding his wife's claims, attacked shipping moving towards Oléron and England. Hostilities were soon abandoned but Marguerite's claim for her legal rights had been pending in court since March 1255. Since the matter still dragged on unsettled in 1259 Marguerite and Renaud appeared before the two kings in Paris soon after the treaty was proclaimed. Henry immediately assigned them a day for the hearing of their case in the court of Gascony in Bordeaux in order to avoid an appeal. However, the seneschal of Gascony was handicapped by a lack of orders from England and the case was delayed. Marguerite and Renaud then appealed to the French court, claiming default of justice because of the delay, and were heard by the Parlement de Paris. The process still moved slowly but it moved, and the results were unfavourable to the English king's desires. He was forced to accept Renaud and Marguerite as the legitimate heirs of Elie Rudel III, and to accept their homage for Gensac in 1262. The affair of Bergerac was even more contentious and long drawn out. Decision was finally given in favour of Renaud and Marguerite in 1267, but their homage was only finally accepted by Edward in 1269.[9] This first appeal proved to be typical of many others. They frequently dragged on for years through a morass of delays, non-appearances, adjournments, special pleadings and changes of proctors before any final judgment was achieved—and accepted.

When Henry returned to England the immediate problems facing him in his struggle with the barons, and the gradual descent of the realm into civil war, blotted everything else from the horizon. The king had no power and the barons had no particular interest in Gascony. Very little time could be spared for the affairs of the distant duchy, nor any serious discussion take place on its new status and the consequences it involved. Despite Edward's real concern with his duchy and his brief stay there in 1260–61, little attention could be given to the problems of Gascony until after the defeat of Simon de Montfort and the reorganization of royal power. Edward himself departed on crusade in 1270, two years before his father's death, but took care to appoint adequate officials in Gascony before he went. He took advantage of the duchy too, for he borrowed money from Louis for his crusading expenses and pledged the proceeds of the customs of Bordeaux as repayment.[10] On his return from the Middle East after the death of his father, he felt it necessary to stop in France and put Gascony in order. He wished to deal in detail and on the spot with the problems which had already begun to develop from the confused and inequitable clauses of the Treaty of Paris.

CHAPTER IV

Edward I: Duke of Aquitaine

More than any other person Edward I, both as prince and king, was responsible for the shape of English rule in Gascony. For the first time since Richard the Lionheart a century before, Aquitaine had as duke an English king who knew Gascony well and spent sufficient time there to understand the people and customs of that turbulent land. Edward has often been called the English Justinian, but until recently both French and English historians tended to overlook his remarkable organizational work in the duchy. It was undertaken during his youth and the first half of his reign when he was at the height of his powers and aided by the most able of his ministers. Some of Edward's initiatives in Gascony illustrate early experiments in policy which were later applied in England in a more fully developed form. As well, the royal encouragement of a highly trained corps of administrators, both lay and clerical, to serve him in many fields was used to provide trusted subordinates in the duchy.

Edward had already had some valuable personal experience of Gascony, and its problems. His father had granted him the land—primarily for its revenues—first in 1249, and more specifically in 1252, although he was never given the title of duke.[1] In 1254 when he came to Gascony as a fifteen-year-old, he not only travelled to Castile to marry Eleanor, but was also introduced to the numerous complexities involved in the rule of Aquitaine. During the fifteen months he spent there he was allowed, under the supervision of King Henry and his officials, to play a certain part in the pacification of La Réole, which had been the centre the previous year of the struggle between the king's men and a faction supported by the king of Castile. Edward's marriage had been arranged to reinforce the strength of the English position in Gascony. Immediately after the wedding Alfonso issued the solemn document which embodied the renunciation of all the

Castilian claims to Gascony, claims which had often served as a convenient excuse for rebellion by ambitious Gascon vassals.[2] It is obvious from the tone of the letters issued by Edward's chancery during this period that he was already attempting to put his own stamp on the administration of the duchy and was not content merely to acquiesce in the arrangements made by his father.[3] Perhaps it was the euphoria of an ambitious and able, but very young man, who suddenly felt himself freed from his father's constant supervision, which accounts for the grandiloquence of his title in the document drawn up in Bayonne soon after his wedding. By this time his father had already left the duchy to return to England by way of Fontevrault, Pontigny and Paris. Edward described himself, for the first and only time, as 'now ruling in Gascony as prince and lord',[4] a considerable exaggeration of his actual status since he held the land without title in homage to his father. During this first visit the prince had direct experience of the bitter political struggles and factionalism, which simmered beneath the surface at both Bayonne and Bordeaux and often erupted into overt violence. Bayonne was forced to accept a mayor imposed by the English ruler and its inhabitants had to take an oath to obey the mayor.

Bordeaux was even more troubled as the Colom and Soler continued their bitter feud. Edward's own desire to gain the real power his father withheld from him helped to encourage the factional struggle. In 1256 Edward made a treaty of alliance with Gaillard Soler in which Gaillard promised to procure for the prince control over the mayoralty of Bordeaux. The king's attempts in 1260 to make sure that the mayors of Bordeaux were elected by all the citizens and not merely one party played into the hands of the Soler since the Colom, over-confident of their power, refused to appear before the king. On 22 October 1261 during a second visit to Bordeaux Edward provided a new series of statutes for the city's reform. These created a comprehensive charter for its government, which considerably circumscribed its independence and forced it to accept a mayor chosen by the prince.[5]

These two visits also introduced the young prince to the constant manoeuvring, the exploitation of both legal and military challenges by such difficult and powerful Gascon nobles as Gaston de Béarn and the lord of Bergerac. Such experience encouraged the king's son to continue the policy initiated by Simon de Montfort during his term as lieutenant, the acquisition whenever possible of royal control of the key fortresses on the duchy's borders. Attempts were made to buy Sault-de-Navailles and Mauléon. Where outright purchase or exchange proved impossible Edward carefully required an act of homage, which included the holder's promise to render the castle to him when it might be needed because of war in Gascony.[6] The year spent in Gascony on this occasion produced some solid results for the organization and better order of the duchy. It is tempting to see in these first tentative efforts the beginnings of the long and fruitful collaboration between Edward and Robert Burnell, who had accompanied the king's son to Gascony as his clerk.[7] Burnell was at this time an as yet undistinguished but ambitious and acquisitive clerk, who rapidly established himself in Edward's favour. His rise, which brought him riches, honours, the chancellorship of England and the bishopric of Bath and Wells, began soon after this voyage to Gascony. Whatever his weaknesses as a materialistic and excessively secular cleric, Burnell was a superb official and royal servant who deserves some of the credit for the enlightened and effective policies followed by Edward during the first half of his reign. He continued to be employed on Gascon business, serving as a commissioner of reform with Otho de Grandison in 1278, and spending much of the period 1286–89 in the duchy with Edward.

Thus when Edward first entered the duchy in August of 1273 as king-duke he already had an intimate knowledge of this section of his realm and some definite ideas on how he proposed to implement his government of it. Homage was, of course, due to Edward as the new duke of Aquitaine, but this need for renewal provided a useful excuse for the rapid setting on foot of an inquiry into the lands, whether fiefs or allods, held of him, as well as the services and duties which those fiefs carried. Holders of fiefs were required to do homage and recognize their obligations under the pain of confiscation. Such an enquiry could provide the king and his officials in Gascony with a valuable survey of what was owed him in revenues and military and other services. The mechanism, which was basically related to the later Quo Warranto proceedings in England, called for a proclamation 'by voice of herald and sound of trumpet' in Bordeaux and certain other centres, requiring the inhabitants to present themselves to do homage and answer specific questions. Lawyers and knights served as witnesses and public notaries were used to put the answers into standard form

43

and attest the resulting document. Much of this register has survived and its entries provide useful guides to the feudal geography of Gascony and to the willingness, or lack of it, of Edward's Gascon subjects to recognize their feudal ties.[8] Most of the work was achieved before Edward left Gascony for England in 1274.

Luke de Tany had been named seneschal of Gascony just before Henry III's death in the spring of 1272. A knight of a Norman family which had been established in England since the Conquest, he had previously been constable of Knaresbrough. He was still in office in Gascony when Edward arrived on his first journey of inspection and was plagued by a series of major problems, the most pressing of which was the insubordination of Gaston de Béarn, who, when summoned to submit to Edward, appealed to the French king in what proved to be a long-drawn-out affair. It is obvious from the tone of the king's correspondence with Luke after Edward's return to England that the king was informed and concerned about matters in Gascony. While the seneschal received a constant stream of orders for the actions to be taken for the better management of the duchy, the king also heard the complaints that issued from the Gascons about his official's high-handed measures. There were problems aplenty: the matter of the rightful possession of the castle of Fronsac which the viscount was demanding, claiming to have been dispossessed by Simon de Montfort; a squabble over the regalian rights of the bishopric of Dax and the encroachments of the officials left to collect the revenues of the see for the king during the vacancy; another struggle with the church at Bazas which complained of the harshness of the seneschal; as well as close to thirty appeals in process at the Parlement de Paris.[9]

By 1278 Edward had become sufficiently concerned about the state of affairs in the duchy to send off two of his most trusted familiars, Robert Burnell and Otho de Grandison, a Savoyard who made a stunningly successful career in Edward's service. They went first to Paris and then to the duchy to enquire into matters there and reform them. They had been appointed in February and a royal letter of 21 March suggests the complete confidence the king had in them. He urged them not to attempt to speed their return to England by failing to give sufficient attention to the affairs of Gascony as 'the king has no one about him whom he believes could know the premises and do his will in the premises better and more advantageously than them, not even if he himself

44

were to attend to the matters there in person'. Ordering them to display the faith of Mary, the Mother of God and not that of Saint Thomas the Apostle, he assured them that he would not in any way revoke or change their actions there, but would regard them as his own deeds rather than theirs. He warned them of the Gascons' reputation for changeableness and suggested that they should make very certain that everything was properly arranged and documented 'so that in times to come they shall not presume in their insolence boldly to contravene their own deeds and so that their own deed and surety may be objected to their face, eye to eye, to repress their malice forever'.[10] The commissioners spent five months in Gascony and wound up the long dispute with Gaston de Béarn, having been empowered to readmit him to the king's grace. They also removed the unpopular Luke de Tany from his office of seneschal and took into their own hands the settlement of many of the minor problems which had exacerbated relations within the duchy. Bordeaux was returned the right of electing its own mayor in the hope that the passage of time and certain marriage alliances had appeased the factionalism in that city, and a new seneschal was appointed.

During the first half of his reign the king achieved the final expansion of Gascony provided for under the terms of the treaty of 1259. Although Edward and his cousin, Philip III, were on good terms personally, the need to force the French to carry out their obligations under the treaty took constant diplomatic pressure, and was often affected by other outside events. Obviously the affairs of Gascony did not exist in a vacuum for either the English or the French king, but remained a continuously important factor in a singularly fluid and changeable situation. The outside interests and concerns of both kingdoms, as well as the general pattern of events, naturally affected the willingness of either side to make concessions in Gascony.

The settlement between the two kings at Amiens in 1279 marked the success of a long series of diplomatic endeavours to force the French concession of the Agenais which had been granted by the treaty of 1259. This claim had been in Edward's mind since he had first done homage to Philip at Melun on his return from the crusade in 1273 and pointedly stated: 'Lord King I do you homage for all the lands I ought to hold from you'.[11] As well, Eleanor of Castile had recently inherited the tiny county of Ponthieu in northern France from her mother, so there was the added question of the French recognition of Eleanor's rights and the subsequent obligation of homage. Both matters were dealt with at Amiens and the treaty agreed there attempted to wipe out many of the festering irritations which poisoned relations along the borders of Gascony. The Agenais was to be turned over to the representatives of the English king and to be held by liege homage in the same manner as the rest of the duchy of Aquitaine. King Philip abandoned his demand for the oath which had originally been stipulated for the vassals in all the territories newly handed over to the English. In return Edward gave up his claims to those 'privileged' in the dioceses of Périgueux, Limoges and Cahors who asserted the right of inalienability from the French king's allegiance. Both kings agreed to an inquiry in Quercy to discover whether it, like the Agenais, originally came as a dower from the English king and thus should return to him. Apart from these changes the Treaty of Paris was reaffirmed by both monarchs for themselves and their successors. At the same time Edward did homage for his wife's county of Ponthieu and agreed to pay a relief of 6,000 *livres parisis*.[12] Despite the agreement by the monarchs the treaty was not fully carried out and the officials on both sides were suspicious and aggressive. There was a further proliferation of appeals to the French Parlement and delays in settling them and in handing over the Agenais. Within two weeks of the peace Jean de Grailly, seneschal of Gascony, was writing to his influential old friend, Antony Bek, to press for the immediate appointment of investigators for the inquiry in Quercy as, he argued, the possible witnesses were old and feeble and likely to disappear, while King Philip would be happy to delay as long as possible.[13] There was a great French reluctance to recognize the English rights in lower Saintonge, south of the Charente, which had also been granted them in 1259.

For the moment, however, both English and French kings had more pressing matters on their minds. The famous uprising of Easter Monday 1282, known as the Sicilian Vespers, dislodged Charles of Anjou, Philip III's uncle, from the island half of his kingdom of Sicily and encouraged Aragonese efforts to take it over. The pope, as suzerain of the kingdom of Sicily, was inevitably concerned, especially Martin IV, who in his earlier career as Simon de Brie had served as chancellor of France and was a fanatical French partisan. Both he and Charles of Anjou, as well as Philip's second wife, urged the French king to join the fight against Aragon. French antagonism towards the Spanish kingdom was fanned by the renewal of the Aragonese claims to lands they had once held north of the Pyrenees. Before matters had progressed to actual war Gascony became the scene of one of the most unlikely charades of the century, the so-called 'duel of Bordeaux'. Charles of Anjou had suggested that a personal combat between the competing kings might serve as a way to settle the dispute over Sicily, and its victor would be recognized as the rightful king. After some negotiation between Charles and Pedro of Aragon the date and place were set for 1 June 1283 at Bordeaux where each king would appear, supported by 100 knights. Nobody approved of this attempt to use the old method of trial by battle as a manifestation of the will of God—not the pope, not the French king, nor Edward. The English king thought it frivolous although he allowed it to take place within his duchy and ordered his seneschal to guard the appointed field and make the necessary arrangements. The contestants themselves seem to have had misgivings and took advantage of a crucial gap in the arrangements—the hour of the encounter had not been specified. Thus, King Pedro arrived at the field in the early morning of 1 June to find no opponents there, ceremoniously claimed the victory and departed hurriedly. The same game was played out by King Charles a few hours later. Nothing had been achieved but both monarchs had saved face.[14]

During this time Edward himself was absorbed in subduing the rebellion in Wales, having been obliged to call on Gascon funds and soldiers to help him,[15] while Philip undertook his fatal 'crusade' against Aragon which brought about his death in 1285.

In the spring of 1286 Edward was once more free to deal seriously with the problems of Gascony and to attempt to achieve reconciliation between Aragon and France, as well as freeing Charles of Salerno from his Aragonese captivity. In addition, the accession of the seventeen-year-old Philip the Fair to the French throne meant that Edward as duke of Aquitaine had to renew his homage for his lands in France. Since the English king intended to spend some time in Gascony—he wished to be close at hand for the delicate negotiations needed on both sides of the Pyrenees, and to deal personally with the outstanding Gascon issues—it was a suitable time to go to Paris, do homage and seek a settlement on the major Gascon problems.

The king with Queen Eleanor and a large household crossed the Channel in mid-May in a veritable flotilla and moved through northern France at a leisurely pace. Once arrived at Paris the king and his retinue put up at the abbey of Saint-Germain-des-Prés and travelled by boat to the frequent negotiating sessions at the French royal palace of the Louvre. There, on 5 June, in 'the hall next to the king's palace', Edward did homage to Philip IV. Bishop Burnell, as chancellor of England, expressed in his opening speech the doubts and hesitations among many members of Edward's council. Was it right for Edward to do homage when the treaty of 1279 had not been fulfilled and many aggressions had been committed by the French against the English territories? Edward had decided to fulfil his duty of homage, but his oath was again carefully hedged, as it had been in 1273. The king swore to become Philip's man for the lands which he held over the water, 'according to the form of the peace made between our ancestors'.[16] Philip was temporarily inclined to conciliate Edward, since the young French king was struggling to put his kingdom in order after the disastrous expedition to Aragon that had caused his father's death.

The ceremony done, negotiations continued during June and July on the three most serious problems concerning Gascony: the proliferation of appeals on the slightest pretext, the settlement concerning the disputed lands in Quercy, and the complete execution of the treaty of Amiens. In July Philip made a considerable concession regarding Gascon appeals to the French court. By a privilege granted personally to Edward I the king of France conceded that when an appellant defaulted or was convicted of an unjustified appeal neither the English king nor his representatives were to be disturbed, and they were to retain all their rights over such an appellant. As well, in case of an appeal for false judgment, the case in future was to be returned to the king-duke and his officials for three months to allow them to amend their judgment and do justice. After this interval the appellant could continue if unsatisfied.[17] Although the terms of this grant were often disregarded on both sides, it provided a possible means of improving the situation and was used fairly frequently. The other issues were dealt with in a treaty proclaimed by Philip at the beginning of August, a few days after Edward's departure. It was equally conciliatory. Philip admitted the English right to the lands of Alphonse de Poitiers in lower Saintonge, south of the Charente, and confirmed Edward's over the privileged in the dioceses of Périgueux, Limoges and Cahors who had recognized his lordship before 1279. Edward in his turn agreed to renounce his claims in Quercy, but was to be compensated with 3,000 *livres tournois* in annual rents which Philip could assign from places of his choice.[18] With these settlements agreed on, the king's stay in Gascony from August 1286 to the end of June 1289 gave him ample opportunity to deal with the Aragonese and free Charles of Salerno. It also allowed him to consider and elaborate on the spot a new and better system of administration for his difficult duchy with its many inherent problems.

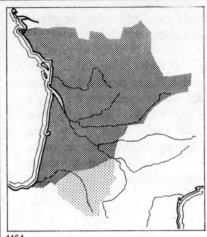

1154

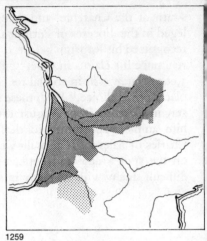

1259

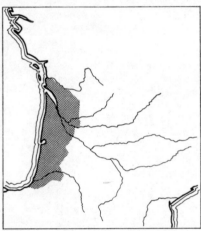

1328

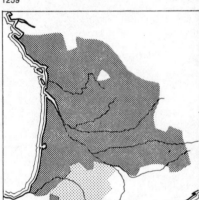

The Principality of the Black Prince

The Duchy of Aquitaine from the 12th century to the 14th century

  Lands under English rule

  Lands recognising English king as overlord

CHAPTER V

The Organization of Gascony: Officials and Their Problems

The crowning achievement of Edward's final stay in Gascony was the proclamation of a series of ordinances in 1289 which codified the responsibilities and rewards of his appointed officials in the duchy. It was a good time for such an administrative reorganization as the king and such trusted subordinates as Burnell had just had three years of personal experience of the problems. They also had before their eyes both the successes and the failures of Jean de Grailly's nine-year term as seneschal. A look at the career, the problems and the duties which faced such an official provides a useful commentary on the terms of the later ordinances.

Jean de Grailly was a Savoyard from the shores of Lake Geneva. His family had close ties with the counts of Savoy and it is likely that Jean was brought to England by Count Peter of Savoy, the English queen's uncle. By May 1262 Jean was already described as a 'knight of Edward the king's son' and had received his first grant in Gascony as well as one in England. A year later he was described as a 'counsellor of Prince Edward' and his career was well under way.[1] His background closely paralleled that of Otho de Grandison who had also been a protégé of Count Peter. Both Jean and Otho established themselves in the group of loyal young men, both knights and clerks, surrounding Edward. When he became king Edward chose his most trusted officials, diplomats and negotiators from this group, which also included such clerks as Robert Burnell and Antony Bek and English knights like Roger Leybourne, Roger Clifford, Luke Tany and Robert Tiptoft. Many of them were to share in Edward's crusading venture of 1270 which forged a close link between them and some, including Jean, kept alive over the years a genuine concern for the crusade. By the time he was first appointed seneschal in 1266 Jean had already made good use of his opportunities, having been given the castle and viscounty of Benauges. Soon after, he acquired the salt-works of Bordeaux, the town of Langon and the toll of Pierrefite on the Dordogne. Grailly joined Edward on his crusade and remained behind as seneschal of the kingdom of Jerusalem for some time after Edward's departure. He was back in Gascony by 1276 and once more concerned in its affairs. In October 1277, while in England, he warned both the king and Antony Bek, 'his very dear and special friend', of the conspiracies plotted by the viscount of Castillon. When he was reappointed as seneschal in 1278 he plunged into an active and exhausting term as the king-duke's senior official.

His duties fell into three main categories. In the first place, he was charged to keep peace and good order in the duchy, a difficult enough assignment in itself considering the inevitable struggles over disputed feudal successions, the turbulent and self-serving manoeuvres of the Gascon nobles and the simmering factionalism of the towns. This task was widened in 1279 when the French agreed to turn the Agenais over to Edward. Grailly was not only named one of the commissioners for the surrender, but was also appointed seneschal of the territory in addition to his mandate in Gascony proper. Secondly, he bore the brunt of the day-to-day encounters with the French officials on the borders or in the disputed areas of the duchy, and felt the weight of the royal ordinances which the French king insisted on applying throughout the whole kingdom. In these matters masterful delay was often the tactic invoked with Edward's approval and encouragement. In 1279, for example, Edward wrote to Jean ordering him to put off by a series of polite delaying manoeuvres any attempt by French officials to collect the *fouage*, or hearth tax, ordered by the French king. If the officials proved to have all the requisite documents giving them power to act, Jean was to claim that bad harvests and the mortality of cattle had forced Edward to put off raising the tax for a year or two. The king added that he was sending Jean suitable letters to use for either term.[2]

Another dragging controversy with the French court which required Jean's presence in Paris centred on the dating clause in the ducal charters granted in Gascony. The original clause had read *regnante Edwardo, rege Anglie*, making no mention of the French king. After a year of debate an agreement was finally reached on a new formula which was acceptable to both the French and the English: *actum fuit regnantibus Philippo rege Francie, Edwardo rege Anglie, duce Aquitanie.* The affair may sound trivial, but it had very practical ramifications as the French king threatened to disregard any charter which did not include his regnal year at the beginning of the dating clause.[3] Edward's forced compliance meant another successful assertion of the French king's superiority over his vassal, even though the vassal was also a crowned king. Such matters of dispute, as well as the numerous Gascon cases on appeal before the Parlement de Paris and the enforcement of the judgments which were finally handed down, required Grailly to spend a good deal of time in Paris, even though King Edward kept an almost permanent staff of trained law clerks there to act in his interests and keep him informed of developments.

When the carrying out of some of Edward's delicate diplomatic initiatives were added to these heavy responsibilities, it is easy to understand the distraught tone of a letter of December 1280 in which Grailly laid his difficulties before the king. He described the extra burdens imposed by the presence in Gascony of King Philip of France, the king of Castile and Charles of Salerno (son and heir of Charles of Anjou). He explained that his absences from the lands in his custody had only come about because of necessary journeys—to Paris for Parlement, to Spain to deal with the king of Castile at Fuenterrabia, and to Amiens as well as to England to be present at Edward's meeting with Philip when they came to an accord on the Agenais. All these trips had impeded his usual activities. 'No wonder,' he added, 'you hear stories about me. I do not know where to turn.' He was now being asked to go to Savoy for an accord between the counts of Savoy and Burgundy and had promised to be in Vienne on 2 January. He ended his letter with a desperate plea for funds to meet the commitments which had been forced upon him, as well as enough for the daily expenses of himself and his household so that 'your men of these parts are not thrown into a pool of pitiful poverty'.[4] His various interventions were usually well managed. He had been sent by Edward to give counsel and assistance to Marguerite of Provence in a meeting at Macon in 1281. The widowed queen wrote to her nephew of her gratitude for the help given her by Grailly and begged for his return.[5]

Grailly, as can be seen, worked hard and with considerable success during his period as seneschal. He played an important part in Edward's continuing diplomatic negotiations and was especially involved in the complex and delicate manoeuvres over

C

the succession of Bigorre 1280–85. This was a dual question: who was the rightful heir to the county? and to whom was the homage properly due? It became one of the most involved of all the tortuous feudal litigations. It had begun with Simon de Montfort's involvement with the Countess Petronilla of Bigorre when he was lieutenant in Gascony and dragged on, contested by the heirs of the countess' many marriages as well as Simon de Montfort's widow. Ultimately the title to the county came to rest in Jeanne of Navarre, wife of Philip IV, and the quarrel over homage, which had finally been adjudicated to the bishop and chapter of Le Puy, was extinguished, since by French law a husband was bound to do homage for the lands of his wife but the king could do homage to no one.[6] In the fifty years of claims, counter-claims, negotiations and legal appeals the homage of Bigorre remained a prime bone of contention between the English and French because of its strategic location. For the same reason possession of it continued to be hotly argued between the counts of Foix and Armagnac.

A perennial problem for any royal official was finding the necessary funds to support him and his household in their multifarious activities. Although Jean de Grailly had been granted a salary of £2,000 his difficulties were exacerbated by the fact that his expenses had to be approved and his wages paid by the Exchequer in London. It often refused to reimburse him for the wages of lieutenants whom he had to install when he was outside the duchy on other business for the king. Grailly fell into the trap which caught so many officials, using his position of power and prestige to increase his own personal revenues—and to cover his deficits—by high-handedness and exploitation. Finally the local complaints reached royal ears. Some time after June 1286 Jean de Grailly was removed from the office of seneschal and in the spring of 1287, when King Edward and Queen Eleanor were actually in the duchy, an inquiry was set up into his exactions and encroachments. Obviously the matter was considered serious as the commissioners included the most knowledgeable officials who were currently with the king in Gascony. There were the reliable Burnell and Grandison, the reformers of 1278, Henry de Lacy, the earl of Lincoln, as well as three Gascons: Guitard de Burg, a knight, now seneschal of Saintonge, who had occasionally served as a lieutenant for Grailly; Guillaume de la Cornere, king's clerk, lawyer and later bishop of Salisbury; and Jean Gerard, canon of Saint-Seurin Bordeaux and also a king's clerk. William of Middleton, bishop of Norwich and lawyer, as the presiding official gave the commission's decision at the end of July 1287. The commission agreed that the seneschal had misappropriated the rights and revenues of high and low justice in Saint-Emilion, Saint-Macaire, La Réole and Villefranche-de-Chapt during his term and was bound to restore them. Their sentence was later confirmed by the king. The verdict of this inquiry marked an abrupt end to Grailly's career in the English royal service. Edward did not confiscate Grailly's lands in Gascony which Jean had turned over to his son Pierre when he himself returned to Savoy, and the king ultimately applied against his debt the arrears of expenses which were owed to him. There is no record of any such coldly furious letter as Edward wrote to a subsequent seneschal, John of Havering, when it was discovered that he had been alienating royal property for his own benefit.[7] Jean was dismissed but not disgraced, though the old link between the king and his Savoyard knight was broken. Grailly appears once more on crusade as a captain of the troops of Philip the Fair and he fought in the final vain and bitter struggle for Acre. In the final mêlée he was rescued by his fellow Savoyard and companion in Edward's service, Otho de Grandison. Jean's last years were spent on the family lands in Savoy where he died in 1301 or soon after, having ensured a firm territorial base for his descendants in Gascony.[8]

Grailly's career as seneschal had been a long one, but his final failure was particularly obvious since it took place while Edward himself was in the duchy. As a royal official Grailly had proved competent and effective, but the king had not solved either the problem of adequate control or the proper payment of royal officials in this far-off corner of his realm.

The king's first concern in 1286 was to set on foot in the Agenais an inquiry about fiefs, services, rents and dues similar to the one carried out in the rest of the duchy in 1273–74, and to ensure that his new vassals took their oath of homage to him. The information garnered both from this inquiry and the one into the misgovernment of Jean de Grailly by commissioners closely linked to the king and to the administrative process was amplified by Edward's personal experience of affairs in the duchy. The king's council, under the presidency of Bishop Burnell, sat at Condom from January until May 1289, preparing a series of ordinances regulating the rights and duties of the king's officials in Gascony. When the king himself arrived at Condom in April he spent a month working with the council to add the finishing touches. The completed texts were ready by the beginning of May, but it seems probable that they were not promulgated until Edward held a final Gascon parliament at Libourne in May and June. The ordinances were designed to serve as a fitting summary of Edward's intentions for the duchy and a prelude to his imminent departure for England.

The texts, which have survived, are detailed and comprehensive and regulate the duties and rewards of officials ranging in importance from the seneschal of Gascony and the constable of Bordeaux to individual castellans and the man in charge of the royal armaments.[9] The seneschal was the ordinary representative of the king-duke's authority, so his choice and the length of his appointment were at the king's pleasure. By the ordinance of 1289 the seneschal's wages were put on a more regular basis for he was now to receive 2,000 *livres bordelais* annually, to be paid quarterly by the constable at Bordeaux. The seneschal's role was at once administrative, judicial, military and, upon occasion, diplomatic. For this difficult mixture the king needed a knight and Edward preferred to appoint someone known to him on whose ability he could count. The seneschal was almost never a Gascon, although like Jean de Grailly he might have Gascon interests. His responsibility towards the king was to give him fidelity, obedience to his commands, the maintenance of his interests and the necessary local information for intelligent royal decisions. Before the seneschal exercised authority in the duchy he was bound to take an oath of office before the people, swearing to be loyal, to do justice to all, to maintain the peace and to respect the established customs. The ordinance specified with great care the seneschal's judicial functions—the assizes which he must hold in person quarterly in the four courts of the duchy—and provided that he must always be accompanied by an adviser versed in the law and customs of the land. It also insisted on his duty to visit and inspect the sub-seneschals and all the *bailliages* and *prévôtés*—the basic administrative divisions—in his district at least once a year. To assist him in what seems to have been, even in its minimum duties, a strenuous position, he was allowed to have a permanent lieutenant for the remote district beyond the Landes.

It is interesting to note that this ordinance envisages the

seneschal's duties as primarily administrative and judicial. Financial affairs were completely outside his competence, for he was strictly forbidden to receive any of the king's moneys from any royal *bailli* except by the consent of the constable of Bordeaux and at his express mandate. Interestingly enough, too, there is no mention of the seneschal himself having any direct responsibility for pursuing Gascon interests at the court of France, only the requirement that he should appoint a competent and informed proctor. Such affairs had occupied much of the time of Jean de Grailly but it may have been the feeling of the king's council that the long absences from his duties, occasioned by the seneschal's presence in Paris, had contributed to the use of inadequate substitutes and to improper administration in the duchy. It seems likely that Edward already had in mind his intention to appoint a royal lieutenant for Gascony who would outrank the seneschal and have the powers of the king himself as long as he was in office. Such appointments were usually made when conditions seemed particularly grave and the man chosen was always an important lord, usually picked from among the king's immediate entourage. On 9 June 1289 before Edward left Libourne he appointed Maurice de Craon, his cousin and friend, to serve as king's lieutenant.[10] The clauses of the patent letter suggest that the king felt the need for a truly personal representative in Gascony to complete the reforms the ordinances envisaged and briefly 'to do every and each thing that we, if we were present in the duchy, would do for the common good, and that of each person'. He wanted to make sure that the royal officials, even the seneschal, had closer supervision than before, for he gave Maurice the power to remove the seneschal and the other officials and clerks if they were found wanting, and also to ensure that his Gascon subjects could find easy redress without the expense and labour of going to England. Since Maurice was also given 10,000 *livres tournois* for his expenses in furthering the royal business, to be paid by the constable of Bordeaux as soon as possible, it is obvious that the king reposed great confidence in his kinsman.[11] From the later record of events it would appear that the duty of representing the king-duke's interests at the highest level in Paris was confided to Maurice as well.

The second ranking official in the normal hierarchy was the constable of Bordeaux, the duchy's chief financial officer, who was also chosen by the king. He was responsible for the collection and the centralization of ducal moneys, and the payment of wages and money-fiefs. Twice yearly he was required to audit the accounts of the sub-seneschals, and those of the *baillis* and *prévôts*, as well as those of the treasurer-receiver of the Agenais. It is obvious that the constable's financial powers were great but, as a built-in check and discouragement to misappropriation, he was strictly forbidden to receive or pay out money or to hear accounts in the absence of the controller or the controller's deputy. Apart from his strictly financial duties, he had certain other functions. Once a year he was to inspect all the royal castles and fortified places in Gascony, Saintonge, and Périgord, to make sure that any necessary repairs were made and that the castles were adequately stocked with the arms and supplies needed for defence. Although not specifically mentioned in the ordinance, the constable was also responsible for the archives of the duchy kept at the Ombrière and had to provide inventories of them on taking up office and leaving it. His rate of pay was considerably below that of the seneschal, only 365 *livres bordelais* a year though augmented by an allocation of 70 *livres bordelais* for his robes and those of his deputy and clerks. Nevertheless, since the constable was normally a clerk he usually profited from various benefices which brought him regular income and marked his progress up the ladder. Richard of Havering, for example, even served as constable of Bordeaux for a second time when he was already archbishop-elect of Dublin.

The constable also had to render his accounts to his superiors and, after some experimentation, the king decided in 1293 that the constable should appear in person at the Exchequer in London once a year to present his account and have it verified. This was not always an easy matter. There had always been irregularities and delays, some due to deficiencies in the local accounts, and some to the extraordinary range of expenses which a constable might claim, though the barons of the Exchequer would regard them with great suspicion. For example, in 1290 Edward specifically instructed those delegated to hear the account of Itier Bochard of Angoulême, whom he had appointed constable the day after the appointment of Maurice de Craon, to accept all reasonable expenses. They were to accept, not only such normal matters as travel through the duchy and repairs of castles and houses but other less predictable items, such as messengers to Aragon as well as to England, presents to the king of Castile and to the king of France (for Edward's passage on his way home the previous years), the two horses and their trappings presented to the new archbishop of Bordeaux on his enthronement, and a gift of a rouncey and a robe to a specially favoured individual.[12]

The seneschal and the constable were responsible for the choice of the many lesser officials. The ordinance was specific about the structure of administration in Saintonge and the combined districts of Périgord, Quercy and Limousin, which were each to have a sub-seneschal and the necessary supporting officials. A separate ordinance for the Agenais provided a parallel structure for this newly acquired territory, with certain differences due to the varying customs. The seneschal there was to be supported by a judge, who also had lesser judges below him, and by a receiver as the finance officer. The seneschal was specifically given the power to appoint and install throughout the duchy sub-seneschals, judges, such lesser men of the legal system as the auditors of causes and the defenders of the king, who upheld the king's rights in the various courts, and the choice of proctors. As well, the seneschal was responsible for the castellans, generally chosen by him, but if chosen by the king then installed by the seneschal.

The charge of a castle and its surrounding territory was originally purely military, and always retained at least a remnant of that concern, depending on current conditions. Castellans, or constables as they were also called, were local knights and nobles. By the time of the ordinance of 1289 they had taken on more administrative functions and the terms of their appointments illustrate this. In several cases custody of a castle was combined with control of the local *bailliage* or *prévôté* as at Dax or La Réole. At Saint-Macaire the castellan, besides guarding the castle and keeping a doorman and a watchman there, collected the custom due and had the town and *bailliage* at farm. The castellan at Bayonne was responsible for the provision of a doorkeeper, a watchman and a prison guard. However, he profited from many of the town rents, such as ovens and weirs as well as the bridge tolls, but had to surrender any returns from whales (frequent in the Bay of Biscay during the middle ages), since these were reserved to the king. Because of their mixed duties castellans were generally paid a certain sum for the castle in their charge, and gained other revenues from the receipts flowing from their other responsibilities. These texts of 1289 not only specified each castellan with his duties and rewards, they also listed two technical experts. There was to be an 'engineer' to take in hand the practical supervision and keeping up to strength of all the royal castles and fortresses, and an 'artillator', a chief of armaments, who was responsible for making and distributing in suitable quantities crossbows and quarrels, bows and arrows, and lances and darts.

As befitted their distribution of responsibilities, the constable was charged with the selection of the *baillis* and *prévôts*, both almost identical lower-ranking officers in charge of a definite territory. These positions were normally farmed, that is, the official paid a lump sum for the receipts and rents from his district and then reimbursed himself by collecting in turn from those liable. Usually the appointment was for one year, but by 1289 greater emphasis was being put on keeping good *baillis* in office, and not just renewing sales or contracts to the highest bidder each year. Besides his financial duties the *bailli* or *prévôt* was responsible for local justice in civil and minor criminal cases, served as police and military officer for his district, received and executed the king's orders or those of his representatives, and tried to maintain the integrity of his domain. In all these multifarious activities he was at least aided by a clerk who was a notary public.

The constable was also responsible for the choice of his deputy, a clerk who collected the custom of Bordeaux when the constable himself could not be present. This clerk also served as the keeper of the seal for contracts in Bordeaux, though this latter rather lucrative function was soon reabsorbed by the controller, whose responsibility and reward it had previously been. The controller was primarily important because he served as a check and a guarantee for the constable's receipts and payments and his office was charged with keeping a complete counter-roll of such transactions. The holder of the office was unique, both in length of service and in the method of his nomination after 1289. In fact, in a period when seneschals and constables came and went with considerable frequency the controller served as a strong thread of continuity for the whole administrative process. For example, the term of office of Master Osbert de Baggeston, king's clerk, ran from 1280 to 1293, while three seneschals and six constables came and went. His successor as controller, Jean Guitard, a clerk and the son of a prominent bourgeois of Bordeaux who was also an enthusiastic supporter of King Edward, was nominated by the city of Bordeaux and confirmed by the king in 1303. He remained in office until his death in 1334, having served under three kings. Although the constable was likely to be a rising king's clerk who was not a native of Gascony, the lower offices in the legal, administrative and financial sectors were practically all occupied by local men. Local lords formed the class from which the greater part of the *prévôts* and *baillis* were chosen, while the most effective were often promoted to serve as sub-seneschals or lieutenants of the seneschal. Local clerks were commonly used as judges, lawyers and subordinate treasurers. These officials were the bulwark of English rule in Gascony, for their self-interest encouraged their loyalty to the king-duke.

The ordinance of 1289 highlights the importance of clerks at every level of the administrative process. Every official from the seneschal down was ordered to have his own clerk, who was preferably to be a public notary. Many of these clerks in the more important posts headed a writing office which was responsible for records and documents. Even in the middle ages incipient bureaucracy seemed to require a veritable train of papers, parchments and rolls as well as the necessary people to write, classify and preserve them. In the fourteenth century the Black Prince bought for his officials, in a single order, 100 dozen parchments, four reams of paper and a two-gallon leather bottle of ink.[13] It is amusing to see a formal royal order to a clerk who had served as a defender of the king in the Agenais insisting that he hand over to his successor 'all the instruments, writings and other muniments'—in other words, his current files—or he would be forced to do so. There were other complaints that strike a contemporary note, such as the king having heard that the clerk in charge of writing the bills of lading for the ships at Bordeaux was charging unduly high prices, damaging the sailors and merchants and disgracing the king. Inquire, wrote the king sternly, and if he is guilty name another in his place.[14]

The Gascon parliament in May and June 1289 served as a fitting conclusion to Edward's two and a half years in the duchy. It is likely that the ordinances were made public at this assembly, and certainly the king acted according to their provisions when naming officials in early June. It would appear that he was trying to give the widest publicity to what was to be expected from his nominees. The heavy emphasis on the judicial structure, the provision for a judge of appeals, and the insistence on the frequent holding of assizes in all the lands of the duchy seem a necessary part of Edward's strategy to cut down on appeals to the French court, by providing within Gascony an adequate network of courts held sufficiently frequently. As well, by carefully regulating the appointment of proctors to the French court and providing for lesser officials to deal immediately with their local French counterparts, the king showed his willingness to try and settle the mutual harassments by legal means, while still declaring his firm intention to maintain his own rights. He must have felt that the regularization of administrative matters by the provision of such a carefully ordered structure and the adequate payment of most officials would help to keep the duchy strong and prosperous.

When Edward left Gascony for the last time in the summer of 1289, after having devoted so much time and thought to the duchy's internal problems as well as to the diplomatic tangles surrounding it, he may well have hoped for a period of peaceful consolidation in his overseas land. Such hopes were soon to be proved illusory. The underlying struggle between French and English officials to extend their influence and define their frontiers at any meeting-point of their respective powers continued and inevitably involved legal confrontations, disputed appeals and the use of force. What was true on the local scale between minor officials also proved to be equally characteristic of the wider struggle between the French king and the English king-duke and their highest advisers. The time of Gascony's relatively peaceful expansion came to an end in 1289, and the legal and military conflicts which followed defined the history of the duchy of Aquitaine for the next half century. They helped to encourage the mutual distrust and growing nationalism, which was to lead into the wider series of conflicts known as the Hundred Years War.

CHAPTER VI

Conflict Begun: The War of 1294–1303

In 1286 the young Philip the Fair had shown himself conciliatory towards the English claims in Gascony, but less than ten years later he encouraged the outbreak of war over the duchy—the first military episode in a struggle which was to continue over 160 years. What caused this sudden change of policy and, having decided on war, why did Philip not push it to its logical conclusions? The war of 1294–1303 has always intrigued historians for they find it singularly difficult to explain. Certainly there had been constant difficulties between the English and French kings over the application of the treaty of 1259, but up to this time settlements had been achieved by negotiation. Now, however, Philip IV was no longer constrained by the legacy of his father's unsuccessful invasion of Aragon, and was insisting with arrogant eagerness on the full extension of his royal powers over every part of his kingdom. Undoubtedly the relative independence of Aquitaine under its king-duke was a source of considerable annoyance to him. Edward was not eager for war in Gascony at this time, since he was far too concerned with events in Scotland and the dangers in Wales. When the quarrel with the French first arose in 1293 and early 1294 he moved quickly to settle matters diplomatically, sending his younger brother to negotiate at the French court. Having accepted in good faith the settlement arrived at, Edward then saw Philip brazenly exploit the arrangement to gain complete control of the duchy by trickery. Obviously the English king could not acquiesce in such a barefaced appropriation of his inheritance. When the inevitable war broke out and the French won the first campaign why did King Philip then draw back from the total expulsion of the English from Aquitaine? To try and gain some understanding of the complex situation it is imperative to look at the causes of the quarrel and its gradual development.[1]

The pretext for Philip's actions lay in a more than usually virulent outbreak of the almost endemic piracy practised by the Breton and Norman sailors on the one hand, and by the English and Gascon, especially Bayonnais, on the other. In the middle ages bad blood between sailors was encouraged by the fact that small medieval ships felt the need to hug the coast whenever possible, and also had to land quite frequently to load provisions and fresh water. Thus the rights to convenient harbours were fiercely disputed and fighting frequently broke out. Pointe-Saint-Mathieu, on the western tip of Brittany near Brest, was one of the favoured landing-places, frequented—and disputed—by all the sailors using the Gascon or Breton route. There were several skirmishes in the summer of 1292, and in the spring of 1293 the Normans, after a preliminary success against ships going to Aquitaine, were met and destroyed by a navy from the Cinque Ports. Philip seized with avidity on this pretext of assaults upon his subjects to put forward his royal claim to all justice within the realm. He cited the attackers to appear at Périgueux before his seneschal of Périgord and ordered his agents to occupy Bordeaux, the Agenais, and the English king's lands in Périgord. In July Edward sent an embassy to Paris with powers to reconcile the differences but nothing was accomplished, since the two kings were diametrically opposed on whether the French king had a *direct* right of judgment over the inhabitants of the duchy, or merely the power to hear appeals. At the end of October Philip summoned Edward as duke to appear before the king's court in Paris in mid-January. In accordance with the necessary form of delivering the citation within the land to which it applied, the document was read publicly at Saint-Astier and Agen on 1 December and at Libourne and Saint-Emilion on 12 December, although at the latter towns the French official was forced to remain outside the gates which had been firmly closed by their English defenders.

Meanwhile Edmund of Lancaster was sent to the French court to see what compromise could be worked out. Edward's choice of negotiator underlined his view of this quarrel as one open to compromise. In naming his brother, obviously the most prestigious of possible ambassadors, he also relied on Edmund's close ties at the French court, for Edmund had chosen Blanche, a niece of Saint Louis and widow of Henry, count of Champagne and king of Navarre, as his second wife. Her daughter Jeanne, heiress to her father's rich lands, had married Philip IV before he came to the throne and was now queen of France, while the dowager queen, Marie of Brabant, was still at court and also favourable to the English connection. Edmund had maintained his footholds on each side of the Channel. Although frequently at the French court he constantly went back and forth to England and served in the early Welsh expeditions. In 1291 Edward had given him the county of Ponthieu, which Eleanor of Castile had inherited from her mother, to hold until Edward of Caernarvon came of age. It was perhaps this natural reliance on the good offices of the three queens and the atmosphere of a family conclave in which reasonable good faith could be presumed that lulled Edmund into an unwarranted trust in King Philip's unsupported word.[2]

Edward had been summoned to appear before the French king and the court of peers in mid-January. By 1 January 1294 he had given Edmund full powers to deal with the problems of Gascony and ordered his officials in the duchy to obey what Edmund should order. The settlement worked out by the queens with Edmund, and agreed to by King Philip, provided that six of the important border locations in Saintonge and the Agenais were to be handed over to Philip along with twenty guilty officials, while the French king would be allowed to put 'one man or two' in other towns and fortresses of the duchy, including Bordeaux and Bayonne.[3] In an effort to solve the problem of the dual nature of Aquitaine once and for all, a marriage treaty between Edward and Philip's sister Margaret was drawn up by which the heir of that marriage was to receive Aquitaine in perpetuity for himself and his heirs.[4] In return for all these concessions it was secretly agreed that Philip was to return the duchy to Edward within a reasonable space of time (considered to be forty days) and was to repeal the summons to Edward to appear in Paris as a disobedient vassal.[5] Walter of Guisborough, the English chronicler who has the most vivid account of the negotiations, wrote that Edmund 'in all simplicity' relied so much on the royal promise that he took no further security. Acting on the authority given him by Edward, Edmund wrote to the seneschal of the duchy to hand over seisin of the towns and agreed strongpoints to the French king's officials. Philip, however, did not content himself with the agreed one or two men but, as Guisborough succinctly phrased it, sent first a few, then many, then an army.[6] The

French king's further behaviour in refusing to carry out the secret terms which he had solemnly agreed to, denying a safe-conduct to Edward for his trip to Amiens to ratify the earlier agreements and then his condemnation of the king as a faithless vassal for non-appearance, followed by the total and immediate confiscation of his whole fief in May is 'inexplicable', even to French historians.[7] Edmund's lame apology to his brother on his return to England that he had been 'a fool or as one seduced'[8] is no doubt true, but it is hard to credit Philip with any more noble quality than crass and faithless opportunism.

This disastrous and most unexpected turn of events rallied Edward into feverish activity. He busily started to gather an army and the necessary supplies, offering pardons for those who would serve him in Gascony.[9] He held a parliament in early June and gained its support to send an embassy to France to forswear his homage and break the feudal tie to Philip. He announced his intention to reconquer Gascony and issued a series of almost draconian demands for financial aid. The king was given the power to seize all the wool, hides and fells in England; to confiscate the alien priories and use their revenues; to seize the money available in the coffers of the abbeys and priories, especially that already collected for the crusade. At a clerical convocation in September the king demanded—and received—one-half of clerical moveables while the November parliament granted a tenth of moveables from the lords and a sixth from the burgesses. This was a sudden and massive increase in financial demands. As the troops were being raised Edward appointed William Leybourne (son of Roger Leybourne, Edward's old friend and steward) as captain of the fleet. Everything was pushed to readiness for a major embarkation at Portsmouth. Edward came there himself, having called a muster of the feudal host for 1 September to sail to Gascony with him. At this crucial moment revolt again broke out in Wales and the king instead marched west with a part of the army which he had destined for Gascony. A smaller force, under the command of John of Brittany, the king's nephew, John of Saint John, who had already been named seneschal, and William Latymer finally arrived in Gascony at the end of October, having been delayed—as was so often the case—by contrary winds.

The campaign of 1294 saw some English successes. The relieving force captured Bourg and Blaye, key towns for the control of the Gironde, where their booty included 2,500 tuns of wine. Having made a vain skirmish around Bordeaux the English force continued up the Garonne, capturing Podensac and finally disembarking at Rions. The town quickly surrendered and the English were finally able to unload their horses from their prolonged confinement on board ship. Here the expedition decided on its strategy. John of Brittany and William Latymer stayed at Rions with part of the English force, while John of Saint John led the rest to Bayonne where siege was set by the end of December. The seneschal was highly regarded by the Bayonnais, whose sympathies were with the English cause, and the inhabitants soon decided to open the gates of the city to the besiegers, forcing the French garrison to take refuge in the castle. Within a week it too had capitulated and John of Saint John could then send an expedition east to capture Sorde (south of Dax) and the stronghold of Saint-Sever. This concluded the winter campaign. The recapture of Bayonne gave the English an important centre from which to carry on the war, Bourg and Blaye at least menaced French control of the Gironde, and the other regained strongholds reassured the Gascons that the English proposed to fight for the duchy.

It is a commonplace in the description of medieval military movements that spring was looked forward to as an ideal time to start campaigning—and spring comes early in the south-west of France. In March 1295 Charles of Valois, King Philip's brother, led a large French army to attack the English footholds on the Garonne. Charles had a special interest in this war. Now a mature man of twenty-five, he was felt by some of the English chroniclers to have specifically encouraged the Norman sailors' depredations and to have added venom to the quarrel as it developed. On 27 March he laid siege to Rions. The morale of the defenders was sapped by Charles' decision to hang in full view of the town walls the Gascons captured in a successful French attack on Podensac. English and Gascons within Rions fell to quarrelling and on the night of 7 April the English commanders and many of their men fled secretly to their ships. The following day Charles took the partially abandoned town by assault, pillaged it and razed its walls. He then marched south to attack Saint-Sever. The stronghold finally surrendered, but resumed its English allegiance as soon as the impatient Charles had returned to France.

While these rather inconclusive campaigns were being waged in Gascony Pope Boniface VIII was busily trying to make peace between the kings and had dispatched two cardinals to both courts with authority to conclude a treaty or at least a truce. Pious pronouncements abounded on all sides, but there was no real desire to find a solution. Edward was still very angry at Philip and was busy searching for alliances in Germany and Flanders. King Philip was equally concerned with further conquest, and fomenting trouble in Scotland and Wales. Some of his plans emerge in the extraordinary treason trial of Thomas Turberville, one of Edward's own household knights. Captured at Rions in April Thomas had agreed to spy for France to regain his freedom. He reappeared at the English court in the beginning of August, claiming to have escaped from prison—he had actually been released by his captors to pass on information and to foment trouble in Wales. In a letter to the provost of Paris, whose prisoner he had been, he warned the French that the king was sending provisions in abundance to Gascony and that another expedition was planned, led by the king's brother and the earl of Lincoln. Thomas had made some contact with the Welsh who might be incited to revolt, although he had apparently been unable to carry out fully his errand to Morgan, one of the few surviving rebel leaders in Wales. In addition, he informed the French that the English sea defences were poor—little watch was kept towards the south and the Isle of Wight had no garrison. His report was dispatched to France around 7 August and he may have received a reply. Towards the end of September Turberville was overcome by fear of discovery and fled from the king's court, only to be captured within two days while he was trying to escape to Wales. It appears that his treason was unveiled by the messenger he had chosen to carry his letter to France, who informed upon Thomas and brought about his pursuit and arrest.

The trial took place in the great hall of Westminster on 8 October and was rapidly followed by a public and ignominious execution. The sentence of the court ran that he was to be drawn and hung and that his body was to be left to hang 'as long as anything of him can remain'.[10] In the thirteenth century treason trials were rare and this case seems to have become very much of a *cause célèbre*, perhaps because the widest publicity was considered advantageous at that moment. The summons for the famous parliament of 1295 had just been issued and the writs of summons

68

to the prelates were prefaced by an attack on the iniquities of the French king who proposed, Edward wrote, 'if the power of his evil concept corresponded to his detestable design (which may God avert) to totally obliterate the English race from the earth'.[11] Turberville's treason had been one of the iniquities planned by the French king and the corpse hanging from its chain at Smithfield could bear grisly witness to the members of the realm gathered in parliament of the dangers to be guarded against and to what ends they might lead.[12] The bitterness expressed by Edward against the French king seems to mark the beginning of anti-French feeling in the court. Edward's resentment was certainly sparked by Philip's legalistic trickery and perhaps by the suborning of one of his own household but the bad feeling lingered. Distrust and dislike of the French festered among such influential classes as the royal clerks, who were the constant element in the never-ending legal discussions with the French, and the fiercely xenophobic merchants of London. The preamble of 1295 marked the first ripple of the vigorous anti-foreign, and especially anti-French, sentiment which the Hundred Years War developed into full flood.

Despite the royal warnings, parliament's response to the king's demands for money was rather grudging. The lay lords offered an eleventh, the burgesses a seventh, while the clergy suggested a tenth. Edward was not pleased, although there was sufficient to raise and send a further expedition to Gascony under the leadership of Edmund of Lancaster and the earl of Lincoln. Its departure was delayed to the end of January by Edmund's illness, only reaching the Gironde in early March. The force landed on the left bank of the Gironde, captured Lesparre in the Médoc, once more skirmished ineffectively outside Bordeaux and then moved upstream to attack Langon. Although the inhabitants opened the town to them the French garrison in the tower held out strongly and were reinforced by Robert of Artois, commander of a new French army. The discouraged English went on towards Bayonne, their one sure stronghold in the south, where Edmund of Lancaster died at the beginning of June. Edmund had always been a most faithful supporter of his brother, though never a very forceful personality, and his death meant still another break in Edward's group of intimates and advisers. The earl of Lincoln took over the command of the force which attempted a futile seven-week siege of Dax, but was forced to return to Bayonne by French concentration at nearby Mont-de-Marsan. Since King Edward and all the major English military forces were concentrated on the campaign in Scotland the small army in Gascony did little more than provide a modest token of the English concern for their continued possession of the duchy.

Meanwhile, Edward's relations with the English lords, both lay and spiritual, were becoming more and more irritable. The king, once he felt that the Scottish menace had been crushed for the time being, was anxious to raise further subsidies to wage war more actively in Gascony. The Gascon war was not popular with his subjects—so far it had brought them heavy financial impositions with no apparent result—and the duchy's fate touched them less closely than the struggles in Scotland or Wales. At the November parliament of 1296 the clergy withdrew behind the recently proclaimed bull of Boniface VIII, *Clericis Laicos*, and refused to give further aid for Gascony, claiming that they could only do so with the permission of the pope. The lay representatives grudgingly agreed to a twelfth and an eighth. The king was infuriated and when the clerics continued their opposition in January 1297 he angrily withdrew the royal protection from them. Since this implied that any injury done to the clergy would have no redress in the royal courts it was an open invitation to the robbery and pillage of clerics and their goods.[13] Gradually a compromise was worked out, although it took some time to bring the angry Edward and the determined archbishop of Canterbury, who was the focus of the clerical opposition, to a reconciliation.

Having thus alienated the clerics and not obtained his desired funds, the king turned to his barons at a parliament on 24 February. He requested them to cross to Gascony, an expedition which seemed to offer little profit or glory and from which they began to excuse themselves. Edward's temper exploded and he threatened them with the duty to go as part of their feudal service, or he would give their lands to those who were willing. The earl marshal, Roger Bigod, spoke up, insisting that his office only required him to lead the host when the king himself was in command and that he did not wish to go without him. The king's strategy had been to send an expeditionary force to Gascony but to lead a force himself to Flanders, so that French interests would be threatened on two fronts. Infuriated, Edward threatened his recalcitrant baron: 'By God, Earl, you shall either go or hang.' The earl marshal's response was swift and equally vigorous: 'By the same oath, O King, I will neither go nor will I hang,' and without seeking leave from the king he withdrew from the meeting.[14] Edward, in this parliament and in his actions during the spring and summer, sparked a major confrontation with the most important elements of his realm. His effort to require feudal military service for his overseas campaigns collapsed in face of their unpopularity. Edward was forced to agree that those who went abroad would only have to go at the expense of the king and on his wages. Once more the affairs of Gascony— and the Flemish expedition which had originally been designed to serve as extra pressure to aid Gascony—helped to develop English domestic policy by the pressure it put on English finances and administrative structures.

Meanwhile the Gascon fighting had trailed off in an embarrassing defeat. In January 1297 a relieving expedition sent out from Bayonne was trapped near Bonnegarde. Many English were killed and John of Saint John, the seneschal, was captured, while supplies destined for the English fortresses fell into the hands of the French. The monastic chronicler recounting this costly loss found artistic satisfaction in depicting it as suitable divine punishment for the king's oppression of the clergy, and pointed out with considerable care that it happened on the very day on which his harsh edict of confiscation was promulgated—a clear case of miraculous involvement.[15] Whether or not divine assistance was needed to account for military incompetence the result was discouraging and this skirmish proved to be the final Gascon military operation of the war.

The course of events in the summer of 1297 also proved disappointing for Philip for the French king was disappointed in his belief that a successful campaign in Flanders, now allied to England, would be easy. Since Flanders was of more immediate importance to French policy than Aquitaine, both kings became more willing to listen to the continuing pressure towards peace, or at least truce, brought to bear by the pope and the negotiating cardinals. By 7 October a truce had been agreed on and proclaimed at Vyve-Saint-Bavon on the basis of each side holding what it possessed on the day the truce came into force. It was to apply to both Flanders and Aquitaine and to bind both kings and their respective allies.[16] Originally designed to last for only three months it marked the end of the hostilities and was renewed until the final conclusion of peace in 1303. Agreement was reached that all matters at dispute between the two kings were to be submitted to the arbitration of Pope Boniface VIII, acting not as pope but in his private person, as Benedict Caetani.

The arbitration brought together at the Curia the proctors and legists for both the English and the French, and also for such interested subordinate parties as the count of Flanders. We are fortunate to have some of the direct reports on the progress of these complex and fiercely contested negotiations which lend considerable interest to the relatively bland terms of the arbitration itself. On the English side there is the record of the important and secret instructions for the defence of the English cause sent to Edward's representatives at Rome soon after the discussions had begun.[17] There is also a fascinating account of a meeting at Anagni, in early August of the Jubilee Year of 1300, between the pope and the English ambassadors, headed by John of Pontissara, the bishop of Winchester, in which the pope seems to have spoken most frankly, voicing his opinion of the French legists such as Flote who were active in putting forward Philip's case.[18]

There was intense activity by the English jurists and diplomats between the signing of the truce and the final peace of 1303 and it is possible to trace the activities and importance of such men as Raymond de Ferrières and Philip Martel who provided the brief for the more prestigious ambassadors to argue. Master Raymond de Ferrières was a Gascon, trained in law, who had served as a king's clerk for more than twenty years, had been a royal councillor in Gascony and served as Edward's proctor at the Parlement de Paris in the contentious years of 1294–98. He had been well rewarded with benefices both in Gascony and England, and received an annual fee of up to 250 *livres tournois*.[19] Master Philip Martel was a professor of civil law, a king's clerk, and became particularly concerned with Gascon matters as the first custodian of the processes and memoranda of the king touching the duchy of Aquitaine. Until his death in 1306 he worked hard to achieve one of two things: either the total denunciation of the treaty of 1259, or, if the king of France was willing to fully execute the terms of the treaties, then to re-establish Gascony and the other lands of the duchy in their ancient statutes and liberties.

The argument of 1298 was based primarily on the memorandum prepared by Master Raymond de Ferrières and sent to the king's council in England.[20] The English argument struck at the very base of the French claims by stating that the title of duke of Aquitaine, or Guyenne in its French form, was applied to an artificial grouping of lands of which Gascony was not even an integral part. The duchy was a fief of the king of France but only the northern dioceses of Limoges, Cahors, and Périgueux belonged to it. Gascony was in reality an allod, that is, land freely *owned*, not held for any homage, service or feudal due, and the Agenais was its dependency. The treaty of 1259, it continued, had no juridical value since the French king could not make a fief out of an allod. This line was difficult to support, as on many occasions the English king himself had turned the allods of his Gascon subjects into fiefs. As a second and stronger line of defence it was argued that the treaty of 1259 was a contract, and therefore was only binding on one party if it was observed by the other. Since the French king had not obeyed his obligations, Edward was not bound to his. Consequently the English king was not a vassal of the French king and thus could not commit treason. If the French king had ever had possession of the fiefs he had lost it by not living up to the terms of the contract. Homage had been conditional and the conditions had not been fulfilled. These points appear to have been put to the cardinals working for the truce as well as to the pope during the discussion before Boniface handed down his sentence. The arguments were cogent ones and rested on accepted principles of feudal law, but the important fact was that Edward had lost the war and King Philip was in *de facto* possession of almost the whole duchy. Edward was willing to make compromises in cession of territory to try and free the remnant of his duchy from any homage or feudal service, and suggested several ways of achieving this. Philip, on the other hand, also put forward a very extreme case and appears to have brought a charge of treason against Edward for having waged open war against him since 1294, and demanded that, as a contumacious vassal, the proper penalty should be applied, i.e., he should be condemned to forfeit his fief. Such a move would provide the French king with full legal title to the fief he had only officially sequestrated for non-appearance at court.

Pope Boniface was in an awkward position, as he made very clear in his discussions with the English in 1300. The power and prestige of Philip the Fair were at their apogee and the pope was already beginning to be enmeshed in the conflict over the extent of papal authority, which was to culminate in the scandalous attack on his person at Anagni in 1303. In July 1298 Boniface opted for the safe decision, a return to the *status quo* before the outbreak of hostilities. The lands of both sides were to be delivered into the hands of the pope until a mutual agreement could be worked out, or a new arbitral sentence was provided to settle the rightful lord. The English king was to restore the ships and goods seized in the original conflicts which had sparked the war. Peace was to be sealed by the arrangement of two marriages: one of King Edward to Margaret, Philip's young sister, to take place at once; and a future wedding of Edward of Caernarvon to Isabella, Philip's infant daughter. A so-called peace of Montreuil in May 1299 merely put the marriage alliances into legal form and arrived at certain tentative agreements about dower.[21] The wedding of the sixty-year-old king to his young bride took place in Canterbury in September. Although it did not in any way affect the continuing impasse between the English and French in Gascony, the marriage is a pleasant oasis in the middle of so much dispute and chicanery and seems to have brought considerable pleasure to Edward. Some of his personal letters to the young queen (and to her physician when she came down with the measles) show a vigorous concern for her health and a real, if brusque, affection for 'our dear companion'. His youngest daughter Eleanor, born the year before his death, obviously held a special place in his affections for, in a letter to Margery de Haustede who was in charge of the children, he complained that, although he had heard from others, she had sent him no news and that 'he trusted her reports more'. He was particularly anxious that she should watch Eleanor, then only five months old, with great care and let him know what she thought of her.[22]

By 1300 Pope Boniface was quite outspoken—at least to the English ambassadors—on his fear of the French and their covetousness, remarking that 'He who has business with the French ought to take great care, for he who has business with the French has business with the devil'.[23] The pope told the English how he had reproached Pierre Flote with the apparent French intention to expel the English king from all his possessions in France. Flote had agreed with a smile that this was certainly true and the French clerks insisted that their king would not be willing to let the lands go for anything. In fact this refusal of the

French king to obey the terms of the papal arbitration and deliver lands he held in Gascony to the pope's hands was a deliberate tactic, for during the long-dragged-out negotiations they took the profits of the Gascon lands and tried to reinforce their political presence there. Edward had been impelled throughout this whole affair by his need for a settlement in Gascony, given his problems in both Scotland and Wales. It was not until 1302 that Philip felt equally constrained by his major defeat at Courtrai at the hands of the Flemings. The peace treaty of 1303, agreed to at Paris on 20 May and ratified by Edward on 10 July at Perth, provided for the return of the duchy in its entirety to Edward while the earl of Lincoln, one of the negotiators, took the oath of fealty as proxy for the king. The preamble, in the usual rather high-flown manner, suggested that the arranged marriages would encourage firm alliance and mutual love between them, so that both kings might be better friends and 'all rancours, injuries, ill-will and hatreds be put away, remitted and pardoned on one side and the other'.[24]

The war had come to an end, influenced in its waging and its settlement by matters extraneous to Gascony, and military peace, though not an end to legal disputation, had come to the embattled duchy. The restitution of Gascony to the king-duke was put into effect by a joint itinerary of English and French commissioners—a procedure used again after the Treaty of Brétigny in 1360—but the French officials encouraged delay. The problems of the earl of Lincoln and Otho de Grandison as the English commissioners were also made more difficult by the initiative of local nobles who had benefited by the general dislocation to take over powers and revenues they coveted. Most of the required fortresses were returned, though the French king attempted to hold on to Mauléon. Nevertheless by the end of 1303 the process of English administrative reorganization in the duchy was reasonably well advanced. English authority was not completely re-established in such outlying districts as the Agenais and the three dioceses whose attachment to the English connection had been brief. The debts incurred for the war overloaded the local finances and made administration particularly difficult. Most importantly the causes of the conflict had not been solved, but were to lead to further extensive and fruitless legal negotiations and ultimately to another war.

What was the real importance of this prolonged but singularly inconclusive incident? From the military historian's point of view it was almost a non-existent war for it had no real battles, no major sieges. Although the French gained parts of the duchy, such as Bordeaux, they were never again to hold until the final collapse of the mid-fifteenth century, they did so by trickery rather than military force. However, this period of hostilities illustrated the enormous change in the pattern of military deployment and finance since the last open hostilities between England and France more than fifty years before.[25] The centralized power of both monarchies had grown immensely over the course of the century and so had the means of raising revenue. The old feudal concept of unpaid military service owed to one's lord for a set number of days as part of the requirement of land-holding had so weakened that it had to be replaced by a system of forces raised and paid for specific periods. The result was a more willing and professional army which made war an extremely costly business. Even the French king's revenue, approximately four times that received by the English king, was not enough to cover the large new expenses. Both kings took refuge in various fiscal expedients: assorted taxes and levies, loans and planned inflation of the currency. Edward's methods included very heavy levies on the clergy, customs duties especially on wool, annual taxes on personal property, and heavy borrowing. Certainly the bankruptcy of the Italian banking family, the Riccardi, was contributed to by the immensity of Edward's demands and the delay in royal repayments. Loans from one's subjects had ultimately to be repaid if their loyalty was to remain constant. For example, the citizens of Bayonne had loaned large sums to John of Brittany and the earl of Lincoln for the campaigns they waged in Gascony and their own expenses. The bourgeois were ultimately assigned in repayment the revenues of the custom on wool, hides and wool fells in certain major English ports and ended with a deficit of only £56 on loans of over £50,000.[26]

Most of the money raised by all these expedients went into the payment of the fighting men's wages. For the first time it became profitable for the upper classes and mounted men-at-arms to go to war. This development (to become so much more visible in the Hundred Years War for which this minor conflict was a kind of opening salvo) was particularly obvious in Gascony. There a singularly poverty-stricken minor nobility found war, paid service, and the occasional pensions or rewards for loyalty—or for changing sides—were much richer alternatives than trying to live off their fragmented and frequently infertile lordships. Thus the effect of these massive efforts to raise money for the conduct of the war, which despite its minor conflicts required a large number of troops in the field for considerable periods of time, was to encourage a considerable redistribution of income. Money flowed from the merchants, the producers of such major crops as wool, and the townspeople to the great lords, whose rates of military pay were very generous, as well as the minor lords and mounted men-at-arms. In England's case, it meant that much of the money raised for the war in Aquitaine profited Gascony rather than England. This imbalance, caused by the fact that the greater number of soldiers raised for the campaigns were themselves Gascons and that English soldiers sent to the duchy tended to spend their wages there, was heightened by the amount of provisions that had to be sent out of England to Gascony. These were required both for the troops and for the maintenance of the beleaguered towns of Bourg, Blaye and Bayonne. As well, the king was bound by the terms of his agreements to replace horses lost in his service, and that too meant a disproportionate investment in Gascon and Spanish horses procurable in Aquitaine. Wages paid were not restricted to soldiers fighting on land. The necessity for transportation of troops by ship to Gascony and the number of naval skirmishes meant wages for sailors, for Edward normally impressed merchant ships both for transportation and as convoys while providing fighting men to man them. The concept of an actual navy at the king's command was still remote, but this minor campaign saw the first appointment of a captain of the English ships at sea. The captain was soon to be transformed into an admiral and to become a vital element in English military structure.

CHAPTER VII

The Years of Prosperity

The frequent military campaigns and the continual legal quarrels over the status of Gascony have attracted the most attention and make it easy to forget that during the first half of the fourteenth century—before the ravages of war and plague became too ruinous—the duchy of Aquitaine was also an important commercial centre astride several major trade routes. It did business with the Iberian peninsula as well as England, Flanders as well as France, and was both populous and thriving. The continued maintenance of English rule in the duchy required local support as well as military forces from England. The Gascon towns, especially Bordeaux and Bayonne, were the cornerstone of the Gascon attachment to the English crown, which provided them with communal liberties and the surest market for their major export, wine. Any discussion of English Gascony must recognize the importance of this commercial link and its influence on the continuing tug of war between English and French.

The rural population of English Aquitaine in 1315 appears to have been in the neighbourhood of 600,000–650,000. Bordeaux, the administrative and commercial capital, is estimated to have had some 30,000 inhabitants at this time—roughly comparable to Toulouse or Montpellier and probably larger than London. No other city in the duchy could match her in population or in importance. Bayonne had a population of perhaps 8,000 while such secondary towns as La Réole, Libourne and Bazas barely touched 2,500 inhabitants each.[1] The fourteenth-century seal of Bordeaux suggests the preponderant political and commercial elements. The three leopards of England stretch over a representation of the bell-tower of Saint-Eloi, home of the great bell which represented the commune's liberties and summoned its citizens. At the foot of the tower appears the river bearing a moon, the heraldic representation of Bordeaux's harbour (still known as

La Lune from its shape), the foundation of its prosperity. Increases in population during the thirteenth century had caused an overflow into the suburbs and new walls were needed for protection. The enormous task of building more than three miles of wall was begun before the end of the century and continued until the end of Edward II's reign. It was an expensive business. During the French occupation Philip IV ordered a tax levied on all goods brought into the city, with the proceeds to be applied to the fortifications. After the English return the king-duke's officials attempted to collect the same tax over the objections of the merchants. The new walls quadrupled the area of the city and were sufficient for Bordeaux's development until the eighteenth century. Constructed to parallel the older walls of the original centre and the suburb of Saint-Eloi previously incorporated into the city, they stretched for more than a mile along the river to take in the abbey of Sainte-Croix and its dependencies at their southern tip. They then swung north and west to enclose Sainte-Eulalie and met and paralleled the old walls at the archbishop's palace. A smaller extension on the north enclosed the Dominican convent.[2]

Looking from the walls punctuated by their square tower gates, the observer would see the forest lying close to the city in almost all directions though clearings with vines and the occasional new town had begun to dot the horizon. To the north and north-west lay the marshes which separated Saint-Seurin and its *sauveté* from the city. Within the walls were the towers and spires of some twenty churches and the onlooker could see the work in progress on the cathedral of Saint-André, reflecting the grandiose ideas of its archbishop become pope. The archbishop's palace adjoined the west end of the cathedral with its entrance gate perpendicular to the cathedral's royal north door. A large court lay between the cathedral and the main building of the palace, while beyond the ramparts stretched an ample garden with vines as well as fruits and vegetables.[3] No wonder visiting royal personages and commanders preferred its open situation to the more crowded confines of the bustling Ombrière, the castle of Bordeaux.

The Ombrière was the most important secular building in the city. It overlooked the harbour at the south-east corner of the original wall and was the centre of ducal administration, the residence of the constable, a prison and arsenal. During the

French occupation a new great hall was begun and completed by the English on their return. Its entrance door, which was approached by a vaulted staircase, was crowned by a rose window and opened into an enormous space divided into two halls. The returning English officials felt the need for further modernization. The old rectangular donjon was preserved but a new tower was built during Edward II's reign. A two-storey vaulted construction, it resembled the tower-houses being built in England. Within this complex and crowded space were located the chamber of the exchequer and accounts, the hall of the court of Gascony, the mint for coining the duchy's money and the chapel with its altars to Edward the Confessor and Thomas Becket. The accounts provide occasional glimpses of the varied concerns and developments. By 1339–40 the chamber of accounts had acquired two calculators with their covering cloth, made in the castle to the model of those in the exchequer at London.

At the same time, realizing that trouble loomed ahead, provisions and the stock of military supplies had been built up. Edward I's ordinance had provided for a chief of armaments to be situated in the castle. In 1332 this office was held by a Genoese, renowned throughout Europe for their knowledge of weapons. Either he or his successor established the first primitive cannons at Bordeaux, mentioned in the accounts of 1336. A skilled iron-smith, also from Genoa, was hired to work in the castle for three years, making quarrels and bolts for the crossbows and guns belonging to all the fortified places in the duchy. In view of an expected French invasion the chief of armaments was also ordered to reinforce Saint-Macaire with every variety of 'engine', as well as saltpetre and active sulphur for gunpowder. He also made sure there were sufficient banners for any fighting forces—fifteen with the arms of Saint George and six with the arms of the King of England.[4] In the same tradition as the royal menagerie at the Tower of London the Ombrière had a lion belonging to the Black Prince when he was in Gascony. Falcons appear to have been bought in Gascony, complete with canvas travelling cases, and undoubtedly formed part of the establishment of any great lord, though some were sent back to England to the king.[5] The castle was the bustling official nerve centre of English government in the duchy. Along the city's narrow streets clustered the houses of the inhabitants. Small hovels alternated with the houses of wealthy merchants and the town houses of such important barons as the Graillys or ecclesiastics such as the bishop of Bazas.

After the treaty of 1303 the primary need for the duchy was the restoration of order and the reimposition of the English administration. Bordeaux had to be considered first as its inhabitants had anticipated the slow workings of the peace negotiators. In early January 1303 Arnaud Cailhau led an insurrection which succeeded in chasing the French officials from the city. The French chronicler, Guillaume de Nangis, attributes this 'presumption and temerity' to the 'ineffective' return of the French from Flanders (in blunter terms, to their disastrous defeat at Courtrai).[6] The period of French occupation had followed on a quarrel between the city and the English seneschal of Gascony, John of Havering, who had neglected to take the customary oath to respect the city's privileges before exercising his office. One faction had entered an appeal to the French court, and in retaliation, King Edward had seized and confiscated the wines arriving in England from the current vintage. The quarrel dragged on for two years and was settled in Edward's favour in 1291, but the struggles and unhealed rancours may have encouraged French optimism for an easy acceptance of their rule. However, despite several conciliatory moves by Philip the Fair to confirm Bordeaux's privileges, French occupation had been precarious and unpopular. In order to quench possible English sympathy within the city during the active phase of the war (1294–96) hostages had been sent to French territory and imprisoned there, mainly in Toulouse and Carcassonne. It appears obvious from the lists, carefully preserved in the municipal archives,[7] that the victims were chosen indiscriminately among the most important Bordeaux families and that they were held in extremely harsh conditions, for some 20 per cent died in exile. News of their sad state continued to filter back to the city and helped to rouse feelings against the French control which only waited for a suitable moment to explode. The uprising of 1303 resulted in short-lived independence for the commune, but it made little difficulty in returning to its original allegiance to the English king after the peace treaty was finally ratified.

The scourge of factional warfare within Bordeaux remained after the peace. This was nothing new, for over the years Simon de Montfort, Henry III and the young Edward had all tried to control it with only relative success. The city continued to be racked by conflict between the opposing parties of the Colom and the Soler who had been enemies for eighty years. They had now been joined by the Cailhau, also divided into two branches, one of which favoured the Colom and the other the Soler. Lesser families attached themselves to one or the other and violence was frequent. The aim was to control the municipal government made up of the mayor and the jurade, or body of jurats. At this time the mayor, although usually a Bordelais, was appointed by the English king. The jurats, who during most of the fourteenth century numbered twenty-four, were chosen from the well-to-do citizens born and living in Bordeaux and were the most important men of the town. Since they picked their own successors when they left office after a year, the possibility of a closed oligarchy was always present. The prize of such office was control of the municipal seal and thus access to the communal funds. After his success as the leader of the insurrection against the French, Arnaud Cailhau was named mayor by the English and controlled the office for five years. In 1308 he was succeeded by Pierre Cailhau, his relative and rival, a move which endangered the Colom supremacy in the jurade. In order to maintain their own position the Colom took advantage of the English absorption in Scotland and the relative weakness of the seneschal to appeal to the king of France.

This process of bitter factional dispute, frivolous appeal to the French and the consequent dispatch of French officials to safeguard the persons and properties of the appellants, thus disrupting English authority, continued for some twenty years and encouraged constant upheaval in Bordeaux. Edward II's reform commission of 1310 made little headway. It is easy to sympathize with the jurats and commune when they wrote to the English king during an attempt at reform in 1311 describing their difficulties:

> Be it known that since the last war all your land of Gascony, and above all your city of Bordeaux, whether by an insufficiency of your officials, or by the presumptuous insubordination of the nobles and the powerful men of the country, has endured a government not only bad but detestable.

They went on to list the 'innumerable murders, homicides, rapes, rapine and other most wicked evils' arising from the conflict between the Colom and Soler factions.[8] The complaint of Elie

Sauciprède to the Parlement de Paris suggests in vivid terms the possible excesses. Elie, a bourgeois of Bordeaux who had also served as a sergeant of the king of France, accused Arnaud Cailhau of having robbed French merchants of more than £30,000 —killing some, imprisoning others, and sending the survivors away in their shirts; of having killed a lawyer of the French king after tearing out his tongue; and of having thrown an unfortunate messenger out the window in fury at his appearance with a French summons for the English seneschal. When Elie himself appealed to the French king Arnaud menaced him and had him banished from Bordeaux 'against God, law and custom'.[9] Elie wanted to challenge Arnaud to a judicial duel. No legal solution was arrived at since Sauciprède was assassinated and Jean Colom and his partisans were thought guilty of it. The appointment of Oliver Ingham as seneschal in 1331 put an end to the worst of the factionalism as Oliver was a strong and able administrator. He was aided in his efforts by the large group of Bordeaux merchants who were primarily interested in improving their commercial position, and thus provided a neutral party.

Despite turbulence, political opportunism and upheaval, the early fourteenth century was a time of great commercial prosperity for Bordeaux, based primarily on the export of its wine. The realistic merchants recognized the value of the English connection which provided them with a secure and eager market for their wine, one in which there was little competition. France could offer no such benefit. This attraction to England was also encouraged by the number of Gascon merchants who spent considerable time in English ports as a natural consequence of the pattern of the wine trade. During the war many Gascon merchants had found themselves forced to remain in England by the exigencies of the war, and they were joined by a considerable number of Gascon lords who had lost their lands by the French occupation and depended rather precariously on the generosity of the royal purse. The king attempted, not always successfully, to exploit these links, perhaps most notably in the case of Amanieu d'Albret, a royal relative and leading noble in Gascony who was the recipient of many valuable royal favours. Unfortunately, loyalty among certain Gascon nobles tended to be based more on present profit than gratitude for past favours.

The towns, however, were a different matter. Bayonne had proved its importance and loyalty during the recent war. Although outstripped as a port by Bordeaux, since the constant shifting of the course of the Adour meant a less consistent harbour, Bayonne was extremely important in the carrying trade to Spain, as well as England and Flanders, and distributed a considerable range of merchandise as well as building and manning ships. Nevertheless, it was the export of wine, primarily through Bordeaux, that was not only the basis of that city's prosperity but also the solid cornerstone of ducal revenues. The customs duties on wine, payable at Bordeaux, formed the major part of the revenues collected by the constable of Bordeaux. The great custom on wine for export was collected from all except the citizens of Bordeaux in regard to wine from their local vineyards, although certain religious houses and nobles had also gained exemption from it. The *issac*, or petty custom, was levied on all wines sold within Bordeaux and its *banlieue* by growers and merchants who were not its citizens. In the thirteenth century the wines that came down from the Haut Pays, that is the country upstream from the Bordelais, had been penalized in favour of Bordeaux. They not only paid the higher custom but also could not be sold until after mid-November when the Bordeaux wine growers had already had the opportunity to dispose of their crop at the best prices.

As the export of wine increased, merchants from as far away as Toulouse, Rabastens and Montauban sought a more equitable share in this valuable trade. A commercial treaty, which was worked out by Jean de Grailly and ratified by Edward in 1285, provided for a fixed duty of 5s. 6d. *tournois* on wine exported or sold outside the district of Bordeaux. If they sold within the city or its district they had to pay the *issac* as well.[10] More and more merchants took advantage of these clauses to become thus 'privileged', ensuring a steady flow of wine from French as well as English lands down the network of tributaries that led into the Dordogne and the Garonne. The prime scholar of the Gascon wine trade has shown that in its peak year, 1308–09, nearly 103,000 tuns were exported. Of this vast amount, some 39,000 tuns came from the privileged merchants of the Haut Pays— only slightly less than the combined total of 31,000 tuns from the Bordelais and the non-privileged Haut Pays and the slightly more than 12,000 tuns from the burgesses, nobles, and ecclesiastics exempt from custom. Some 12,000 tuns were loaded at the Gironde ports downstream from Bordeaux and another 9,000 tuns at Libourne. Between 1305 and 1330 the level of exports was very high, for the average for the years for which totals are available is close to 85,000 tuns. This meant valuable revenues for the English king.[11]

It is impossible to estimate the exact amount of Gascon wines going directly to England, though it was certainly a sizeable percentage of the exports, and the king also benefited from a custom on it when it was landed in England. The old royal right of prise, that is, the taking of two tuns from each loaded ship at a fixed sum, no matter what the current price, was superseded in 1302 by the terms of a charter granted to the Gascon merchants. A new tax of 2s. a tun was imposed, but all others, including the prise, were dropped. In return for the acceptance of this custom the Gascon merchants doing business in England were given personal protection and granted extraordinary privileges. They had already been granted the privilege of remaining in England for three months instead of the usual forty days, now they could live where they pleased, without having to lodge with local citizens as most aliens were forced to do. They could sell wholesale to any citizen or foreign merchant in the kingdom, and were given legal protection for their contracts, a guarantee of speedy justice and assurance of Gascon representation on any inquest.[12] The king in return expected absolute fidelity from them. Despite the reiterated royal favours, local communities, jealous of their own rights and seeking commercial advantage, often infringed their privileges.

Several hundred Gascons came to England each year on business connected with wine—great merchants, agents, ship captains —and they were to be met in all parts of the kingdom, at all the great fairs and all the important ports. London was at this time the principal centre of Gascon commerce and some Gascon merchants even had permanent homes there, while a fortunate few were admitted as citizens. There was also an important Gascon community at Sandwich, where four of its members brought in 1,000 tuns of wine a year. Bristol developed its importance for the Gascon trade during the course of the century. In these ports the merchant could rent a warehouse for storing and selling his wine for periods as short as a week or as long as three months, although some had permanent installations. These warehouses proved to be more than mere business establishments. They were temporary enclaves where Gascons ate, slept, and entertained their friends and fellow-countrymen. Such concentration, especially in the anti-foreign atmosphere of fourteenth-century England, aroused local suspicion, heightened by the problem of language. Gascon was not easily intelligible to the average Englishman, not even to those who knew Anglo-Norman, and most merchants tended to rely on bilingual couriers to ease this difficulty. The undercurrent of anti-foreign feeling is obvious in London's excuse for not sending the service requested by the king in 1296. It felt its efforts were required to guard the city from the aliens in its midst, those 'of divers tongues from abroad who pretend to be your friends and ours, and whom we do not trust'.[13]

The possible commercial profits, as well as this latent hostility, encouraged English merchants to challenge the privileged Gascons. They began to go in person to Gascony to arrange the shipping of the wines they had bought in the duchy and occasionally to maintain a factor there. The shift in the balance was rapid. At the beginning of the century, the non-Gascon merchants had no more than 25 per cent of the trade, while by 1330 the citizens of London alone imported as much each year as the whole group of Gascons.[14] The wine merchants were not the greatest capitalists of their time and individuals did not normally handle very large quantities. Nevertheless they engaged very regularly in a business which called for experience and expert knowledge, and were members of a closely-knit community where prestige and reputation were important factors. They even made allowance for specialized markets, as in the case of the Gascon wine merchant who made a contract with Master Elias and another Jew of London for seven tuns of wine 'made according to the Jewish rite', for which they had paid in advance.[15] Such a merchant was forced to deal with large sums—his profits were high and so were his risks. Usually required to extend credit, he often had difficulty in persuading his clients, even the king, to settle their debts with any promptness. During the course of the century both military campaigns and the effects of plague were added to the natural hazards of occasional bad seasons for the vintage. All helped to reduce sharply the quantity of wine exported from Bordeaux, but made the trade much richer as the price of wine continued to rise. It was inflated not only by relative scarcity, but also by huge increases in freight costs, as the valuable cargoes had to be protected by convoys and armed guards against marauding navies and pirates.

Trade was not only one way. Gascony was also a valuable market for English cloth, leather and above all for grain, as she was not self-sustaining. The profits to be made from wine encouraged everyone from the archbishop to the smallest tenant to plant all possible land to the vine. It served as an inducement to clear the forests which abounded in Entre-deux-Mers and near Bordeaux, for vines provided a quick cash crop, even if the grants often included some form of sharecropping. For example, one of Edward's last concessions before he left the duchy in 1289 was to Master Hodinus of Beverley who received some 155 acres to hold as a perpetual fee for himself and his heirs in the forest of Benon, south of Bordeaux. He had two years to clear the land, and three years to plant vines and was bound to cultivate the land and work the vines, according to the usual formula, 'with hoe and knife and whatever else was necessary for them'. He was to pay 6d. annual rent, 2d. of *esporle* (the Gascon name for the payment owed to the lord on change of lord or tenant and which signified feudal tenure), as well as paying 2d. for the dinner of the guard appointed on the day of vintage. The seventh part of the fruits were to go to the king and to be taken to his adjoining property.[16]

Along with a special care for the wine trade and encouragement to the vineyards which supported it, the English kings were anxious to foster the smaller towns beyond Bordeaux. Such places as La Réole, for example, struggled for privileges and exemptions so as to maintain their independence and jealously cherished local power. In addition, during the period from the beginning of Edward I's reign to the second Anglo-Gascon war in 1324, the kings were also energetic creators and encouragers of bastides, the 'new towns' of the south of France, whose traces are most obvious in the county of Toulouse, the Agenais, and along the frontiers of Périgord. There has been considerable argument whether bastides were created primarily for military and tactical reasons, or for the increase of population and commerce.[17] The weight of the evidence, including the fact that many bastides had no ramparts, or only built them during the war years of the fourteenth century, suggests that they were seen primarily by their founding lords as a useful means of extending their political influence and encouraging trade. The desired result was an increase in both power and revenues, and bastides founded by the kings tended to be erected where royal power needed reinforcement. For example, after Quercy had fallen into the hands of the English king, Edward wrote to his seneschal in July 1290 that since there was a great lack of places in Quercy in which the seneschals and *baillis* could hold assizes or exercise justice, the seneschal was to take counsel with one of the king's clerks to provide a strong place where a bastide could be made in which the royal officials could hold assizes and carry out their tasks of jurisdiction.[18]

Essentially a bastide was a planted town and usually developed from a charter of *pariage*, that is a division of lordship between two or more powers. The interested parties were, on the one hand, the holders of the land where the new town was to be built and, on the other, the king or a lord who made himself responsible for the laying out of the town and subsequently for its protection and administration. A charter of liberties was one of the features, and attractions, of a bastide.[19] They paralleled rather closely the charters granted to new towns in England at the same period, except for the forms of town government which illustrated the regional variations. The inhabitants whom a new bastide hoped to attract were tempted by concessions which freed them from arbitrary feudal taxes and servile obligations, gave them freedom to trade and dispose of their property, provided for markets and tolls, and set up a municipal government with its own seal, administered by consuls or jurats, usually under the final supervision of the lord's *bailli*. Sometimes the charter even limited and defined the military service expected. The attraction of the bastide for the serf, or questal man as he was known in Gascony, was obvious. Their lords were often less enthusiastic and a couple of royal orders illustrate their concerns. Thus Edward in a letter to the prelates and barons of the Agenais agreed to set up a joint inquiry as to whether jurisdiction had been usurped by royal officials and the consuls of towns and bastides from the rightful possession of the prelates and barons. At the same time he also reissued a grant made by Burnell and Grandison in 1278 that no new bastides would be made to trespass on the jurisdiction of the barons of the Bazadais, nor would their questal men be received into bastides, nor their lands and woods be given forcibly to these new creations.[20]

Despite such natural hesitations the *pariage* was a mutually advantageous process if the new town prospered. The landholder gained from a growth in population and a more intense exploitation of the land which increased his revenues. The lord too made financial gains but, more importantly, gained political influence, frequently in disputed or even rival territory. Thus the creation of a bastide was often used as a political weapon for the covert extension of power in disputed territories. Since 1252 the French kings had encouraged royal penetration into Gascony by entering into a considerable number of *pariage* contracts with Cistercian monasteries in the lands between the Garonne and the Ariège.[21] Such centres of French influence, administered by French officials, were a continuing irritation to English seneschals and *baillis* and a threat to peaceful and consistent ducal government. They frequently provoked a counter-current of seignorial bastides in an attempt by the local lords to maintain the balance of power.

Some of the bastides in Aquitaine were founded or inspired by English officials working there: Roger Leybourne, friend of Edward and lieutenant of the king in Gascony from 1269-72, founded the town which bears his name, Libourne; Jean de Grailly, lord of Benauges, founded Cadillac in 1280 to provide a river port near his castle; while in 1287 the bastide of Baa was named in honour of Robert Burnell, bishop of Bath. The three towns suggest the range of possibilities for such foundations. Libourne grew and prospered because of its ideal location as the centre for the wine trade on the Dordogne—and it remains important in the wine trade to the present day. Cadillac, on the other hand, although a useful new port on the Garonne, was over-shadowed by its more powerful neighbour, Saint-Macaire. It survived, but was never of more than moderate importance. The new town of Baa was even more unfortunate, and its fate was characteristic of the one-in-three of these new towns that did not succeed. Founded to encourage the clearing of the land in the forest close to the southern limits of Bordeaux which the king had recently bought, it was planned as a major settlement. Master Gerard de la Tour, who has been described as a 'veritable urban architect', supervised its layout and first construction.[22] An access road was opened and a church and royal house built. The town was near the route of Saint James, that is the road south to Bayonne and Compostella, but apparently the commercial advantage foreseen from this proximity did not accrue. The Gascon Rolls tell the sad story of the two men who had been granted land in Baa and built a house there 'at great cost and labour'. Because the main road to Saint James did not run through Baa, as they had expected, they were allowed to have an alternate

89

grant near the road to Langon, the main road to Toulouse, and were allowed to move their house there setting up a place to brew beer. In subsequent years Baa, never successful, disappeared so completely that it is now almost untraceable.[23]

Although few bastides vanished so completely, many remained small or middle-sized, not even filling out the areas originally traced for them. Such present-day villages as Lisle-sur-Tarn or Monpazier, which owe their beginnings to foundation as a bastide, betray their origins and illustrate the original patterns less overgrown by modern accretions than such continuing commercial successes as Libourne. The town sites were normally laid out in a gridiron pattern with rectangular building lots and a central market-place, lined by arcaded overhangs known as *cornières*. The main roads drove straight to the corners of the market-place, while the church usually had a separate area a little aside from the market square. Some bastides acquired walls and fortified gates during the troubled years of the fourteenth century, and in the border districts many of the churches were also fortified. There were, of course, a number of reasons to account for the success or failure of a bastide. On the rivers, Gascony's arteries of commerce, bastides could flourish in fairly close proximity, serving as collecting centres for the increasing shipments of wine. In other less-favoured sections many founders had over-estimated the pressure of population growth and underestimated the opposition of the neighbouring lords. The irritated bishop of Rodez who excommunicated all the inhabitants of Villefranche-de-Rouergue, vainly hoping to inhibit its growth, merely adopted an unusual weapon for his attack.[24] In southern Gascony the poor adventurer often preferred to journey through the Pyrenean passes to the urban centres of Navarre, Aragon and Castile than to settle in the local bastides whose future did not seem bright. As late as 1337 the inhabitants of the valleys of Lavedan and Barèges in mountainous Bigorre sought reassurance that they would not be transported against their will to bastides such as Flavacourt, except for cases of crime or debt.[25] Despite such failures and local quarrels, most bastides were useful to the king and often brought substantial financial advantages as well. In the Agenais, for example, two-thirds of the *baillis'* revenues came from the bastides.[26]

The towns with their commercial vitality and export trade, the bastides with their encouragement for development and

increased population in the less peopled countryside were important elements in the prosperity which Gascony enjoyed in the
early decades of the fourteenth century. Unfortunately it can
only be described in general terms. No Bordeaux bourgeois left
a personal archive like that of Francesco Datini, the celebrated
merchant of Prato, to give us an insight into his personal life
and deepest concerns. We can only guess at the vigour and com-
plexity of the life led by so many inhabitants of the duchy in
these self-confident years of their greatest prosperity and influence.

CHAPTER VIII

Clement V, a Gascon Pope

One unexpected event temporarily lifted Gascony to the centre
of European politics and provided a sudden flow of wealth and
power to the natives of the duchy. In his cathedral of Saint-
André on 24 July 1305 Archbishop Bertrand de Got listened to
the reading of the official letter from the cardinals announcing his
election as pope and took the name of Clement V.[1] His pontificate
is best known for its settlement of the papal court in Avignon,
commencing a period of over seventy years in which the popes
did not return to Rome. His decision was influenced by the extremely unsettled situation in Italy as well as the troublesome
matters at issue with King Philip the Fair. The French king's
desire to have a posthumous trial of Pope Boniface VIII and
his mass arrest of the Templars and demand for their sup-
pression were highly charged and difficult matters. In addition,
Clement's wish—so natural in someone from the disputed
duchy—to see real peace achieved between the kings of France
and England also suggested the importance of remaining close
to the political centre. Avignon was an independent city, part of
papal territory, separated from France by the river Rhone but
well situated to act as a nerve centre in complicated diplomatic
negotiations.

Clement's pontificate also opened an extraordinary era of
favouritism for the men of southern France. The seven Avignonese popes were all men of the Midi. Most of them passed their
lives and made their careers in Aquitaine or the neighbouring
French territories. They knew from harsh experience the problems
at issue between the French and English kings and generally
looked at them from the point of view of men of the *langue d'oc*.
French policy was often unduly favoured, since three of the popes
had served the French king at one time in their careers. The
appointment of cardinals during this period suggests some of the

biases. The Avignon cardinals included sixteen northern Frenchmen, only two Englishmen, fourteen Italians, five Spaniards, one
from Geneva but ninety-five from the Midi. Many of these were
drawn from Aquitaine in its widest definition fourteen Gascons,
fourteen from Quercy, four from Foix and an astounding thirty-
one from the Limousin.[2] Each pope, with the honourable exception of Benedict XII, tended to reward his own relatives and
closest supporters and the Limousin party was reinforced by no
less than three popes. Such a situation provided encouragement
for ambitious Gascon clerics to turn towards Avignon, hoping
for benefices and rewards at the papal curia. Pope Clement
himself appointed thirteen Gascon cardinals, four of whom were
his relatives, and the Gascon nobility exploited any claim of
relationship to gain papal grants of revenues or lands or papal
assistance in their struggle with their secular sovereigns.

Bertrand de Got had been elected pope after a long-drawn-out
and divided conclave. He came from a noble family of the duchy
whose principal lordships of Villandraut and Uzeste lay almost
at the border of the Bordelais and the Bazadais, some twenty-five
miles south-east of Bordeaux. Born in the middle of the century,
Bertrand was a younger son and destined for a career in the
church. He studied law at Orléans and Bologna and returned to
Gascony to work as a royal clerk, on one occasion serving as
King Edward's proctor at the Parlement de Paris and being
rewarded with suitable benefices. His career was advanced by his
elder brother Béraud who, on being appointed archbishop of
Lyons, chose Bertrand as his vicar-general. When Béraud became
a cardinal in 1294 he had his brother appointed a papal chaplain
and may have had some influence in his appointment as bishop
of Saint-Bertrand-de-Comminges, a small rich bishopric in the
foothills of the Pyrenees which attracted many pilgrims as it was
an important stage on the route to Compostella.

Both brothers were much involved in Boniface VIII's efforts
to stop the war between England and France. Cardinal Béraud,
along with Cardinal Simon of Palestrina, was dispatched by the
pope on a formal peace mission to the English and French kings,
while Bertrand was sent on a personal errand to King Edward
early in 1295, carrying pledges of the pope's sincere affection and
his desire to arrive at a reasonable settlement. An unknown
correspondent reported to the king meeting Bertrand at Nantwich
and trying, rather unsuccessfully, to discover the exact content of

D*

his message. The letter-writer laid stress on Bertrand's love for Edward and also recommended Gérard, Bertrand's servant who had previously been with the king, because he could provide prompt and full information on what happened in France.[3] When Boson de Salignac, archbishop of Bordeaux, died in 1299 Bertrand was transferred to that see, so pleasantly close to home. He was immediately catapulted into the difficult attempt to hold the balance between the English and the French kings, which was to plague his later career as pope, for Bordeaux was then occupied by the French. The archbishop's revenues had been seriously diminished by the war and the French occupation, and the French seneschal was ordered to make a compensating payment to the archbishop. This generosity did not inhibit Bertrand from declaring in Paris in 1302 that he was not bound to do homage or to take an oath of fidelity to the king of France for his archbishopric which he held only from the pope.

During Clement's first three years as pope he made three separate stays in or near Bordeaux, for one of his most marked qualities was his excessive attachment to his family estates and all his relations. The papal visits brought prestige to the city but also expense and great concern. John of Havering had just been reappointed seneschal and reported to England on the arrival of the new pope in Bordeaux and the problems it had caused. The pontiff had to be greeted with suitable formality and given an impressive bodyguard, but the seneschal's major concern was the maintenance of peace and order. Bordeaux was full of important Frenchmen seeking interviews with Clement, but the recent French occupation of the city and the insurrection that ended it had not been forgotten on either side. Feelings between the French and the citizens of Bordeaux ran so high that John explained that he had the city patrolled by day and night to forestall trouble. The pope proved a costly visitor. The seneschal had to provide Clement with twenty tuns of wine and such delicacies as deer, herons, bitterns, sturgeon and dolphins (probably captured in the Bay of Biscay). The accounts also listed the more prosaic carcasses of beef and pork for his household. As well, the seneschal presented the pope, on the king's behalf, with a cross of gold bearing a crystal and gold figure. Those around the pope also benefited. The papal physician, the famous Master Arnold of Villanova, received a personal gift of a tun of wine, especially suitable as Arnold wrote a popular text on the many varieties of medicated wines and the diseases against which they served as a protection.[4]

When Clement returned to Bordeaux in May 1306 and remained in the province until March 1307 the effects on Bordeaux of being the temporary official centre of the church were not altogether happy. The magnitude of the retinue which followed the pope and the cardinals to Bordeaux taxed the resources of the city to the utmost. The pope installed himself within the familiar walls of the archbishop's palace while the cardinals and the branches of the curia took over sections of various religious houses. This influx was swollen by representatives of lay and spiritual powers from all over Christendom wishing to do business with the curia, as well as by a disorderly horde of place-seekers and hangers-on. Inevitably the city suffered from over-crowding, unexpected traffic and a rise in prices, all of which roused vocal complaints from its inhabitants. The effects were even felt in England where wine supplies were down because 'by reason of the pope's staying in Gascony, wine had not been brought thence to this country in the usual quantities'.[5]

Surrounded by relatives and friends—and few others could penetrate to the pope's presence—Clement gave innumerable proofs of the strongest facet of his personality, his amiable but excessive generosity. Examples abound: grants to the secular as well as the clerical members of his family and to the nobility of Gascony, particularly the Albrets, do not seem surprising. More unexpected are the considerable grants given to relatives of John of Havering, who seems to have put to personal advantage his proximity to the pope at this time. Two of the sons of the English seneschal were clerks. The more notable, Master Richard, was serving as constable of Bordeaux under his father. Both became papal chaplains and received generous grants. When Master John of Havering died at the papal court at Bordeaux in the autumn of 1306, Clement immediately transferred to Richard some of his brother's benefices, and later appointed him to the archbishopric of Dublin. The seneschal, however, was allowed to acquire papal benefits for more than just his sons— there were grants for his nephew, the nephew of his son-in-law, and for clerks in whom John was interested in England. It appears that there was a genuine link of affection between the Gascon pope and the English seneschal who had conducted him so ceremoniously on his first papal journey through the duchy, for from Avignon the pope in 1309 offered an indulgence of twenty days, good for three years, to all the faithful of the diocese of Dublin who would pray for the soul of Sir John of Havering, father of their archbishop elect.[6]

Papal generosity was also displayed towards his old see. His cousin and successor, Arnaud de Canteloup, was almost immediately made a cardinal, and was succeeded in turn by another Arnaud de Canteloup, a nephew, who presided over the archbishopric at the height of its ecclesiastical influence and territorial power. One of Clement's first acts was to remove the archbishopric from any subordination to the primacy of Bourges, a matter dear to the pride of the archbishops of Bordeaux. Bordeaux was now named the primatial see of Aquitania Secunda with metropolitan authority over Agen, Périgueux, Angoulême, Saintes and Poitiers—an ecclesiastical jurisdiction which did not correspond with political realities. The pope also defined most generously the rights of the archbishop within his own province, gave him the right of nominating three canons at Saint-André and two at Saint-Seurin, and confirmed various old privileges while adding new ones. He also added to the archbishop's territorial possessions, bequeathing him his own manor of Pessac.

Clement had always been sickly and was very ill for much of his pontificate—the modern conjecture is that he probably had cancer[7]—and this may have accounted for his lack of force. As pope he is best known for his failures, especially his weakness in withstanding Philip IV, which seriously compromised his credibility as an arbitrator between the French and English kings. The pope did succeed in persuading King Philip to pardon the inhabitants of Bordeaux for their rebellion against French rule in 1303. In another grant inspired by the commonplace brutalities of war, the pope empowered the archbishop of Bordeaux and the bishops of Aire and Dax to absolve from excommunication those men of the duchy who came to them as penitents because they had slain many enemies or rebels by the sword, mutilated and beaten others, wasted churches and ecclesiastical places by fire and ruin, or committed fire, spoliation or rapine 'in accordance with custom of enemy against enemy'.[8] There are signs that Clement tried to balance his concessions to Philip with special favours to Edward I and his son. During his early years as pope he complacently allowed royal financial levies on the English clergy. The English king was given many privileges and special dispensations for the benefit of his royal clerks and Edward I's confessor was even named a cardinal. When the Council of Vienne (1312) insisted that the clerical tenth could only be used for crusading purposes, Edward II looked to the pope for a loan, using as his negotiator a papal nephew, Bertrand de Sauviac, to whom he made generous grants.[9] Discussions went on between the king and the Curia for eighteen months with Edward making concessions and gifts to the Got family. Not long before Clement's death (1314) a loan of 160,000 florins was made from papal funds, but by the pope as a private person, so that repayment would go to his heirs. Originally intended for Edward's struggle against his barons the money was ultimately used for the expedition against the Scots which culminated in the disaster of Bannockburn. The repayment of the loan was based on the assignment to the pope and his heirs of the tolls of Bordeaux and Marmande and of the revenues of Aquitaine, in itself a threat to proper financial management in Gascony. By 1318 Edward had succeeded in getting a general quittance of repayment, although in reality only part of the sum had been repaid.[10] These financial manipulations, which bore heavily on English clerks as well as the unfortunate Gascons, roused considerable fury in clerical circles in England. In a diatribe against Pope Clement's greed, the author of the *Life of Edward II* exclaimed angrily: 'after this may it never happen that a man so near to us ascends the papal throne'.[11]

The means used to attract this loan suggest how the English and French kings vied in their attempts to sway the pope by generosity to his relatives. Another papal nephew, also Bertrand de Got, was named viscount of Lomagne and Auvillars by Philip IV and given all confiscations from heretics there. The viscounties were later advanced to a marquisate. Edward II gave the same nephew the castle of Blanquefort and Puyguilhem, the bastide of Monségur, and an appointment as his proctor at the papal court.[12] Bertrand's sense of self-esteem was flattered as French sovereign and English king-duke wooed his favour and support. The Gascon noble's ideal of being rich, sought after and irresponsible has rarely been so completely fulfilled. Such attitudes played havoc with the maintenance of order in the duchy.

Apart from his unhappy involvement in French and English politics Clement had real intellectual interests. He added the final volume of decretals to the collection of canon law, founded universities at Orléans and Perugia and displayed an unusual concern for Greek and Oriental languages. In perhaps the most unexpected act of his pontificate he created John of Monte Corvino, the devoted Franciscan missionary to the Mongols, the first archbishop of Peking. John had been serving in China since 1294 and continued his labours with considerable success until his death in 1327. It is tempting to see the creation of this new archbishopric as a delayed result of the visit of the Nestorian monk, Rabban Cauma.[13] As ambassador for Argon, Khan of the Mongols, Cauma made an extensive tour of the princes of Europe and came south from Paris in 1287 to visit Edward's court at Bordeaux. At this time Bertrand de Got, as a rising royal clerk, was much occupied in business for the English king. The monk was well received by Edward and celebrated mass in the Oriental rite for him and the court though the king pointedly reminded him to report to Argon that in the European countries all Christians followed one profession of faith. Did the memory of this unusual occasion and the consequent desire to extend the prestige of the Roman rite in that far-off land perhaps encourage Clement to set up this new see?[14] On the pope's death in 1314 his body was brought back to the Gascony he loved, to be buried in the church at Uzeste he had benefited and beautified, surrounded by the lands of the relatives he had enriched.

Inevitably the existence of a pliant Gascon pope was the most striking feature of Gascony's ecclesiastical life but the local religious structure, though less visible, maintained its importance.[15] The archbishop of Bordeaux was not only the leading ecclesiastic of the duchy, he was also one of the most distinguished seigneurs of the Bordelais. His see was worth 12,000 florins—a major contrast with that of Bazas, valued at 1,800 florins, and poverty-stricken Bayonne at a mere 300 florins.[16] By the middle of the century his income from a variety of sources came to some 4,000 *livres tournois*. The archbishops had normally been local men and for the greater part of the fourteenth century they were related in one way or another to the Got family. Exceedingly conscious of their dignity they worked assiduously to assure their freedom of action. Thus, the archbishops continued to maintain fiercely their exemption from homage to either French or English king, their rights to exercise sole justice in their lands and their efforts to extend their holdings and their influence. Their activities as landlords and political figures are reasonably well known, their religious influence and individuality cannot be traced.

Although the archbishop's seat of power was in the cathedral, he was not concerned in its day-to-day routine. The cathedral of St-André in Bordeaux, for example, was ruled by a chapter of twenty-four canons who elected their own dean.[17] Despite occasional references to the 'abbey' of Saint-André the chapter was never a monastic institution, although for about sixty years its archbishops required it to follow the rule of Augustinian canons. Clement removed this requirement soon after his election to aid the recruitment of new members. The pre-eminence of Bordeaux in the fourteenth century is noticeable in the manner in which this chapter served as a springboard to promotion, since it provided two popes and four cardinals, as well as four archbishops for the see. Although the canons' power and estates were not as extensive as those of the archbishop, they probably possessed more land in the immediate vicinity of Bordeaux. Their primary recruitment was local, for the stalls of the chapter had always been filled by the younger sons of important families. Such arrangements were made possible because, except for three canonries reserved for appointment by the archbishop, the chapter itself elected its new members. Over the years greater emphasis was gradually placed on university training in theology or law as a requisite for a non-noble candidate. The chapter's seigniory of Lège, near the Teste de Buch, must have been a welcome refuge for their moments of relaxation. Its forest was used for the hunting of stag or boar by the canons or their guests, as well as the lesser sport of hares and rabbits. They could go fishing on its coast and enjoyed rights of flotsam, jetsam, and shipwreck, profitable matters which often had to be upheld by legal action against enterprising intruders.[18]

The chapter of Saint-Seurin struggled to uphold its privileges and importance on the basis of its antiquity, claiming that its church had been the first episcopal seat. Its rivalry with the chapter of Saint-André was long-standing and bitter and its revenues were only half as great. Since it remained outside the city walls even after the fourteenth-century extensions it was somewhat overshadowed, but it maintained an active life. In 1309 it moved to encourage further university training among its canons, allowing an annual subsidy of 30 *livres bordelais* for any canon who had completed his statutory year of residence. He was now to be allowed to study in any of the advanced faculties, not merely theology. Showing an interest in physical health, it put Master Bernard of Rocamadour, a Bordeaux physician, on an annual retainer of 15 *livres bordelais* for his services as doctor for the canons and their households.[19] The dean of Saint-Seurin frequently played an important part in the political life of the duchy and was usually appointed to the king's council along with a representative of Saint-André.

By the fourteenth century the abbeys had retreated from the forefront of religious life, nor were their abbots usually men of political prominence. Sainte-Croix, within Bordeaux, remained rich but had lost influence and prestige. Outside the city, La Sauve-Majeure, the great Benedictine abbey set in the middle of the dense forest which covered most of Entre-deux-Mers, served a double purpose. It encouraged the clearing and settlement of the forest for which it was named and also served as a useful stage on the route to Compostella, attracting pilgrims of all social ranks. The new town of Créon—still a prosperous market centre —witnesses its success. During the early fourteenth century the abbey continued to extend its tilled lands, especially its vineyards, and gathered some seventy priories under its rule, swelling its revenues. The most remote was Burwell in Lincolnshire, founded by a grateful English pilgrim.[20] Even the abbey's ruins, now fortunately well cared for, leave a striking impression of what a monumental place it must have been at the peak of its power when it had more than 300 monks and a network of dependencies.

New outlets for popular piety had become influential as the friars came to Bordeaux in the thirteenth century and gained an important foothold. The Dominicans, Franciscans and Carmelites were the most influential of these orders and gifts and legacies testify to their popularity. Popular religious sentiment appears most clearly in the confraternities which proliferated in the fourteenth and fifteenth centuries. Some fourteen of these pious associations are recorded for the fourteenth century, but they appear so fleetingly in the records that it is difficult to trace their growth, purpose and practices, or even be sure of their basic nature. There is the intriguing example of the confraternity of Saints Abden and Sennen which appears in the records in 1331–32. Certain citizens of Bordeaux declared that the confraternity was founded to honour God, Holy Church, the blessed martyrs Abden and Sennen *and* to maintain fealty to the king-duke and give aid to his ministers so that they could do proper justice. Its members appealed to the king to confirm their statutes since some in the city were objecting to them. Edward III ordered an inquiry to be made by the seneschal and constable into the confraternity and also requested a copy of its statutes, but his decision does not appear. Obviously the confraternity's aim, which the king baldly described as intended to stop trouble in the city, was not purely religious and may merely have been another manifestation of continued factional struggle.[21] In the fifteenth century certain trades gradually developed professional confraternities, but the pious associations of the previous century are less clearly delineated.

It is possible to describe the institutional patterns of religious life but it is hard to penetrate below the surface. Clement V, because of his position, correspondence and share in major events, can be perceived as an individual but the local ecclesiastics are only names and abstractions. What religious beliefs really moved the townspeople who lived in the shadow of the many churches or the peasants toiling on their fields to the sound of the bells of parish or abbey? There are occasional hints of popular piety: the passion for processions and pilgrimages, the generosity expressed in wills—though not before—and the panoply of funerals closely linked with social status and prestige. Nevertheless as yet the picture can only be a rendering of the superficial features of a generally accepted pattern of life.

CHAPTER IX

Conflict Continued: the War of Saint-Sardos

When Edward I granted the duchy of Aquitaine to his son in the spring of 1306 he may have hoped that a new era of peace would develop there.[1] Superficially all seemed well. The treaties ending the war had provided for the restoration of the duchy to its pre-war state and for the tightening of the bonds between the kings by a further reliance on marriage alliances. In reality the situation was not so happy. The French were seriously delaying their restoration of parts of the duchy, especially the castle of Mauléon, a vital strongpoint near the border of Navarre, and Edward had refused to do personal homage until the treaty was fully carried out. The stage was set for a re-enactment of the difficulties which had led to the first war, since none of the basic issues had been even partially settled.

Certain new factors were to make Edward II's reign almost as unfortunate in Gascony as it was in England. Edward of Caernarvon, who acceded to the throne in 1307 at the age of twenty-one, lacked his father's organizing ability and his talent for picking competent ministers. The young king's unbridled favouritism towards Piers Gaveston, the son of a Gascon knight of Edward I's household, and later the Despensers, alienated the leading barons and fuelled a growing unpopularity further magnified by general social disdain for Edward's awkward conduct and unkingly amusements. The war with the Scots took much of the country's energy and money and the royal prestige was further weakened by the disastrous defeat at Bannockburn in 1314. It is not surprising that a series of upheavals rocked the country and that this internal chaos precluded serious concern with Gascon affairs. In contrast to his father's personal knowledge, Edward II had no experience of the duchy. He was forced to rely on councillors and officials mainly trained under his father's regime: they served him loyally but were not able to suggest new initiatives to deal with recurring problems. No wonder one of his advisers gloomily portrayed the business of Gascony as 'a great sea, filled with wreckage and having no port of refuge'.[2]

At the time of the prince's appointment as duke the king also reappointed the existing seneschal and constable of Bordeaux. Sir John of Havering and Master Richard his son were an experienced team of administrators who remained in the duchy until 1308. In contrast, at least some of the difficulties experienced in Gascony during the remainder of the reign came from the rapid turnover of the officials appointed from England. Amanieu du Fossat, a loyal Gascon official, warned the king in 1319 of the damage caused by this policy. He reminded Edward that a seneschal could hardly make the necessary first tour of the duchy in a year, since he had to take the required oath to the people and receive their fealty. 'When he has gained knowledge of the country and the people and ought to remain to serve the king and the people better . . . to reform the country and put it in better state, then, Sire, he is taken away.'[3] Amaury de Craon was an exception to the general pattern. He was an important noble, equally accepted on both sides of the Channel. His father, Maurice de Craon, had served as lieutenant of the duchy for Edward I, and the family was related to the king through descent from a half-sister of Henry III. Amaury was also hereditary seneschal for the French lands of Anjou, Touraine and Maine. Appointed seneschal of Gascony in 1313, at a time when relations between Edward and Philip IV were at their most friendly, he remained in office until 1316 and served again in the same office between the summer of 1320 and the beginning of 1322, in the meantime advancing Edward's interests in Paris. There seems little doubt that he was instrumental in appeasing the mutual hostility which was beginning to colour the relations between the two kings, fanned by the growing hostility of their officials.

The constables of Bordeaux were not changed as frequently as the seneschals but included some inappropriate choices. For example, the appointment in 1309 of such a man as Amerigo Frescobaldi, who exercised power through his deputy Ugolino Ugolini, was evidence of the subordination of Gascon interests to royal needs. In the end the position proved disastrous to the Frescobaldi, Italian bankers on whom the king depended for large loans, since they came to be regarded with even greater suspicion because of their Gascon connections with friends and relations of Gaveston. Bernard Cailhau, of the important and powerful Bordeaux family, was Gaveston's nephew and served as financial agent for his uncle. Such links seemed both too close and too dangerous in the eyes of the Lords Ordainer. An order for the arrest of Ugolini and any other Frescobaldi agents in Gascony was carried out in December 1311 when the seneschal not only captured Ugolini and four other agents at Marmande but also seized some damning letters from Amerigo to his partners. Amerigo had prudently ordered his agent to immediately send out of the duchy all the money and goods he could. They were to buy large amounts of wine—on credit if cash was lacking—even if the prices were too high, as Amerigo anticipated the swift departure of the company from Gascony before demands for payment could be presented.[4] Their high hopes of support from Edward and Gaveston were frustrated for Ugolini and the others were shipped from Bordeaux to imprisonment in England. Ultimately the Frescobaldi had to flee the realm with the king's debts to them unpaid and soon fell into bankruptcy. It is obvious that they only valued the position of constable of Bordeaux for the stranglehold it provided on all the revenues of the duchy. Such a misuse of funds meant that Gascony's real needs, even the basic payments for its administrative requirements, were often neglected.

During this turbulent reign the very real need for some continuity in the government of the duchy was provided through the lower ranks of officials who were normally Gascons. The English king was served long and faithfully by such men as Albert Mège and Jean Guitard who knew their homeland and its problems intimately. Master Jean Guitard was a native of Bordeaux, a king's clerk who had served in the household of John of Brittany in 1297. In 1303 he was appointed controller, the second ranking financial officer of the duchy and remained in that office for more than twenty-five years. During this period he often served as deputy for the constable and performed assorted financial duties for the king-duke. Master Albert Mège, the son of a physician and a king's clerk, filled a great number of confidential functions in Gascon government. He was a public notary, the clerk of the Ombrière in Bordeaux, and was often associated with Jean Guitard in attempts to collect extra subsidies for the king.[5]

During these difficult years one organ of the administration which allowed for considerable Gascon influence on the government of the duchy first comes into prominence. The council of the duchy, which gave advice to the seneschal as the king's representative in the same manner as the king's own council in England, is known to have existed at least since the thirteenth century, but orders addressed to the councillors and requiring their advice become far more general at this time. The council was presided over by the seneschal and the constable, to whom were added a considerable number of local councillors. They included important local clerics, some representatives of the bourgeoisie of the main towns, king's clerks trained in the law and some local barons who were paid annual salaries and granted expenses for the times they had to be away from home on the king's business. The variety of individuals who were councillors between 1307 and 1317 is interesting.[6] They range from Amanieu d'Albret, probably the most important baron of the duchy; the mayor of Bayonne, and the brother of the mayor of Bordeaux; Arnaud Guilhem of Marsan, the brother of Piers Gaveston and once seneschal of the Agenais; to such local clerics as the archdeacon of Bazas and a canon of Lectoure as well as king's clerks and proctors such as Master Guilhem de Cazes and Master Bernard Pelet, prior of Le Mas d'Agenais, who was described in one letter from the king in 1312 as 'our chief councillor'.[7] Master Bernard was also responsible for the preserving of the form of a councillors' oath in which each was required to swear to give good and faithful counsel according to his conscience, to maintain the rights and state of the king, and to excuse himself openly from acting in any business touching other people to whom he is bound by other oaths.[8] The king obviously hoped, as he wrote to Amanieu d'Albret, that the seneschal would thereby receive 'sane counsel and opportune aid'.[9] His hopes were not always realized, but the council undoubtedly formed a useful forum for the Gascons to express their major concerns about the problems of the duchy.

Sporadic efforts were made to attack the worst weaknesses of the administration. In 1310 the king's commissioners chosen to deal with outstanding issues with the French at Périgueux were also expected to deal with the reform of Gascony. The group was distinguished and knowledgeable, as it included John of Brittany, the bishop of Norwich, and Guy Ferre, who had served as seneschal.[10] Nothing much seems to have come of the reform effort, although the commissioners were horrified by the dreadful state of the archives after the years of French occupation and neglect, but this was a more important issue for their arguments with France than for the immediate problems in Gascony itself. The second attempt at reform was more substantial and was achieved under the aegis of Amaury de Craon during his second term as seneschal. The original lines seem to have been drawn up at Amiens in the summer of 1320 when Edward made his hurried trip to France to do homage to Philip V and appear to have been a genuine effort to reform the royal officials. Amaury as seneschal was given power to dismiss all officials, except those appointed for life, and only to reinstate those recognized as capable and faithful. Specific abuses such as too many sergeants, men exercising more than one office, and lack of residence were to be dealt with by the seneschal and the council. Amaury's own ordinance insisted on the need for the seneschal to have a good chancellor to aid him in his work, and tried to bring order to the whole complex network of judges, proctors and appeals, as well as the necessary clerical support for all these courts.[11] It was the constant English hope that if the courts in Gascony provided quick and reasonable justice there would be fewer appeals, though in practice French officials were dangerously eager to encourage unjustified appeals. The final ordinance for the reform of Gascony, provided by the king in 1323, was perhaps encouraged by the royal need to win confidence, loyalty and Gascon support in Scotland. In this document considerable emphasis was placed on the need of subordinate officials to be appointed under the seal of Gascony—a loophole which the French officials had been exploiting, since judgments of any official appointed by the king himself could be directly appealed to Paris. Edward repeated the need for the creation of a suitable clerk as chancellor and listed the officials of the duchy and the wages they were to receive, occasionally giving the name of the current occupant. But the commissioners who had been named to seek reform and armed with this ordinance—the invaluable Amaury de Craon and the bishop of Ely—had not been appointed primarily to improve matters in Gascony, but because relations with France had again reached a crucial point.[12]

The pivot around which all of Gascony's political affairs revolved between 1259 and the Hundred Years War was the relation between the English and French kings and their differing interpretation of the exact status of the duchy of Aquitaine. The French royal officials had no doubt as to how the requirements laid down by the treaty of 1259 were to be interpreted. They moved in every possible way to weaken the control of the king-duke by endeavouring to treat him as merely one of the peers of France who was obviously and essentially subordinate to the French king. The awkward reality of having a duke of Aquitaine who was also a crowned king interpreting homage in its most restricted feudal form, meant inevitable legal, and ultimately military, conflict. When Pope Boniface's arbitration and subsequent peace treaties put relations in Gascony back to pre-war status the stage was set for continuing difficulties. The French manipulation of the weapon of appeals from the ducal courts in Gascony was aided by the extraordinary changeability of the Gascons, whose consistent aim was to work for their own immediate advantage. Aggressive French officials encouraged appeals by any dissatisfied litigant to the Parlement de Paris, which normally favoured the French side of the case. One of Edward I's most respected lawyers, an expert on Gascon questions, spoke out bitterly on this matter:

> Of what use is it for Englishmen to go to law against the king of France in his kingdom, against his whole council, and against you who are our co-judges? Certainly none![13]

For the English king the performance of homage was always the sticking point, since it was a sign of inferiority. The English king found this requirement increasingly irksome, especially when royal sovereignty was becoming more entrenched and extending to more fields. At the same time France passed from a period of having kings who ruled for extensive periods—Philip IV, for example, was king for almost thirty years—to having four kings within the twenty years of Edward's reign, so that the distasteful ceremony had to be frequently repeated. English feelings were further exacerbated by the continued French assistance to the Scots, with whom Edward had great difficulty and against whom he was not very successful.

Both Pope Clement V and John XXII tried to use their papal office to bring peace between the two kings. Pope John (1316–34) was less exclusively Gascon in his outlook than Clement. Although considerably more favourable to the French kings than to Edward he was not their total creature. John had served as chancellor of Charles II of Anjou and been bishop of Avignon, so he knew well the complications of the English–French dispute. He tried desperately to make the French and English kings keep peace in their domains in southern France, since the constant battling often meant the sack of church lands and wanton violence against individual ecclesiastics. There was, for example, the papal complaint to Edward about the violence done to Isnard de Montaut, guardian of the Franciscans at Agen and papal legate to Foix and Armagnac. On coming to Valence his efforts to enforce the procurations owed him by a local chaplain were fruitless, so Montaut excommunicated the recalcitrant cleric. No sooner had Isnard left the town than its *bailli*, the enraged chaplain and his clerk attacked him, grievously wounded his servant, and dragged them back to Valence where they displayed them like public criminals, as well as robbing them of their papal letters, horses, and belongings. Fortunately the aggrieved clerics were rescued by Amanieu du Fossat, a lieutenant of the English seneschal, who arrested the malefactors and sent the chaplain off to be tried at the court of the bishop of Agen.[14] On the other hand, the pope also reproached the king of France, urging him to reprove his officials for their encroachment on properly English jurisdiction by the encouragement of uncontrolled appeals to Parlement. The result of this, the pope wrote, was to suspend by long delays the regular course of justice to the profit of those who stirred up disorder and trouble in the country.[15]

Unfortunately the Avignonese popes, despite their desire for an Anglo–French settlement and a crusade, were in no position to do anything more effective than to multiply exhortations to the kings to seek peace. The decline of their prestige and the dangers of their local attachments are made particularly obvious in the case of Jourdain de l'Isle, a particular protégé of John XXII. Jourdain held lands in the Agenais where he was a co-seigneur with such Gascon lords as Alexandre de Caumont and Amanieu d'Albret. Aggressive and ambitious, he was in constant conflict with these lords and with the seneschal who tried to enforce English jurisdiction. He launched several appeals, claiming maltreatment by the seneschal, and the pope wrote countless letters in his favour, not only to Philip V and Edward but to the important men at both courts. The case dragged on for some five years until Jourdain made the fatal mistake of killing two French royal sergeants. He was condemned to death by the

Parlement de Paris and hung in 1323. As a sign of the inefficacy of papal protection the French officials dressed him before his execution in a robe with the papal arms—a symbolic but scandalous insult according to the manners of the times. John XXII's real weakness in influencing practical politics was made embarrassingly manifest. By his headstrong and unreasoning support for an unworthy character the pope had actually helped to aggravate the conflict between the two kings. He had himself encouraged the useless appeals for which he reproached Philip and attempted to threaten Edward by innuendo, urging him to manipulate his justice in Gascony in order to win the support of even his most turbulent subjects.[16]

The legal efforts to arrive at some compromise between the kings were no more successful. Two meetings, known as 'processes', were held, one at Montreuil in 1306 and the second at Périgueux in 1311. Neither achieved anything, since the claims put forward by the rival commissioners merely displayed the unbridgeable gap between them. For example at Périgueux each side put forward a series of articles as a basis for discussion. Both claimed that they merely sought the fulfilment of the earlier treaties and of Boniface's arbitration but the conclusions each drew from the same material were dramatically opposed. The almost laughable weight of the French demands and their continued insistence on the total subordination of the duke to the king suggest that they were not really interested in achieving any compromise but merely gaining further hearing for their most extreme case. These attempts foundered on a basic disagreement on just what these 'processes' really were. The king of England and his advisers considered them as bipartite commissions, a method founded in Gascon custom for the regulation of disputes arising in contested frontier districts between Gascons and French subjects. Each side elected one or two judges and then proceeded in an amiable conference of equals. The French position, on the other hand, was rooted in their indefatigable emphasis on the superior position of the French king as suzerain with royal jurisdiction over all usurpations within the realm. They would only recognize the two kings as equals during periods of war or truce when the feudal tie no longer existed. The insistence of the French king, expressed through the continuing intransigence of his officials, was rooted in the unshakeable French policy that the sovereign could never be judged by a subject, and therefore the English king as duke of Guyenne must be totally submissive to French demands.[17]

Frequently the English king had to acknowledge French theory, but attempted to minimize its effects by the judicious use of personal consultation in a family atmosphere. Edward's visit to Paris in 1313 is an example of what could be achieved in this manner. Official diplomatic efforts had been continuing, despite the failures at Montreuil and Périgueux, to smooth over the most acute difficulties in regard to the duchy and, on this occasion, the king himself crossed to France to speed and conclude the negotiations. The visit was punctuated by formalities and amusements: the knighting of Philip's sons, a banquet given by Charles of Valois and, on a more serious level, the crusading vows taken by both kings at Notre-Dame on 6 June. In the intervals Edward and his advisers discussed Gascon business with Philip and, as a mark of goodwill for Edward's visit, considerable concessions were achieved. The French king remitted all the penalties for acts committed against him by Edward or his father, pardoned Edward's officials in the duchy for any excesses committed by them in the exercise of their functions and withdrew certain fines imposed on towns and individuals in Gascony.[18] In addition he renewed the regulation of appeals to Paris by the men of the duchy, originally granted in 1286, and encouraged a settlement of the violent dispute between Amanieu d'Albret and a recent seneschal, John Ferrars. This had been appealed to Parlement but was settled by Albret's withdrawal of his appeal and Edward's subsequent grant to him of 20,000 *livres tournois*. (It was undoubtedly relevant that Amanieu was a relative of both Edward and the pope which, added to his leading position in the duchy, much increased his bargaining power.) The impetus of Philip's more conciliatory approach carried over into the hearings before Parlement on the 'day of the duchy of Aquitaine'. Amaury de Craon as seneschal, Master Guilhem de Cazes, judge in the Agenais and Gascon councillor, and Master Austence Jordan, king's clerk and royal proctor at Parlement, attended as part of their duties, but on this occasion they were joined by Queen Isabella. Perhaps her presence, as well as the warmer atmosphere, was responsible for more decisions in favour of the king-duke and against the appellants than in any other such session. In addition, ten appellants renounced their appeals and the seneschal was granted permission to punish five aggressive Gascon lords for their crimes, even though they had appealed and were technically withdrawn from his jurisdiction.[19]

All these legal and diplomatic ventures bring into some prominence a group whose traces in the conduct of affairs are often hard to follow. The king's clerks were the 'faceless civil servants' of the later middle ages. Their names are plentifully scattered through the administrative documents, but they themselves are almost always in the shadow, making it difficult to estimate their influence accurately. They were responsible for many facets of the royal administration, both in England and Gascony, and frequently developed into experts in specific fields. Edward I had early seen the value of a cohesive group of intelligent and well-trained men and had steadily recruited Gascon as well as English clerks to serve him, needing their specialized knowledge of the duchy and of his quarrels with France. There was a regular ladder of promotion. At the beginning of his career the aspiring clerk might simply be used for specific and unrelated missions. If he acquitted himself well he might rise to the level of a permanent 'king's clerk', engaged by contract and with a fixed salary. The most able and fortunate of these became in Edward I's day clerks of the wardrobe, attached to the king's own household. Later they fanned out into the other departments of government. Gascon king's clerks more commonly followed the route of service in the lower levels of administration, with perhaps a turn as judge in one of the network of courts in the duchy, a period as royal proctor at the Parlement de Paris where they worked with the clerks and legists from England whom the king kept permanently stationed there, and ultimately as a member of the council of Gascony. A few were even appointed to bishoprics. The calibre of these men was remarkably high.[20]

The eighty-year legal and diplomatic struggle with France from the treaty of 1259 to the outbreak of the Hundred Years War encouraged the use of some of these clerks in what appears to have been an embryo diplomatic service. Considerations of prestige required that diplomatic missions be led by distinguished lords, perhaps seconded by one or two bishops who owed their sees to successful service with the king but, then as now, behind the personages were the expert advisers. In the middle ages these were drawn from the king's clerks, usually trained in the law, who knew the state of the questions to be discussed and were well able to construct legal arguments and to brief their principals. It is obvious in tracing the names that recur in such appointments that these men often specialized in a particular diplomatic field. By the end of Edward I's reign Gascon affairs had become so important and so voluminous that it became essential to have an English clerk, resident at the king's court, to be in charge of all the files dealing with previous negotiations, who was described as 'keeper of the processes'. The career of Master Elias Joneston, who was first appointed in 1306 and served for thirty years, has been uncovered by diligent scholarship.[21] Unlike his predecessor, Master Philip Martel, whose clerk he had been, Joneston himself was not active in pleading the Gascon case. He was almost exclusively the archivist and expert charged with keeping and setting in order the amazing volume of documents concerning Gascony and making good the gaps caused by war and enemy action. Others, such as Master Thomas Cobham, whose service to the king was ultimately rewarded with the bishopric of Worcester, served more visibly in expounding the English point of view to the French king and court, but Joneston's advice on such matters was constantly sought. New registers and calendars were compiled since complaints had poured in from the negotiators that they could not argue with the French unless they had adequate records to buttress their demands. But all this diplomatic activity and legal struggle, so often fruitless and time-consuming, could be overturned by an unexpected flare-up of violence at a crucial point.

Such was the affair commonly referred to by the rather grandiloquent title of the War of Saint-Sardos.[22] The priory of Saint-Sardos, located in the Agenais just south-west of Villeneuve-sur-Lot, had been founded by the Benedictine abbey of Sarlat. The mother house had 'privileged' status which it claimed extended to all its dependencies, despite the treaty giving the Agenais to the English king. The abbot of Sarlat argued his case in Parlement as early as 1285, and again in the Process of Périgueux. After the accession of Philip V the abbot made a *pariage* with the French king on the condition that a bastide be built there. This was bitterly opposed by the local lords, especially Raymond-Bernard, lord of Monpezat, whose castle was the priory's close neighbour. In December 1322 the French Parlement declared that the King was within his rights in building this bastide and the French seneschal of Périgord set 16 October 1323 as the official date for the recognition of its status as a royal bastide. The night before the ceremony the men of the lord of Monpezat raided and burnt the bastide and hung the French official from the stake bearing the royal arms. Such a flagrant act of hostility was bound to incite a vigorous reaction and the English officials recognized the impending danger, although it appeared at first that it might be smoothed over. Adam of Lymbergh, then constable of Bordeaux, wrote to the king at the beginning of December of 'the great need and peril of the duchy'. French commissioners had begun to inquire about Saint-Sardos and he had heard mention of a French summons to Ralph Basset, the seneschal. Adam had felt it expedient to go immediately to Bourg and Blaye 'to comfort the people' and, more importantly, to see that they repaired their walls. Basset, in a private letter to Hugh Despenser, expressed the frequent English distrust of their Gascon allies, raising grave doubts about the loyalty of even the king's councillors, for he felt they had been 'seriously corrupted by the French',[23] an estimate in which he was proved correct.

The continued intransigence of Basset and the lord of Monpezat, who refused to answer any summons and not only disregarded but opposed the carrying-out of the decisions of the French court, meant that skilful diplomatic negotiations were essential if peace was to be maintained. In addition, there was continuing irritation at the French court by the English king's long delays in doing homage. When Louis X (1314–16) came to the throne both kings were absorbed in their own difficulties. The English defeat at Bannockburn, the prolonged and ineffective French campaigns in Flanders, the general failure of crops and the consequent famine of 1314–15, the widespread discontent in France which erupted in the provincial leagues of 1315: all meant that Edward found it easy to escape doing homage to Louis X. Philip V became king in 1316, but judicious delays and eloquent excuses succeeded in putting off the ceremony for another four years. When homage was finally performed at Amiens in 1320 Edward took refuge in the usual reservations about its nature. Charles IV succeeded his brother in 1322 and the question of continually delayed homage added further irritation to the perennial disputes over rights and complaints against officials. The affair at Saint-Sardos was merely the last of a series of minor clashes made impossible to overlook by the intransigence of the local Gascons and the ineptitude of the English negotiators. The king's half-brother, the earl of Kent, and Alexander Bicknor, archbishop of Dublin, when sent to the court of France not only temporized about the status of the castle of Monpezat, which King Charles was demanding be surrendered to him, but also allowed excuses for a further delay of homage to be put forward at a most inopportune time. Charles IV had really been remarkably patient: his confiscation of the duchy and of the county of Ponthieu on 1 July 1324 for non-performance of homage was a natural decision.

The only real fighting of the 'War of Saint-Sardos' was at La Réole which was besieged at the end of August by Charles of Valois, once again commanding the French army. He had a powerful force with many supporting 'machines' which Edmund of Kent and his English army could not withstand. After five weeks of battering and the non-appearance of English reinforcements Edmund agreed to the surrender of La Réole and a six months' truce. He was then allowed to leave for Bordeaux.[24] The military side of the war was over. The loss of La Réole, added to the peaceful defection of the Agenais and Saintonge to the French king, meant that English Gascony had shrunk to a narrow coastal strip between Bordeaux and Bayonne and the land around Saint-Sever.

A distinction needs to be made between the war of 1294 and this war of Saint-Sardos. Unlike his father's underhanded behaviour, Charles IV's occupation of the duchy was legitimate under feudal law when a vassal had refused homage. Legally, however, his lands should be returned to him when he had fulfilled the necessary conditions. Until Edward did homage Charles' legal right to hold the lands and take their revenues was acceptable. It was important to arrive at some agreed conclusion to this impasse and Pope John XXII added his voice to those seeking a peace between the two kings. The English negotiators had not progressed very far at the French court and, at the pope's suggestion, Queen Isabella was encouraged to join them to try and influence her brother, King Charles. This accorded very well with Isabella's own desires as her situation in England was becoming more difficult daily as the king fell progressively under the control of the Despensers. The queen had begun to serve as a rallying-point for a nucleus of lay lords and bishops opposed to Despenser greed and bad government. At the beginning of March 1325 Isabella left for France and a possible treaty was hammered out by the end of May.[25] By its terms Edward was to regain his duchy as soon as he had done homage, although the French king reserved the lands he had conquered. The required ceremony was set for Beauvais in mid-August. It would appear that the king genuinely proposed to fulfil this agreement, but the Despensers were not anxious to see both king and queen out of the realm and beyond their influence. At a suspiciously convenient time Edward fell sick at Dover and Queen Isabella suggested at Paris the acceptability of Prince Edward's performance of the required homage. The French king agreed if King Edward would give his son full seisin of the duchy. This too roused argument in England where the motives of the French king were suspiciously scrutinized, for the English worried whether some misfortune might befall the prince 'exposed to the astute and greedy French'.[26] By the beginning of September the decision had been reached and Edward granted his son the duchy of Aquitaine. The prince then crossed to France accompanied by Bishop Stapledon, in whom the king still retained some confidence, and did homage to his uncle King Charles before the end of September. Although the duchy of Guyenne was officially restored to its new duke in November Charles exacted a payment of 60,000 *livres parisis* for the conveyance of the fief as well as continuing to occupy all the lands (including the Agenais and La Réole) captured by Charles of Valois during the course of the war.[27] King Edward was resentful and felt that he had been tricked by his fugitive wife into agreeing to an unsatisfactory treaty and alienating the duchy to his son while both queen and prince remained overseas. Early in 1326 the king confiscated the queen's possessions and took back into the hands of his own officials the administration of Aquitaine. This move provoked King Charles into calling a halt to the withdrawal of French troops and re-occupying the duchy.

However, Gascony had become a minor side-issue as events in England so obviously led to confrontation and catastrophe. By the end of 1326 the revolt headed by Queen Isabella and Mortimer had succeeded in dislodging the unfortunate Edward II from the throne. The fourteen-year-old Edward III formally acceded on 27 January 1327 and by 22 February a diplomatic mission had been appointed by the queen-regent to arrange a settlement for Gascony.[28] A new and expensive treaty on 31 March 1327 gave Edward back his duchy but in a most attenuated form, since the French king continued to hold the Agenais and the Bazadais. To the payment of 60,000 *livres parisis* agreed to in 1325 was added an indemnity of 50,000 marks for the damages caused by the war. As a slight concession, eight prominent men of Gascony, condemned to death by the French king had their penalty commuted to banishment. These included Sir Oliver Ingham, the previous seneschal and a protégé of the Despensers.[29] In the end this ban was abrogated.

Thus at the accession of the king in whose reign, and at whose initiative, these sporadic conflicts were to develop into that wider and more continuous conflict known as the Hundred Years War, the duchy of Aquitaine—or Guyenne, which becomes the more common name—consisted only of a relatively narrow coastline, barely fifty miles wide. It stretched from Saintes and the mouth of the Charente to Bordeaux, and from there down the Landes to Dax, Bayonne and the foothills of the Pyrenees. The youthful king-duke had legitimate reason to doubt the good faith of a suzerain who had continued to absorb the peripheral territories of the duchy, while making no attempt to restrain the aggressions of his officials or to smooth the sensibilities of a brother sovereign. This pattern could not continue indefinitely.

CHAPTER X

Henry, Earl of Lancaster and the Beginnings of the Hundred Years War in Gascony

The first years of the reign of Edward III seemed to presage a further prolongation of the grinding, inconclusive disputes over homage and appeals, unsuccessful legal conferences and continued French encroachment in Gascony—a mere repetition of the pattern which had governed French-English relations since the 1290s. The French king and his advisers may well have believed that the successful policy of extension of royal sovereignty over Aquitaine by the manipulation of legal weapons, reinforced by the sanction of confiscation, would soon lead to the total absorption of the duchy as it had already led to major territorial gains. Certainly, the advisers and administrators of the young English king tended to look back nostalgically to the happier era of Edward I and proposed to confront the problems of the present with the remedies of the past. Despite this element of conservatism in both French and English bureaucracies, the fundamental approach to the issues and the methods used to solve them was about to change drastically.

The death of Charles IV in February 1328 marked the end of the Capetian dynasty since the three sons of Philip IV had all died without male heirs. The peers of France had already decided in 1316, when Louis X died leaving only a daughter and a posthumous son who died soon after birth, that no woman could inherit the crown of France. They had chosen Louis X's brother as king, a procedure which was repeated in 1322. The new question was whether the crown could pass through a female to her male heir. It was an unexpected by-product of the papal enthusiasm for marriages between the ruling families as a way of ensuring peace that one of the closest males to the French throne was Edward III himself as the son of Philip IV's daughter. The legal issue was a proper subject for dispute, but the practical realities of fourteenth-century politics ensured that the French decision would be that such a situation was incompatible with French law. Edward was only fifteen, still under the control of his ambitious and immoral mother, whose conduct towards her husband and her lover had shocked the French court. Although a peer of France and a grandson of Philip IV, Edward was a Plantagenet and the king of England, inevitably a rival and perhaps an enemy. Almost as a formal gesture, Edward's claim to the French throne was put forward at this time but, given the current unsettled state of England, it was more a matter of recording the possibility for the future than making a serious decision for the present. Philip of Valois, son of the Charles of Valois who had twice led armies against Gascony, cousin of the last three kings and a man in the prime of life with a reputation as a chivalrous and able knight, was speedily accepted as king.

The accession of Philip VI in 1328 meant that the obligation of doing homage again pressed on the English king, and the French were naturally anxious that the bond should be acknowledged as swiftly as possible. According to the *Grandes Chroniques* the envoys whom King Philip sent to England in 1328 (including Pierre Roger, already important at the French court, and the future Pope Clement VI) stayed a long time. They wished to speak with the young king but instead Queen Isabella 'gave them unsuitable responses in the manner of a woman'. Indeed, according to one version:

> She said to them, so it is said, that her son who was born of a king ought not to do homage to the son of a count. And that Philippe de Valois who calls himself king of the French should watch what he does, and that her son was nearer and closer to the holding of the kingdom of France than he was.[1]

During this interim the revenues of Gascony were seized into the French king's hands as a form of reprisal and a final summons was issued to Edward. It was obvious that, unless homage was done, Edward might suffer a final confiscation of his duchy—a move which in the still unsettled early days of the reign would have been impossible to counter—so in May 1329 Edward crossed to France to meet Philip at Amiens.

The kind of hard bargaining which went on between the legal experts on both sides, while the two kings indulged in the usual ceremonious festivities, is suggested by Edward's letter of

30 April ordering his treasurer and chamberlains to collect from all departments of government:

> all bulls, charters, letters, instruments, rolls and memoranda necessary for the defence of the king's right in all the processes between him and his ancestors, their ministers and subjects, and the kings of France and their ministers and subjects in the court of France and elsewhere, and lately begun and still pending, and in all uncompleted agreements, and all questions newly arisen from wars, resistances and rebellions, excesses and disobediences and from all other offences whatever.[2]

It was essential that the king's proctors and lawyers should have the requisite documents to argue their case. The weight of baggage, both material and intellectual, which must have accompanied such encounters, each of which further swelled its records, provokes memories of the chain of Marley's ghost. On 6 June in the cathedral of Amiens Edward did homage to Philip VI for Aquitaine but the ceremony was not conclusive, since it was marked by protestations on both sides. Edward reserved his rights in the whole duchy of Gascony which he claimed had not been fully restored to him, while Philip in his turn reserved his rights to the lands his father had conquered during the last war. No oath of fidelity was taken and the unsolved difficulties left standing between the kings give point to the remark of the chronicler Knighton that 'they were made friends only in appearance'.[3]

King Philip was not satisfied with the ambiguous ceremony at Amiens. Embassies criss-crossed the Channel fruitlessly, but French pressure continued and Edward, seriously beset at home, yielded in March 1331. He agreed to recognize by his letters patent his obligations as a liege vassal. Even another ambiguous 'process' set up by the two kings was unable to resolve the disputed matters, for the newer insistence on national claims could not be accommodated in the old framework designed to settle feudal rights and duties.[4] The impetus of goodwill which had momentarily inspired the kings relapsed yet again into the usual interminable bickering.

The legal activity and apparent attempts to find solutions did not really affect the hostile behaviour of both sides and their determined efforts to search out every advantage. Edward had begun early in his reign to reinforce Gascony and, after the breakdown at Agen, was convinced that he would have to maintain his rights by force. As early as 1330 he had written to his officials in Gascony, urging them to put the duchy's defences in order and to look for support among the Gascons themselves, since he feared an imminent attack but proposed to defend the duchy.[5] The French king was also planning for possible war as is shown by a number of documents of 1327–30, especially one of 1329 laying down the requirements for a force against Gascony. It was estimated that the king would require 5,000 mounted men-at-arms and 16,000 foot soldiers, of whom three-quarters would come from Languedoc.[6] As well, King Philip had been encouraging devotion to the French cause by extensive gifts to such strategically useful supporters as the count of Armagnac and Gaston, count of Foix, who was also viscount of Béarn. Very much in the pattern of the history of the last eighty years, the final dispute came over an appeal to the Parlement de Paris. The lord of Navailles, whose castle of Sault-de-Navailles was a vital stronghold for the English on the frontier of Béarn, had complained that English officials had ravaged his lands. Parlement commanded that he should be compensated and sent French troops to seize and hold the castle of Puymirol until the money was paid. The inhabitants resisted and the French had another 'rebellion' to add to their list of grievances. On 24 May 1337 Philip VI ordered the confiscation of the duchy, citing in general terms the rebellions, excesses and acts of disobedience committed by the duke of Aquitaine, but using as a specific reason, not the disputes in the duchy itself, but the English harbouring of that rebellious French vassal, Robert of Artois.[7] Edward's answer to this was not only the normal defiance and disavowal of homage which, in the usages of the time, was a necessary formality before he could wage war on his suzerain the king but, more importantly, the dispatch of this communication not to the king of France but to 'Philip of Valois usurper'.

The pattern which had prevailed since the treaty of Paris nearly eighty years before had finally been discarded. Edward had decided that attempting to use legal means to enforce his rights was useless. His father and grandfather had been handicapped in their struggles by their subordinate feudal status towards the king of France: he would cut this Gordian knot by claiming not only his rights in Aquitaine, but the actual throne of France. Such a claim at once put an end to the endless squabbling about sovereignty for he would be both duke and sovereign. As well, his claim could lend a valuable air of legitimacy to any war he waged, could imply that he was fighting as rightful king and thus had the support of God. It is impossible to estimate how seriously fourteenth-century men took Edward's claim to the throne of France. It is fair to say that the very real desire to feel that one fought on the side of right, since God upheld the right, helped to encourage their belief in the justice of their cause in a matter which was legally disputable and excessively complex. Whether King Edward actually believed his own publicists is perhaps more debatable. In any case, the problems of Gascony which had already been instrumental in influencing English policy had now led to that long-drawn-out quarrel which was to convulse the two kingdoms for over a hundred years.

So much has been written about the Hundred Years War in all its aspects that it would be superfluous to attempt to paint an overall picture.[8] Guyenne was never the main battlefield and, for at least the early part of the war, the campaigns were sporadic and the devastation sparse. The facts of geography conditioned many of the campaigns. Invasion normally came by the river valleys, Gascony's main avenues of communication, while the Gironde, although more or less open to raiding navies, was the normal highway for military and logistic support from England. Bastides and fortified towns which commanded a river crossing or a salient strong point were of extraordinary value to both sides. They protected their inhabitants from casual attack, but their strategic value laid them open to frequent assault. Thus La Réole, which commanded the middle Garonne, changed hands eight times during the war. The side which held Libourne and Fronsac controlled the lower reaches of the Dordogne, while Bourg and Blaye were the keys to the Gironde and the vital communication between Bordeaux and England. The area of the Bordelais, which can be described as the heart-land of the duchy, was spared both the destructive *chevauchées* of English forces and the attentions of the wandering companies of mercenaries during most of the fourteenth-century. For many of its noble families the war meant lucrative employment and the possibility of riches to be gained by the sword, while Bordeaux itself profited from the higher level of commercial activity encouraged by the presence of so many fighting men.

The initial campaign of 1337–40, when King Philip's troops

came to Gascony to put into effect the seizure of the duchy, was primarily a series of minor skirmishes and surprises. Since Edward was particularly concerned with his elaboration of alliances in the north he was fortunate that his current seneschal in Gascony was experienced and able. Oliver Ingham, a knight from a solid Norfolkshire family, had first served in Gascony under the earl of Kent in 1324, and had acted as seneschal during the war years of 1325–27. His obvious abilities had led to his reappointment by Edward in 1331 despite his period of support for Mortimer. He then served as seneschal until 1343 and was named as king's lieutenant and captain during this period of active fighting. He died in 1344, soon after his return to England. Knighton characterized Ingham as 'an upright knight, elegant and bold, and did well against the French considering his resources'.[9] His task was a difficult one. The French troops, under the command of the count de l'Isle, approached down the valleys of the Garonne and Dordogne in 1338. They took possession of Saint-Macaire, attacked Libourne and Saint-Emilion, captured Blaye and engaged in a seesaw struggle for Bourg. Although Bordeaux was surrounded by French troops and needed defence, it was not formally besieged. Nevertheless, continual watchfulness was necessary and military preparations had to be made. Closer to the frontiers, Penne-d'Agenais surrendered and Tartas, in the Landes, was seized. King Philip had already written in the summer of 1337 to Gaston de Foix suggesting that 'we wish and it would please us that all the damage which you can do to the viscount of Tartas you do, from our part and in our name'. Since the current viscount was Guitard d'Albret who actively supported the English, the French king was delighted to turn Gaston's warlike proclivities into such a convenient channel. By the beginning of January 1338 Guitard was dependent on the charity of the seneschal and the king, having lost everything.[10]

Although military activity was not constant, the seneschal was faced with the need to maintain contingents of armed men for the defence of the duchy and this obligation weighed heavily on its meagre resources. The retinues recruited by such men as Bérard d'Albret and Jean de Grailly, to mention only the most important, amounted to almost 1,200 men in the years 1337 40, and these had to be paid at the going rate. The detailed requisition given Bernard d'Escossan, lord of Langoiran, by the deputy of the constable of Bordeaux in 1341 illustrates the current daily wages: 16 *sous bordelais* for the baron himself, 6 *sous bordelais* for a mounted man and 12 *deniers* for a foot-soldier. Such a lord of middle rank as Bernard d'Escossan had provided during the previous year for a contingent for the seneschal under Bernard's own command, a small guard for the castle of Langoiran and a larger group for Podensac. Bernard still sought payment of wages for the service of his mounted men and foot-soldiers at the siege of Montlaur and at Montendre and Puyguilhem in 1338. In addition, as was normal in such indentures, he was to be repaid for the loss of three horses killed in the war.[11] Such straight-forward expenses for wages were only part of the financial cost. By 1342 Escossan, for example, had been granted by the king high and low justice with its profits in a number of parishes near Langoiran, while Bérard d'Albret was given the castle of Puynormand for himself and his heirs.[12] More expensive still was the general practice of bribing important barons to change sides. For example, in 1339 King Edward granted Gaston de l'Isle, a member of the powerful de l'Isle family, a yearly pension for life of 2,000 *livres tournois* out of the issues of the duchy, a follow-up to Ingham's acceptance of Gaston in the king's service with as many armed men as he could bring, and at the usual wages, 'from the day he left the service and obedience of the French king for as long as the king and the seneschal shall please'. In addition, the king promised to make good any loss of castles and territories as well as pardon the forfeitures due because of Gaston's adherence to Philip of Valois.[13]

These individual examples suggest the enormity of the seneschal's financial difficulties. As early as Michaelmas 1339 the duchy's revenues received by the constable amounted to only 59.5 per cent of the total expenses. Some subsidies came from the English treasury, but the amounts of money owed to Gascon lords for the troops maintained by them had become staggering as early as 1341. Such forced loans, in a situation where only 12–15 per cent of the money owed to the troops in a year was usually paid them, meant that the affected Gascon lords had great difficulty in collecting their wages. The problem has been worked out in great detail as it affected the cadet branch of the Durforts, one of the most important families in the duchy.[14] It took long and active complaint to get any results, even when the necessary bills had been granted. In fact it was almost essential, because of the straitened financial situation of the duchy, to go to London in person to get major sums settled. Such a trip was often very expensive. In 1342 the king ordered the keeper of the hanaper to deliver the charters and letters, which had been made under the great seal for the men of Aquitaine, free of all fees. His reason was that many had 'long been staying in the city of London and elsewhere in England at considerable cost for the prosecution of their affairs so that at present they have not the wherewithal to pay the said fees'.[15] By the time payment was finally made the unfortunate complainants frequently owed the whole sum to Italian merchants who had advanced them money against their expectations.

The effects of such difficulties were underlined by Bernard-Ezi d'Albret when he reported to the king and council at Westminster in December 1341. He personally was owed £14,692 and he drew to the council's attention that little of the duchy remained in the king's hands outside Bordeaux and Bayonne, that many troops were deserting because they had not been paid, and that he himself wished to be discharged from his office of lieutenant.[16] Although the truce of Espléchin, arranged in the autumn of 1340, suspended hostilities in Guyenne as well as in the north, it was merely a pause. The French garrisons remained in menacing proximity to Bordeaux whose inhabitants were naturally apprehensive of what might happen when the truce expired.

For the next five years, however, Gascony was not a centre of interest. Except for the naval victory won at Sluys, which destroyed the greater part of the French fleet and assured England control of the Channel for some years, the first years of the war had been costly and unsuccessful for England. Edward returned from the Low Countries disappointed but determined to reorganize, refinance and re-equip so as to achieve success in the war on which he was insistent. The quarrel over the succession to Brittany after the death of Duke John III in 1341 provided a further opportunity to carve out still another sphere of influence in France by espousing the cause of the dead duke's brother. England needed a friendly neighbour in that coastal province for the safety of the convoys to Gascony and Edward crossed to Brittany to wage an inconclusive campaign in the autumn of 1342. Another truce brought that fighting temporarily to an end with little achieved.

By 1343 Edward's mind had turned again to Gascon affairs

and he was anxious to have trustworthy advice. A letter of 6 April to Oliver Ingham, still seneschal in Gascony, ordered him to come to England with speed to give counsel and advice 'but as secretly as possible so that others observing his departure may not take the occasion to come to the king'.[17] Anxious deputations of Gascons were only too frequent at the English court and usually involved unwelcome demands for payment of money owed or pleas for further help in the duchy. In 1344 just such a group of loyal Gascon barons and representatives of Bordeaux came to the king's court to put the case once more for the need of assistance for the duchy if the king's position there was to be maintained. On this occasion their requests and Edward's strategic decisions were in accord. Henry of Grosmont, earl of Derby, had already been decided on as the new commander for a major effort in the south.[18] He had previously travelled on related diplomatic missions for the king; to Castile, to attempt to achieve at least the neutrality of that kingdom, whose well-equipped and permanent navy could threaten English shipping if allied with France, and to the papal court at Avignon, for the futile peace negotiations arising out of the truce of Malestroit.

Henry of Grosmont was already an outstanding figure in England. Cousin and contemporary of the king and high in his favour, he was heir to the great earldom of Lancaster which his father had gradually regained and re-established after the execution of Thomas, earl of Lancaster in 1322, and the subsequent forfeiture of his estates. Henry was judged one of the outstanding personages of a reign which abounded in chivalric figures. In many ways he appears cut to Froissart's favourite pattern: the noble and courteous knight, good-looking, fond of hunting and jousting and proud of his armour and his skill in dancing. But the earl possessed more important qualities than panache. He was recognized as a fine military commander, who had served his apprenticeship in the Scottish wars since 1330, for a French chronicle described him as 'one of the best warriors of the world'.[19] He proved to have a good grasp of strategy and tactics and an instinctive understanding of the value of bringing dissidents to loyalty by a judicious use of leniency and rewards. And, in an unexpected but not altogether unprecedented display of versatility, he was also the author of a devotional treatise in French, *Le Livre de Seyntz Medicines*, written in 1354 while he was still on active service. His death of the plague in 1361 was a major loss for the kingdom.

The terms of the indenture made between Edward and the earl in March 1345 give considerable insight into the powers and the expectations of his appointment as king's lieutenant.[20] The earl was to head a contingent of 500 men-at-arms, 500 mounted archers and 500 foot archers. Of these 250 men-at-arms, who were to include eight bannerets, ninety-two knights and 150 squires, and 250 of the mounted archers were to be of the earl's own retinue. The king would provide the rest and pay the wages of all at the usual fixed tariffs. They were to be mustered at Southampton ready to embark by 14 May, when the six months for which the wages were to be prepaid were to begin. The king would provide the shipping for the earl, his men, his horses and provisions both going and returning and, under certain safeguards, would pay for horses lost in his service. The earl was equipped with major powers: to make truces, to deal with all rebels and dissidents and to pardon them if advisable, to supervise, and if necessary, replace all the king's officials except the seneschal and constable.

The king had already taken care to appoint a new seneschal only a few weeks before.[21] His choice was Ralph, baron of Stafford who was also Derby's son-in-law, and it was no doubt felt that the two would work well together. The current constable of Bordeaux was John Wawayn, an experienced king's clerk. Certain special concessions were made to the earl to encourage him in his campaign. He was given the lucrative right to have the full profit of any prisoner taken or any cities or castles captured without any percentage being reserved for the king. In addition the king agreed to come to his aid in one way or another if he was besieged or attacked by too great an army for his strength and to protect the earl's rights in any inheritances which might fall in during his absence. This last concession may have been inspired by the knowledge of the imminence of the death of the earl of Lancaster for Henry succeeded to his father's title in September 1345. The difficulty of assembling the 150 ships that were needed to transport this major force held up the departure. When the fleet was in readiness by mid-June the winds were contrary and it was not until 23 July that the expedition finally left Falmouth to arrive in Bordeaux on 9 August 1345.

The earl seems to have had his plan of action already conceived and, perhaps through Stafford who had crossed to the duchy earlier, had arranged for the support of the most important of the Gascon barons loyal to the English connection. Certain families were the important local underpinning of the English strength, the location of their castles was of strategic importance, and their support essential. They included such men as the Albrets, the Pommiers, the Graillys, the Montferrands and the Durforts. The main lands of the Albret family lay between the Adour and the north of the Landes, but Bernard-Ezi had also been gathering important lordships in the Bordelais. His younger brother Bérard was lord of Vayres, Vertheuil and Gironde, had bought Rions and been granted Puynormand and Cubzac, all places of importance for the safeguarding of Bordeaux and the rivers. The Pommiers' family castle was near La Réole and the family had been loyal to the English for over a century. Pierre de Grailly held Benauges in Entre-deux-Mers and Castillon on the Dordogne, while his brother Jean, the Captal de Buch, was also lord of Castillon-de-Medoc. Bertrand de Montferrand's clifftop castle dominated the marshes at the confluence of the Dordogne and the Garonne as well as one of the roads to Bordeaux. In 1341 he added to this strategic spot the castellany of Blaye, often called the key of the Gironde. Arnaud de Durfort held two strong castles within six miles of Agen, at this time the only points in the Agenais still in English hands.[22]

Almost immediately after disembarking the earl moved upstream to Saint-Macaire where he joined Stafford, who was besieging Langon. From there he made a sudden and unexpected march across country to Bergerac. Within fifteen days after landing he had surprised the French army, seized the unwalled suburbs of Bergerac by a rapid dash across the bridge spanning the Dordogne, and had received the surrender of the main part of the town. Here Derby's natural instincts, allied to political and financial realism, avoided unnecessary brutality, for when Bergerac's defenders offered to surrender and asked mercy Froissart reported that the earl's comment was 'who prays for mercy should have mercy' and accepted their surrender.[23] Bergerac was a rich prize in every way. It has been estimated that the earl himself collected booty worth 52,000 marks in the capture of the town, much of which was later used to build his great palace of the Savoy. From the strategic angle, Bergerac commanded the middle valley of the Dordogne so that whoever held it had both an important fortress and a secure base for expeditions into the surrounding territory. By 11 September the earl had appointed Bernard-Ezi and Bérard d'Albret as co-captains of Bergerac with a garrison of some 1,500 men. With his base thus safeguarded Derby took the major part of his force and moved northwards where on 21 October he won another resounding victory at Auberoche, east of Périgueux.

By the beginning of November, having re-established English strength on the northern frontiers of the duchy and having even taken Angoulême, he returned to the south to deal with La Réole. This town, which had been in French hands since 1324, was too important and too close to Bordeaux to be allowed to remain in French hands once English power began to be re-established. With the active assistance of certain bourgeois of the town, La Réole soon submitted voluntarily and was rewarded with a series of grants including the ratification of its characters and liberties, the much desired exemption from the custom of Bordeaux and the right to sell its wine in Bordeaux at any time of the year, and the permission to levy a tax on every barrel of wine, wheat, pastel or other merchandise going up or down river before the town. The money received from this toll was to be used first to repair the castle to its pristine state, then divided so that one half be used to build and complete the town's fortifications and walls, while the other half went to the king for the castle and the royal works.[24] The earl set up his winter quarters in La Réole, pacifying the places already acquired and arranging for their defence. Meanwhile Stafford had captured Aiguillon, halfway up the Garonne towards Agen. The way was now open for English expansion into the east and south-east where French garrisons were small and the inhabitants could be persuaded to join the winning side.

However, the French were not willing to let their recent conquests escape them so easily. In March 1346 King Philip's son John led a large army to besiege Aiguillon. Sir Walter Manny and Pembroke were made responsible for the defence of the town, although their efforts were supplemented by the earl's efforts at La Réole who made sure they received reinforcements and supplies. His own fighting force was too small to allow him to lift the siege himself. By mid-August Lancaster marched towards Bergerac and held a council with the Gascon lords on the tactics to be adopted. The French asked for a truce but, since the English already knew of King Edward's landing in Normandy, they refused it. John decided to raise the siege and march north to join his father but he arrived too late to share in the battle of Crécy (26 August). Meanwhile the Anglo-Gascon force went on into the Agenais, capturing Villeréal and other towns. It settled the defences of Aiguillon and Tonneins, and then returned to headquarters at La Réole where another council was held and a division of forces decided on.

Two Gascon forces were set up to operate in the south and east. The Albrets were deputed to regain the Bazadais—a matter of concern to them because of their holdings in the Landes. With John Wawayn, the constable of Bordeaux, they worked skilfully on the members of the English party within Bazas to encourage the town's return to the English obedience. Meanwhile, Gaillard de Durfort, who had important holdings in the Agenais and had only returned to the English allegiance in 1345 after Lancaster's first successes, was encouraged to extend the English power there. Many of its bastides did opt for the English side. Such gains could be ephemeral, for they depended on the continued ability of the English to reinforce Gascony adequately. The judgment as to which side to espouse was a matter of intelligent self-interest for the inhabitants, particularly in the remoter sections of the duchy with no real tradition of loyalty to the English king-duke. The case of Gaillard de Durfort exemplifies common practice. On returning to the English allegiance he was rewarded with an annuity of 2,000 gold crowns from rents in the duchy; in order to secure these rents he speedily captured Miramont and Castelsagrat in the Agenais and Molières and Beaumont in the Sarladais.[25] His gains encouraged other towns, castles and nobles to return to the English obedience. Such a chain reaction helps to explain the rapid transfers which took place once one side had established even a temporary ascendancy. It was encouraged by wise rewards which suggested further conquests by those rewarded.

The French threat having been removed, Lancaster himself moved north to Saintonge in mid-September, attacked and took Saint-Jean-d'Angely. From there he moved into Poitou where the towns were not expecting attack and took both Lusignan and Poitiers in the first week of October. Although the French regained Poitiers the next year, the acquisitions in the Saintonge remained under English rule for a much longer period. After returning to Bordeaux, Lancaster left for England during December and surrendered his appointment on 1 February 1347. Among other marks of the king's favour he was granted the castle, town and castellany of Bergerac 'which he had lately taken by a stout assault' with the additional privilege that the king would pay for the expenses of its defence.[26] The expedition had added further prestige to Lancaster's reputation and had revived Gascon confidence in the English ability and will to hold the duchy. As well, the successes of 1345–56 had been won at very little cost to the Gascon countryside. Battles and raids had spared the centre of the duchy and the appearance of booty, and prisoners to be ransomed had taught Bordeaux that war could have distinct financial advantages too. The very real gains made in the Agenais and the Bazadais were achieved by the intelligent use of the important Gascon barons on whom the earl had relied heavily.

Lancaster's success in extending the frontiers of the duchy made the previous pattern of a standing army, mainly made up of infantry and occupying purely defensive positions, both expensive and inadequate to deal with the newer conditions. Under the pressure of war England had begun to work out a new model of compact and specific retinues, made up of mounted men-at-arms reinforced by English archers, and under the command of a lord who was responsible for ensuring their appearance. The earl helped to transfer this pattern to Gascony and Gascon lords were encouraged to provide such retinues on short-term commissions and for specific needs. Such a system could make better use of the military resources of the duchy in a more economic fashion. Economy was essential, since the English government found itself required during these years to provide almost half of the total revenues needed. The finances of the duchy, badly depleted by the need to pay pensions and grants to ensure loyalty in addition to soldiers' wages, were further cut by the catastrophic drop in wine shipments. These resulted from devastation in the vineyards, French control of the Haut Pays, and the ravages of both the Black Death and the lesser bouts of plague which followed. Since so much of the duchy's revenues came from the custom on wines the lesser quantity meant a precipitous decline in receipts.

The effects of the Black Death in Gascony are not well documented.[27] In its progress across Europe after Genoese sailors had brought it to Marseilles, it followed the natural path up the Garonne and arrived in Bordeaux by July 1348. Information is scanty, but obviously Bordeaux, like many cities, was hard hit. The king's own daughter died there on her way to Castile to marry King Pedro. Of the twenty canons of Saint-Seurin twelve died, for example, while of a bourgeois family with six children only one daughter survived.[28] The catastrophe of the plague throughout France and England was sufficient to force an interlude in campaigning, and the truce arranged in 1347, immediately after the fall of Calais, was extended beyond its original limit. It was only at the end of 1349 that the earl of Lancaster returned to Aquitaine for a quick raid through French territory as far east as Toulouse. Little is known about the expedition and although it appears to have been a flashy success, producing much booty, it had no permanent effect. Lancaster had served the king well in Gascony and continued as one of his most reliable and capable councillors and military leaders. In an unprecedented move the king elevated the earldom of Lancaster into a dukedom in 1351, and Henry, now Duke of Lancaster, was the first man outside the immediate royal family to carry that title. He continued to serve the king on military campaigns and diplomatic missions for the rest of his life. When he died in 1361, leaving no male heirs, his title and the duchy of Lancaster passed to Edward's third son, John of Gaunt, the husband of Henry's younger daughter Blanche, whose beauty and goodness inspired Chaucer's *Book of the Duchess*.

Perhaps this connection makes it less surprising that the education and culture as well as the piety of such a fourteenth-century noble as Henry of Lancaster could be so many-sided. It is certainly unusual that such a great lord would combine a life of extreme military and diplomatic activity with the composition of such a sincere and attractive, if repetitious, book of piety, as *Le Livre de Seyntz Medicines*. In his epilogue the duke describes his work as having been begun and completed in 1354, a period when he was busy on royal diplomacy in Avignon. He makes excuses for any errors in his French (more properly Anglo-Norman, still in use among the upper classes), since he was English and not much acquainted with French, and for the fact that he was not a good writer since he learned late and by himself.[29] The greatest interest of the book for the modern reader is not in its extensive use of symbolism, so beloved by medieval writers and preachers, or in its profound piety expressed in fourteenth-century forms, but in the concrete detail and specific examples taken from his own experience. These go far beyond the conventional pious disclaimers and hackneyed comparisons of much sermon literature. Duke Henry was very much a man of his time and class with many very secular habits. He loved the singing of man or woman or nightingale, the sound of instruments or the cry of the hounds. He admits ruefully that in his youth he had boasted of his beauty, his height and gentle birth, had taken pride in the shapeliness of his arms and hands and the handsome rings on his fingers.[30] He had delighted to stretch his stirrup at tournaments and to dance elegantly. His intentions were sinful, he admitted, adding realistically 'and perhaps still would be if I was as hot and as young as I was'. He shared the general passion for acquisition of lands or riches; 'if only I had had all my life as much covetousness for the kingdom of heaven as I have had for £100 of land'. He reflects on the fact that his feet, though reluctant to go on pilgrimages, always took him happily to find the best morsels of food and good wine, but now he suffers because they have swollen from all the food and drink and he is plagued by gout.[31]

But not all the material is so personal. The book is full of comparisons, some of which are medieval commonplaces, such as the body as a castle with the heart as its donjon tower, but several are more individual and suggest his own experience in town and country. He talks of the salmon going upriver to spawn, and how their young must return to the sea before they can truly be called salmon. He mentions how the surgeons of the schools at Montpellier were given the bodies of executed criminals to dissect in order to discover how the veins and nerves work within a man, and wished that the soul could be thus dissected to show its wickedness. His experience in his own voyages may have suggested his dissertation on the sea. It terrifies some, he says, but sailors and fishermen, who are used to it, are happier there. Like a sailor in debt, who fears to leave ship because he will have to go to prison, the duke describes himself as afraid to land from the sea of this world because of his fear of being condemned to the prison of hell for his sins.[32] In the longest and most detailed of all these similes he compares his heart to a fox's hole to which his sins retreat, and describes the three ways of getting the foxes out. The vivid use of the detailed description of the destruction of foxes, generally detested as vermin, here applied to the hunting out of sins illustrates both his own personal knowledge of such a country sport and his ability in a pious treatise to go beyond the current platitude.[33] His final comparison of the heart to a city market-place where all roads meet afforded him great scope for the work of the capital sins. He draws a vivid picture of the crowded scene he must have so often observed, with the cooks and innkeepers incessantly crying their wares, the women better dressed than on Easter, the men drinking in the taverns, and the constant brawling and quarrelling among the citizens and merchants, while the local lord inflexibly asserts his rights and his officials collect the tolls.[34]

The practical, observed element even remains strong when the duke comes to discussing remedies for sin in what now seems a far-fetched rhetoric. There is the value of goats' milk in spring, because of the herbs the goats have eaten, the method of making rose-water to sponge one who has a high fever, a recipe for making capon broth in the medieval equivalent of a double-boiler. It is difficult to accept the medieval treatment for fits of frenzy which recommended that a red cock be cut open and placed still warm on the head of the patient, but this is one of the few places where his relation of current practice differs from what might be described as timeless commonsense learned by experience.[35]

Le Livre de Seyntz Medicines adds an unusual element of personal reality to a fourteenth-century figure whom it might otherwise be tempting to dismiss as one of Froissart's two-dimensional heroes, but Lancaster was not alone in such piety. Gaston Fébus, Count of Foix, an outstanding leader of chivalric society in the second half of the century, wrote a similar devotional work, *Le Livre des Oraisons*, some thirty years later. The comparison between the two books suggests the difference in the personalities. Gaston Fébus was a man of extreme passion—he had even his only son murdered in a fit of rage—and his book is much less intelligible to a modern reader. Moved by his remorse and a guilty conscience, he wrote *Le Livre des Oraisons* as a long-winded cry, declaring his abominable sins and his need for forgiveness.[36] His work has none of the careful organization of Lancaster's, nor the lifelike everyday examples which still make the English-man's book rewarding reading. Both men see themselves as sinners in need of pardon, both totally accept the religious framework of their day and both were cultured men of action, but the English duke exhibits a balanced personality and a less frenzied piety which are more sympathetic to modern eyes.

Lancaster's final departure from Gascony in 1350 meant that the military situation which he had improved and stabilized began to deteriorate when the French regained strength. Lusignan and Saint-Jean-d'Angely soon slipped out of English hands. When Jean, count of Armagnac, was appointed lieutenant-general of the French king in Languedoc and the surrounding provinces in 1352 his desire to safeguard his own lands and to counteract any new strength among his neighbours buttressed his vigorous attempts to re-establish French control. He recaptured Aiguillon and by the end of 1354 had asserted a superiority which once again threatened the possessions in Gascony of the English king and his Gascon supporters.

CHAPTER XI

The Black Prince: King's Lieutenant in Gascony

The festivities surrounding the birth of King Edward's seventh son Thomas in January 1355 provided an opportunity for a group of Gascons, led by the redoubtable Captal de Buch, to express their alarm over French aggression. Their complaints also encouraged the restless prince of Wales to suggest the value of sending one of the king's own sons to support the Gascons in their war and encourage them.[1] The king's appointment of his eldest son as his lieutenant in Gascony in July 1355 began the extraordinary fifteen years which saw both Prince Edward and the duchy reach their heights of glory.

The Black Prince—the nickname is inescapable although it was never used by his contemporaries—made an indelible impression in Aquitaine. Local folklore has romanticized innumerable towers, castles and springs by associating them with the travels of the Black Prince—frequently with as little regard for historical reality as is displayed in identifying the resting-places of Queen Elizabeth or George Washington. The prince's contemporary, Froissart, was his first and most generous propagandist, though many other chroniclers also praised his military skill, his elegant and luxurious court and his open-handed largesse, always a popular medieval virtue when described by subordinates. Surprisingly, more modern Frenchmen have also fallen under his spell. The novelist Stendhal talks of his 'reign' as the 'glory and delight of Bordeaux', and praises him as a hero 'so modest, so generous and so great who seems to symbolize the virtues of another age'. A modern Occitan patriot vigorously rebuts the idea that the Black Prince could be considered an Englishman. He is convinced that he was an Occitan in the middle of an Occitan court, sharing its dream of the revival of a great Aquitainian kingdom.[2] In the midst of such a romantic haze it is difficult to find the reality of this almost mythical figure but it is important to observe his activities in Aquitaine on which the foundation of his legend rests.[3]

At this time the prince of Wales was particularly eager to take an active part in pursuing the war. Since the truce of Calais in 1347 most fighting had ceased, although Edward III continued to menace France by his intrigues with Charles the Bad of Navarre and the contenders for the duchy of Brittany. The possibility of an English invasion was never far from French fears. The French refusal at Avignon in the winter of 1354–55 to ratify the treaty of Guines, which would have given Edward the sovereignty he wanted in a widely extended Aquitaine in return for his renunciation of all claim to the throne of France, implied an inevitable return to hostilities, for which both sides prepared.

By the end of December 1354 King John had imposed a *fouage* —a hearth tax—in Languedoc to finance preparations against an imminent English passage to Bordeaux and invasion of the county. The situation struck the French king as so urgent that he told his seneschals that the aid did not require consent and should be collected even when opposed.[4] By the beginning of May 1355 orders were being given in England for preparations for the Black Prince's expedition, although the indenture between the king and the prince naming him king's lieutenant in Gascony with full power was only signed on 10 July 1355.[5] The expedition was delayed by the difficulty of finding enough shipping for such a major force. As always, it is almost impossible to be exact about medieval numbers, but the most detailed history of the expedition suggests that about 2,600 men and an unestimated number of horses were shipped overseas.[6] The emphasis was on mounted men and archers and it appeared from its make-up that the prince saw his army as a raiding force not concerned with siege warfare. Edward was accompanied by members of his household and administrative staff and supported by some of the military leaders of the realm who had fought with him at Crécy. These included the earls of Warwick, Oxford, Suffolk and Salisbury, Sir Reginald Cobham and Sir John de Lisle, all leading contingents of their own, and knights such as Sir John Chandos and James Audley, who were the prince's close friends and advisers. Chandos especially continued to gain in status and prestige during his years of service with the prince in Gascony and had the greater reputation, but Audley appears to have been the most affectionately regarded by the prince.

The fleet finally set sail from Plymouth on 8 September and seems to have had a quiet voyage, as a note appears in the cartulary of Saint-Seurin for 16 September declaring that the prince at the head of a great army entered Bordeaux on that day. The prince was careful to observe the necessary formalities on his arrival. On 21 September he took the oath as lieutenant of Guyenne in the cathedral of Saint-André before the mayor and citizens of Bordeaux, swearing to be a good and loyal lord, maintaining all the city's customs and privileges, while the citizens in their turn took the oath of fidelity to him. The ceremony was witnessed by the group of Gascon lords who were the main support of English rule and its most enthusiastic local military leaders—Bernard-Ezi and Amanieu d'Albret, Pierre de Grailly and his brother Jean, Captal de Buch, Bertrand de Montferrand and the lords of Pommiers, Lesparre and Mussidan—as well as four canons of the cathedral chapter. To avoid bad feeling with Saint-Seurin the prince also attended a solemn mass there and took up his sword and banner from its altar in accordance with the local belief that such a gesture would ensure him victory against his enemies.[7]

The prince had settled himself in the archbishop's palace where he had a right of hospitality, the more easily enforced at this time as Archbishop Amanieu de Lamothe, son of the lord of Roque-taillade, spent most of his time at the Curia in Avignon. The archbishop's accounts, kept by his procurator general, detail the costs of moving the archbishop's household, renting a new house for them, and making presents to the prince's officials to ensure the safety of the archiepiscopal wine and wheat.[8] By 5 October necessary protocol had been observed, the horses had been sufficiently rested, counsel had been taken with the accompanying English lords and the lords and barons of Gascony. General agreement was reached that the lands of the count of Armagnac should be attacked and, with this decision, the force under the prince's command set out on its first *chevauchée*, heading to the south and east.

The history of the raid has been written in great detail and the English chronicles contain letters from the prince himself and Sir John Wingfeld, head of his household, to the bishop of Winchester. They served as summary victory bulletins for the English at home.[9] It is obvious from these statements, as from the diary-like account in the chronicle of Geoffrey Le Baker, that the raid was a great success on its own terms.[10] It was a remarkable tactical and logistic achievement as the prince and his force swept south and east across enemy territory, devastating Armagnac and southern Languedoc all the way to Narbonne. Despite the destruction of the bridges by the French troops based in Toulouse, the prince's force crossed both the wide and rapid Garonne and Ariège upstream from the city astonishing the French. Burning and pillaging along the way, they captured and burnt the important towns of Carcassonne and Narbonne, although their inner castles held out, before swinging back towards their own land. There were minor skirmishes between the French troops and the prince's army but no pitched battles and no sieges. Speed and surprise were the weapons which the prince used most effectively, and the army was safely back in Gascony by 1 December loaded with booty and encouraged by its success.

The *chevauchée* did not in reality extend English power. It merely demonstrated the possibility of such a lightning strike which, although it did not change the fundamental political alignment, struck terror into the local population and, by the devastation it inflicted, impoverished the inhabitants, thus diminishing French revenues. In the midst of the wanton killing and destruction the occasional spark of kindness was considered a miracle and was worth remark. The story was told of Bérard d'Albret who broke into a house in a small village near Carcassonne from which all the men had fled. He found a woman in labour who was so terrified by his appearance that she immediately delivered a baby boy. With remarkably quick wit she begged the intruder that, for the love of God, he would have the baby baptized and act as its godfather. The knight took the boy to a nearby monastery and with some of his fellow knights shared in its baptism and gave it his own name. Bérard then returned the infant to its mother who besought him successfully that 'for the love of his godson the city should be saved from all destruction'.[11]

The results of the raid were satisfactory for both the prince and his Gascon supporters. The prince had taken advantage of the extreme rivalry between Gaston Fébus, count of Foix, and the count of Armagnac, whose lands adjoined, to meet with Gaston Fébus during the course of his *chevauchée*. Since the count of Foix was also the ruler of Béarn on Gascony's south-east frontier, it was politic to ensure Gaston Fébus of his goodwill and encourage a certain neutrality towards the French connection. The Gascons themselves, both those with the prince and those whose lands had previously been menaced by Armagnac, were delighted with the results, while Bordeaux and its inhabitants basked in the reflected glory of the prince and the presence of an army loaded with booty. However, the prince was not willing to rest on his laurels. Once the Christmas festivities were over he initiated a series of wide-spread small-scale campaigns which were undertaken by a number of small commands. While the prince made his headquarters at Libourne, where he was joined by Elie de Pommiers and Bernard-Ezi d'Albret, other Gascon lords, such as the Captal de Buch and Montferrand, ranged north-eastward towards Cognac and Péri-gueux. Meanwhile English commanders harried the middle Garonne valley. The resultant pressure on the count of Armagnac was consistent enough to keep him on the defensive for the time being.

King Edward's general strategy of having several forces operating in France had prompted the dispatch of the earl of Lancaster in the summer of 1356 to lead an active and successful raid through Normandy, even coming within seventy-five miles of Paris. The efforts of the earl and the Black Prince do not seem to have been co-ordinated, as it was not until the beginning of August that the prince departed from Bergerac on his second great raid. The spring had seen the build-up of supplies, armament and horses in England, destined for shipment to Gascony. The prince had been particularly anxious to have a sufficient stock of bows, arrows and bowstrings for this expedition and had sent one of his men to England to buy 1,000 bows, 2,000 sheaves of arrows and 400 gross of bowstrings. Because of the king's requisition of arrows none were to be found for the prince so his agent was ordered to Chester to seize all the arrows he could find still in the hands of the fletchers. The agent was also to force the fletchers to continue making arrows for the prince until his needs were met.[12] In the end his own army was not as large as he had expected as he had received news in Bergerac that the count of Armagnac proposed to invade Gascony soon after his departure. The seneschal, the mayor of Bordeaux and Bernard-Ezi d'Albret were therefore sent back with a large contingent of troops to ensure the duchy's safety. Despite this division Gascon men-at-arms still formed a major part of the prince's army, though his archers were generally English or Welsh. The line of march led north through Périgord, the Limousin and Poitou for the prince later stated that his aim had been to find the French king's son at Bourges where he also expected to get news from his father. Some inconclusive skirmishing outside of Bourges, which was strongly defended, was soon abandoned. A small French force was encountered at Romorantin, which was ultimately taken, and Marshal Boucicaut made a prisoner. From there the stages of the prince's march led him to the Loire at Tours, but he could not cross since all the bridges were broken. Confined south of the river and thus precluded from any rendezvous with Lancaster's forces north of the Loire, the prince turned south on his homeward march till his way was blocked near Poitiers by a large French army bent on battle.

The battle of Poitiers, which was perhaps the most important single encounter of the Hundred Years War, figures prominently in all the contemporary chronicles and in a description by the Black Prince himself in a letter to the people of London, while succeeding historians, strategists, and propagandists have discussed it in exhaustive detail.[13] The French army with King John in immediate command had been pursuing the prince's force for some days. Neither side seems to have been particularly well served by its spies, since the French were only twelve hours behind the English army at La Haye on 13 September. There can be little doubt that the Black Prince was trying to avoid this battle. The French king had a much greater force, at least two to one by the most conservative estimates, and the prince would have been happy to slip back to Bordeaux unchallenged and with no danger of losing his rich store of booty. The two armies finally found themselves facing each other in the fields of Maupertuis, a few miles south-east of Poitiers, near the river Miosson, and immediate battle appeared inevitable. At this juncture Cardinal Talleyrand de Périgord appeared, pursuing to the end his papal commission to attempt to make peace.[14] The cardinal was an important figure in the Avignonese Curia, a respected civil lawyer and a friend of Petrarch. As a younger son of the count of Périgord and a grandson of an earlier count of Foix he was intimately connected with the French-English struggle in Aquitaine and had been a great supporter of King Philip VI. The cardinal put himself forward as a go-between and besought the two armies, actually entrenched in their battle positions, to hold off for a day while he rode between the two forces seeking to avoid the conflict. The English were short of provisions, as well as much outnumbered and tired from continued marching. According to at least some of the chroniclers, the prince was willing to make considerable concessions to ensure their escape. The French, however, were so convinced of their strength and the certainty of their victory that they insisted on total surrender, which the English naturally refused. The cardinal withdrew, his offers rebuffed, accused by both sides of favouritism and of having allowed the enemy to improve his position.

The final English council on Sunday evening decided on an attempt to withdraw, with the baggage train retiring first over the Miosson, but the whole army was to be ready to fight if attacked. Early on Monday, 19 September, the earl of Warwick led the baggage-train over the river; but the French, seeing the movement in the English camp and urged on by the bitter rivalry between the two marshals Audrehem and Clermont, both seeking to prove their greater valour, decided on an immediate attack. The English tactical position had been carefully designed and made excellent use of the terrain. The archers were well installed behind hedges and vines, enabling them to rake the French, attacking up a slight slope. As at Crécy, and later at Agincourt, these archers were to turn the balance, although the battle was hard fought and the outcome in doubt for some time. The Gascon contingent formed a major part of the men-at-arms and fought valiantly. The Captal de Buch was one of the heroes of the occasion for, with a small group of knights and mounted archers, he executed the flanking movement and attack on the French rear which began that army's rout. Sir John Chandos, who served throughout the battle as the prince's chief of staff, when he saw the Captal's banner appear behind the French troops urged the prince to an immediate attack. It is interesting in the light of the legend of the Black Prince as a supreme general that, according to Froissart, it was Chandos who both saw the crucial moment and encouraged the prince to seize it.[15] The fighting was heavy and the French found it difficult to make headway against the English archers. The rather large and undisciplined French army, already deprived of its leaders by the death of Clermont and the capture of Audrehem, was further discouraged by the withdrawal of the dauphin Charles, under his father's orders, quickly followed by his brothers Louis of Anjou, John of Berry and their men. King John himself fought valiantly to the end, supported by his youngest son Philip, but was finally captured. Froissart delights in giving a colourful account of the battle and makes very clear the scene of indescribable confusion as knights and men-at-arms rioted among themselves to claim the French king seeking the honour and above all the financial reward of such a captive.[16] King John was finally rescued from this perilous situation by Warwick and Cobham and taken to the Black Prince while the fleeing French were pursued to the walls of Poitiers.

The battle of Poitiers was a major French disaster. Although their losses on the field were relatively high the real shock was the capture of the king himself and of so many leading French nobles. As the *Chronique Normande* puts it: 'it was not the mortality of this battle that was so great as the discomfiture'.[17] The formal courtesy with which the prince received the king and his insistence on serving his royal captive himself with great humility cast a superficial gloss of politeness over the desperate situation in which the French found themselves. Ransoms from noble captives were an important financial benefit for any medieval soldier but the possession of the king himself and so many of the highest nobility of the realm meant not only enormously high financial profits but also the possession of the major pieces in the diplomatic chess game.

The morning of 20 September the Anglo-Gascon army began its jubilant march towards Bordeaux with its distinguished prisoners and dreams of future wealth. In addition, as Froissart is careful to remind us, they were carrying immediate rewards as well:

As may be imagined, all those who accompanied the Prince of Wales were much enriched, in wealth as well as in glory, not only by the ransom money which they obtained but also from the quantities of gold and silver plate, rich jewels, whole trunks full of belts heavy with gold and silver fittings, and furred coats. No one set much store by armour, for it was in plentiful supply; the French had come as richly and magnificently dressed as they could, as if victory had been a foregone conclusion for them.[18]

The march was made at reasonable speed as the main part of the army crossed the Dordogne by 2 October while the prince and his royal captive waited in Libourne to arrange a ceremonial entry to Bordeaux. According to a register of the Abbey of La Sauve, which is believed to have harboured the king for at least a night, the prince entered Bordeaux officially on 5 October. It would appear that Cardinal Talleyrand refused to be discouraged by his failure before the battle, since by 12 October he too had come to Bordeaux on negotiations for peace.[19] Bordeaux suddenly became one of the capital cities of Europe since it harboured the king of France and so many French nobles, as well as the distinguished retinues of the Black Prince and his supporting English commanders. The Gascons revelled in their moment of importance and enjoyed the festivities which marked the winter months. Some of them also improved their financial situation by allowing the prince to purchase their French captives at fairly high prices. For example, Bertrand de Montferrand was paid 17,000 crowns for the count of Auxerre.[20]

The duchy of Aquitaine, which for so long had been a secondary, rather disregarded theatre of war, starved for supplies and forces, suddenly became the residence of a captive king, and a centre of much diplomatic activity. Soon after his return to Bordeaux the Black Prince had sent his chamberlain Sir Nigel Loring back to England, undoubtedly to report to the king in person the stirring events which had taken place. Loring must also have been expected to serve a general propaganda function, as the prince's letter to the citizens of London suggests that they should ask his chamberlain for any further information.[21] On 17 December Loring was given a secret instruction by the king to take back to the prince, dealing with the negotiations for peace or truce. The royal dissatisfaction with the papal policy towards England was clearly expressed, while the impossibility in the current state of knowledge of drawing accurate boundaries for Guyenne and the need of getting more accurate local information were stressed. Finally the king, fearing that he could not ensure the safety of the prince and his valuable prisoner in Gascony, felt it was advisable they should both come to England as soon as the truce had been established leaving enough men to guard and govern the duchy.[22] By the end of March, Cardinal Talleyrand and his fellow negotiator had arrived at a truce and the prince announced his plans for their departure.[23] Gascon pride and, quite likely, ambition were offended by this move. Albret and the Captal de Buch seem to have been the spokesmen for the displeased Gascon barons. They reminded the prince that the king was presently in a handsome, well-fortified city and that they themselves had worked so hard to capture him that they could not accept his removal. The prince appeared to agree with them, but quoted his father's command and promised them generous rewards. According to Froissart, it was Chandos and Cobham who knew best how to deal with the greediness of the Gascons and arrived at a sum of 100,000 francs which the prince would pay the Gascons before he left.[24] On 23 April the prince, his royal captive, and some of the Gascon lords, led by the Captal de Buch, sailed for England. Albret, the lord of Pommiers and his brothers, and the lords of Lesparre and Rauzan were left to guard the country.

France was in a state of upheaval from the shock of defeat. The nineteen-year-old dauphin Charles had the difficult task of trying to establish his authority as regent so that for the moment the danger of organized military activity by the French was minimal. The greater danger was the freebooting devastation caused by the mercenary soldiers banded together in units known as 'Free Companies'. With the suspension of formal warfare these men no longer had employment or pay, they pillaged and burnt the countryside, using the castles they held as a base to menace the surrounding territory while extracting payment (*appatis*) for 'protection'. These Companies were generally referred to as English, partly because many had a large number of rootless English and Gascon members and such English soldiers as Robert Knollys, Hugh Calveley, and Matthew Gournay made their fortune as their commanders. Like locusts, they stripped the countryside. Harassed inhabitants tended to seek refuge in forests or marshes and, particularly along the frontiers of Périgord and Quercy, fortified their churches so as to have a place of refuge for themselves and part of their goods. The vivid letter of the prior of a small house in the diocese of Sens sums up the experiences of many. Pillaging English soldiers in 1358 had stripped his priory of all its goods, drunk its wine and carried off its oats, while he and his neighbours hid in the woods. Later they took all his clothes and ate the priory's pigeons while the safe-conduct he had bought was of no use, because the captain was captured. He was faced with the need to make another settlement to protect the priory's grain fields. The end of the letter suggests the common despair of the countryside: 'I am writing this behind our barn . . . because I do not dare write elsewhere. Do you who live in cities and castles ever see trouble equal to my trouble?'[25]

Under such difficulties it is not surprising that people turned to unusual remedies. Thomas de Pizan, physician and astrologer to King Charles V of France and father of the author Christine de Pizan, used magic in an effort to expel the English companies from France. An unknown contemporary described his procedure minutely. Thomas made five hollow metal images of naked men and on their foreheads wrote the names of the English king or one of the captains. On the jaw and breast he placed astrological characters. Earth had been obtained from the centre of the kingdom and each of its four quarters which was then used to fill each figure. At the proper astrological moment each was buried, face down with its hands behind its back in one of the regions, while an incantation was recited asserting this to be the perpetual burial and total annihilation of the captain, the king and all their officials and adherents, 'so long as this work shall endure by God's will, Amen'. The reporter obviously considered this a purely scientific procedure and concluded with pleasure that within a few months all these companies had fled from the kingdom. Unfortunately, the Companies were not so easily disposed of.[26] They were to be a scourge to much of France for many years, although Gascony itself escaped the worst of their depredations till the disasters of the fifteenth century.

The prince's trip to England with his royal captive was un-eventful. After their formal entry into London on 24 May 1357 with all the pageantry and symbolism so characteristic of such medieval occasions, King John settled down quite happily to a captivity marked by considerable luxury and freedom. The spotlight turned to the English diplomatic efforts to wring the last drop of advantage out of the distinguished pawn in their possession. The Black Prince rejoiced in showing his generosity to all and sundry who had been on his service in Gascony. The grants provide an interesting miscellany: pardons for criminal offences, manumission of a bondman of the prince and all his issue, for such good service. Grants of manors were made to such friends as Chandos, annuities to men who had fought around the prince's person at Poitiers, while the prince's baker received 10 marks yearly for life from the prince's mills and ovens at Macclesfield.[27] Such easy generosity had its own dangers. In September 1357 the prince had to warn the lieutenant of his justice in Chester that some of the men to whom he had given rewards were suing for further grants, taking advantage of the fact that the prince and his council were so 'closely occupied in business of importance and have to a great extent forgotten the above gifts'. The lieutenant is to be careful to honour only one warrant.[28] By 1358 when the Gascons who had come with the prince to England had started to return home they too were given gifts or money. Before the leader of the Spanish contingent at Poitiers left, the prince had bought from him his prisoner the count of Auvergne for the value of 5,000 old crowns of France, as well as provided money to replace ten horses lost in the war. Albret received nearly £270 for no specified reason.[29]

The matter of greatest importance for the English in the years following the battle of Poitiers was the settlement of a peace treaty exploiting their advantage. King John was not a good negotiator. He was too anxious to obtain his freedom, too willing to feel that his subjects would be happy to beggar themselves to pay his ransom. The two preliminary treaties of London in 1358 and 1359 showed these weaknesses most obviously. The proposed agreement of 1359 would have so dismembered the kingdom of France and burdened its truncated territory with such an astronomical ransom for the captured king that the Regent and his advisers refused to accept it.[30] Edward III took advantage of this breakdown to launch still another invasion of France. Accompanied by the prince of Wales he moved into northern France in the autumn of 1359. The expedition was not a success. The attempt to capture Reims was an ignominious failure, and the campaign, although harassing much of the north-east of the realm, achieved no real victories. In fact, it revived French confidence by undermining the legend of the invincibility of English armies. Even the weather worked against them, further disorganizing the invaders, and it became obvious that a settlement was essential. On 8 May 1360, after brief discussions between the dauphin and the prince of Wales, preliminary agreement on peace terms was reached at Brétigny near Chartres. King Edward had lost prestige and bargaining power through this abortive invasion and the new terms were more favourable to France. Edward was still to receive an extended Aquitaine, stretching almost from the Loire to the Pyrenees, in complete sovereignty and absence of *ressort* as well as the English holdings in the north—Calais, Ponthieu and the county of Guines. In return he would renounce his claim and title to the kingdom of France, as well as any residual rights of sovereignty over the ancient English lands of Normandy,

146

Anjou and Maine. King John's ransom, previously set at four million crowns, was reduced to three million (£500,000). Six hundred thousand crowns were to be paid at Calais within four months after the French king's arrival there and this would ensure his freedom. Upon this payment, and before the king was set free, the treaty would be formally ratified. The remaining payments were to be made at the rate of 400,000 crowns a year and until they were completed French hostages, including princes of the blood, great feudal lords and representative bourgeois from certain towns would remain in England.[31]

The agreement was implemented rather rapidly. In early July King John was taken to Calais—it is a revealing sidelight on the comforts available during his period of captivity that it took sixteen carts to transfer his baggage from London to Dover. The down payment, for which Edward agreed to accept 400,000 crowns instead of the required 600,000, was paid by 24 October. The treaty was formally ratified and the king freed. King John made considerable efforts to try and keep up the ransom payments. The remainder of the first instalment was paid before 1 March 1361 and annual payments continued to be made till John's death in 1364, although they were always less than the agreed sums. Before the breakdown of the treaty more than half of the sum had been paid, a remarkable inflow to the English Exchequer.[32]

However, in the ratification at Calais one clause of the original treaty, that dealing with the mutual renunciations which by the original terms were to come into effect at once, was made the subject of a special agreement.[33] According to this, the renunciations were postponed until specified lands in Poitou, Agenais, Périgord and Quercy had been transferred to the king of England. This was supposed to occur by 24 June 1361, or at the latest by 1 November, and mutual oral renunciations would then follow. During the interval the French king was to abstain from using sovereignty in these lands and the English king would not use the title of king of France. It was this clause which was to cause all the later difficulty since the expected renunciations were never made. It would provide the loophole by which Charles V would agree to accept appeals from the Gascon lords in 1368 and cause the re-opening of the war. There has been much argument over the responsibility for this. The panegyrists of Charles the Wise claim that it was his astuteness which insisted on the saving clause and provided the possibility for a future overturning of the treaty, but this seems an inflated claim. Edward III must bear the responsibility for the delayed renunciations, which the French offered to make but before all the promised territories had been surrendered. Since the English king's only weapon to ensure their delivery was the withholding of his own renunciation, the matter continued to drag. The renunciations had to be mutual and it would appear that Edward was lulled into over-confidence in regard to the necessary fulfilment of this article of the treaty by the ease and magnitude of the English military victory.

The French were naturally anxious to repatriate their hostages, for fear of the concessions which they might be tempted to make, since the slow payment of the ransom instalments had made the princes of the blood very impatient. In November 1362 they agreed to all the English demands: the immediate cession of the disputed lands with certain castles in Berry as pledges, and a further immediate payment of 200,000 crowns which would release the hostages. Their agreement was rejected in France as too abject a surrender. When Louis of Anjou broke his parole, his father, King John, chivalrously returned to London in person to act as the required hostage.[34] The French king died there in April 1364.

The Treaty of Brétigny–Calais was to prove merely a pause between hostilities rather than a permanent peace treaty. During the brief years between 1362 and 1368 the Black Prince was to reach his height of glory as prince of Aquitaine. He was to be known throughout Europe for his elegant and luxurious court and was to win further plaudits for his victory at Najera in his quixotic invasion of Spain. Gascony, absorbed once more into a larger Aquitaine, basked for a while in his reflected glory only to find the costs were heavy and its own particular interests neglected.

Manuscript illumination of a confrontation between Edward I and the Archbishop of Canterbury.

Effigy of Philip IV the Fair from the abbey of Saint–Denis.

Effigy of Sir Oliver Ingham, seneschal of Gascony and King's lieutenant there at the outbreak of the Hundred Years War.

ved head of the Black Prince from
k Minster.

igy of Bertrand Du Guesclin,
nstable of France, from the abbey
Saint-Denis.

Effigy of Charles V from the abbey of
Saint-Denis.

Naval battle off La Rochelle as illustrated in Froissart.

Drawing-up a treaty, late fourteenth century.

Richard II gives the duchy of Aquitaine to John of Gaunt, from Froissart.

Henry VI appoints John Talbot, earl of Shrewsbury, constable of France.

BÉNAUGES

A nineteenth-century view of the castle of Bénauges, fortress of the Graillys.

A nineteenth-century view of the city-gate of Bazas.

View of the central square and
cornières of the bastide of
Montpazier.

Bordeaux: Pey Berland's Tower.

Seal of John Streatley, constable of
Bordeaux.

A Gascon vineyard worker of the
fourteenth century.

Ceremony of surrendering a town, late fourteenth century.

CHAPTER XII

The Principality of Aquitaine

The Black Prince was already intimately linked with Gascony by his successful military campaigns. At the time of his appointment in July 1362 as prince of the newly created Principality of Aquitaine he was given full powers there subject to the requirement of liege-homage to his father.[1] The principality he was to rule had expanded enormously under the Treaty of Brétigny and once more included Poitou, Saintonge, the Angoumois, Périgord, the Limousin, Quercy, Rouergue, Armagnac and Bigorre as well as the Agenais and those Gascon lands which had formed the permanent core of the English duchy. Only Béarn, now ruled by the count of Foix, the redoubtable Gaston Fébus, refused to recognize either English or French sovereignty.

The rule of this large territory posed a number of military and administrative problems. Many of the districts newly attached to the Principality had a long tradition of fidelity to the French king and resented the change in allegiance. The administrative pattern, originally designed for a much more compact unit, needed to be adjusted to the new circumstances. With the great increase in the number of *senéchaussées* the choice of good local officials became even more crucial. The new ruler of Aquitaine needed to show himself a man able to govern as well as to command. A French historian summing up the Black Prince's qualities recognized his abilities as an extraordinary strategist and general but argued that he was neither a statesman nor a wise politician and was quite incapable of organizing or administering the territory he had been granted.[2] It was perhaps characteristic of the prince that he moved more quickly after his appointment to ensure the presence in Bordeaux of his goldsmith and two embroiderers than he did to make certain that his officials already serving in Gascony were given enough money for their own expenses until his own arrival.[3]

F

The pacification and transfer of the towns and fortresses of the newly acquired provinces to the English commissioners, called for under the terms of the peace treaty, had been made the responsibility of Sir John Chandos, who was actively engaged on this mission from July 1361 to the end of March 1362.[4] It was a delicate operation which required both tact and firmness, which Chandos seems to have displayed. It is a striking testimony to Sir John's ability that it was an enthusiastic local historian of the Rouergue who praised his wisdom, disinterest and lofty character as compared to the harshness and cupidity of most English officials and the profligacy of the Black Prince.[5]

Meanwhile in England the prince had caused a sensation by his marriage in October 1361 to Joan of Kent, the very recent widow of Thomas Holland. Daughter of Edmund Earl of Kent, the half-brother of Edward II who had been executed in 1330, she had spent her early years at court with the kindly Queen Philippa. She was considered one of the most beautiful and charming women in England, as her nickname the Fair Maid of Kent suggests, and was certainly the most ardently courted. Her secret marriage when very young to Thomas Holland, who then left England for some time, was followed by a marriage to the young earl of Salisbury. When Holland reclaimed his wife the marriage to Salisbury was annulled by the pope.[6] Joan inspired many of the chroniclers to gossip and romanticized stories, reflecting the influence of the romance literature on historical writing of the fourteenth century. Since several so-called histories were designed to glorify a particular king or lord such stories were often adopted with more concern for their artistic effectiveness than their historical reality.[7] The king could not have been particularly pleased at his heir's marriage since it provided no diplomatic advantage, but at thirty-one it was certainly time that his son married. A further source of concern may well have been the fact that Joan was two years older than the prince. Although she had already borne several children, would she be able to provide him with heirs? It would appear that on the prince's side at least it was a love match, although it is interesting to note that when Joan died nine years after the prince she asked to be buried at Stamford, next to Thomas Holland, rather than at Canterbury with the prince.

The prince and princess and their household made ready to go to Aquitaine after the Christmas festivities of 1362. The preparations were extensive as the prince was accompanied by a retinue of 250 men-at-arms, including three bannerets and sixty knights, and 320 archers—a very large company for peacetime.[8] The Patent Rolls suggest the difficulties of shipping and victualling such an expedition since wheat and oats were to be requisitioned for 1,000 horses. By the beginning of March the sheriff of Devon was ordered to buy still more supplies in Cornwall and Devon for the sustenance of the prince, his company and their horses.[9] The expedition finally left Plymouth on 9 June and landed at Lormont on 29 June. One of the immediate necessities was to ensure the taking of homage from all the prince's Gascon vassals. During much of July the cathedral of Saint-André was filled for these ceremonies. Arnaud-Amanieu d'Albret, son of Bernard-Ezi who had died in 1359, and the most important of the Gascon barons, led off on 9 July and was followed by other lords of the second rank such as the Pommiers and the Lamothes. Later in the month it was the turn of the towns, many of whom insisted on the recognition of the fact that their appearance in Bordeaux should not prejudice their ancient right to take the oath in their own town on the first tour of a new lord or his official.[10] Much of the rest of the year was devoted to carrying through this process in such parts of the principality as Bergerac, Saint-Jean-d'Angely, Saintes and Poitiers. In the Christmas season of 1363 the prince was to be found at Agen on the same errand. He remained there all January while a great number of lords and knights travelled in one of the worst winters of the century to take the necessary oath. According to the chroniclers the conditions were unprecedently bad from December to March. The cold froze the vines down to the roots, blighted the fruit trees and killed many sheep and lambs. Thick ice formed, even on the swiftest rivers, and made the moats of castles a convenience rather than a discouragement for brigands. Wine froze so hard in its pots that it had to be broken and sold in chunks to be melted on the fire.[11]

On 12 January 1364 Gaston Fébus, count of Foix, came to Agen to see the prince. It was an important occasion as Fébus was a major power in the south-west and could be a redoubtable enemy.[12] The count's oddly assorted territories illustrate both the confusions of feudal geography and the opportunities it provided for political intrigue and opportunism. Gaston owed homage to the king of France for the county of Foix and its dependencies, to the king of Aragon for fiefs in Roussillon and Castillon, and to the duke of Aquitaine for Marsan and Gabardan. The homage of the viscounty of Béarn was a matter of contention. In the previous century the viscount of Béarn had done homage to the duke of Aquitaine but Gaston, by judicious exploitation of French and English attempts to purchase his support, now insisted that Béarn owed homage to no one. Fébus, a year younger than the Black Prince, was the type of successful and capable feudal prince who used diplomacy as his primary weapon and took to arms only as the means to a specific end. Froissart wrote glowingly of the count's court at Orthez, dealing discreetly with Gaston's killing of his only son when the count was in one of his towering rages—the event that led him to write the *Livre des Oraisons* already mentioned. Among his contemporaries Gaston was highly reputed for his passion for the hunt and his skill was reflected in his magnificent treatise, *Le Livre de Chasse*, probably written during the last four years of his life.[13] It seems appropriate that he died of a stroke after an arduous bear-hunt in the woods near Orthez on a hot day in August 1391. His fondness for hunting surfaced even in his political manoeuvres with the Black Prince. During a flowery and totally inconclusive correspondence in 1365, when the prince was trying to enforce the performance of homage for Béarn and Gaston was making a series of excuses for his non-appearance, the count begged the prince that all of Chandos' dogs, and all others possible, should be available when he finally arrived so that Gaston could show off 'a little of my science'.[14]

His policies were determined by the strategic location of Foix, which was an important element in southern Languedoc, while Béarn, with its fertile lands along the Gave de Pau, was marked by the concern of its inhabitants for good commercial relations with England. Both lands had much Pyrenean territory and Béarn controlled some of the best mountain passes but they were widely separate. There was a continuing antagonism between the counts of Foix and the counts of Armagnac as their expansionary interests inevitably came into conflict. The county of Armagnac, which spread south-west of the Garonne from its centre at Auch, was the centre of Armagnac power but there were also detached lordships, often acquired by marriage. For example, in 1304 Count Bernard of Armagnac had married the heiress of Rodez and his attempts to consolidate these scattered territories, an unsuccessful claim to Béarn and disputes over Bigorre had brought him into continuing struggles with the count of Foix. Count Jean d'Armagnac (1319–73) had married into the fringes of the royal family of France, for his second wife was Béatrice de Clermont, great-granddaughter of Louis IX, and the alliance was further strengthened by the marriage of Jean's daughter to the future duke of Berry.[15] Naturally Armagnac's appointment as French lieutenant-general for Languedoc encouraged Gaston of Foix in a policy of neutrality, or even veiled enmity to France, since it provided an excuse to attack his rival's territory.

After the French defeat at Poitiers Gaston had found it both convenient and interesting to leave the scene temporarily, using the excellent excuse of going on crusade in Prussia. He not only avoided immediate political problems with the French, but also seized the opportunity to hunt reindeer in Norway and Sweden. Gaston was accompanied by his cousin the Captal de Buch and the two distinguished themselves by their military activities in Prussia. On their way home they enhanced their reputation for chivalry by rescuing the duchesses of Orléans and Normandy from the market of Meaux where they had taken refuge from the assault of the Jacquerie, the peasant uprising in France. When Fébus returned to his own lands in October 1358 he discovered that Armagnac had not only been busy consolidating his own position, but had also been putting forward claims to Bigorre. Despite efforts by papal legates and Marshal Boucicaut to make peace war broke out between them in 1362. By this time the count of Armagnac had gained valuable Gascon support, including that of Arnaud-Amanieu d'Albret, his nephew. However, on 5 December 1362 the battle of Launac (a few miles north-west of Toulouse) resulted in a decisive success for Gaston Fébus. Not only were Armagnac's forces routed by the count of Foix, but the count of Armagnac himself and many of his leading followers, including Albret, were captured and held for very stiff ransoms on which Fébus was totally intransigent. Armagnac was required to pay 300,000 florins, Arnaud-Amanieu 100,000 and his cousin Bérard 10,000. Gaston demanded 600,000 florins in all from his captives and seems to have been unusually successful in collecting most of it, since at his death he had 700,000 florins in his treasury at Orthez. This financial strength compared favourably to the revenues of the Black Prince himself and was very much greater than any other Gascon lord. In addition to Armagnac's growing absorption in royal policy, this helps to explain Gaston's political preponderance in the Pyrenean Midi in the second half of the fourteenth century, and his ability to attract the poverty-stricken Gascon lords to his side by pensions or fief-rents.[16] For all these reasons the appearance of Gaston Fébus at Agen on 12 January 1364 was important for the English administration. He did homage to the Black Prince as representative of the English king and as prince of Aquitaine in his own right, but stated specifically that his homage was only for Marsan and Gabardan. All he would concede regarding Béarn, in response to Chandos' direct question, was that he would do what ought to be done if it could be truly proved to him that he held Béarn from anyone.[17]

During these first years of the principality no signs appeared of the fragility of the new state. Froissart explains that he cannot describe 'the feasts, the honours, the processions, the stays, the comings and goings . . . In the beginning all loved and honoured him as their lord as they said his kingdom was the greatest of the world'.[18] Such enthusiastic statements, however, are not of any help in the effort to describe in detail the prince's administration, nor are there adequate records. Once the principality was set up and the prince had taken charge the long-established links with the royal administration in England were cut off. The prince appointed the officials for the principality, the Exchequer at Bordeaux controlled its finances and, with the notable exception of Gascon appeals to King Edward and the English Parliament, the principality was a self-contained unit. Its records were kept in Bordeaux and remained there after the prince's withdrawal only to disappear in the centuries following its capture by the French. Thus the administrative picture is of necessity a mosaic with a fair number of missing pieces. The general outlines are reasonably clear, but there is not the wealth of documentation that accompanies many other periods of Gascon administration.

One of the charges against the prince, vociferously made by Froissart, was that many of the troubles of the principality, and the fragile loyalty of the Gascons, stemmed from the haughtiness of the prince and his English followers and their refusal to allow the Gascons any share in the government.[19] It is worth looking at this claim more closely. It should be remembered that the senior officials of the duchy, the seneschal and the constable, had always been English or, at any rate, not natives of the duchy.

Minor officials, on the other hand, had usually been natives. With the creation of the principality and the personal presence of the prince the seneschal of Gascony became a minor figure, no more important than the other seneschals who had originally been subordinate to him. Sir John Chiverston, for example, seneschal when the prince first arrived, is a rather shadowy figure. The office of chancellor was newly important under the prince, as is illustrated by the calibre of the men appointed to it. Master John Streatley, a man with an extraordinarily wide experience of Gascony and its problems, was the prince's first choice. A doctor of laws, Streatley had already served twice as constable of Bordeaux, from 1348–50 and 1354–61. After the battle of Poitiers he had followed the prince and King John to England and remained for some time in London, being present for five sessions of the king's council. When war was resumed in 1359–60 he returned to Bordeaux to deal with the duchy's finances, and then was sent north to assist Chandos in the territorial takeovers. His appointment as chancellor recognized his knowledge and indispensable competence. In 1364 he was replaced by Master John Harewell, one of the prince's clerks who had been serving as constable of Bordeaux. Harewell remained as chancellor till 1370, being rewarded with the bishopric of Bath and Wells 'for his services to the king and the Prince of Wales in Aquitaine'. The final chancellor of the principality was a local ecclesiastic, Bishop Peter of Périgueux, but he died in office in April 1372 and seems to have had little influence.[20]

When Chandos accepted the surrender of the new territories he often instituted new officials at the same time and he retained many French officials in lesser positions. The appointed seneschals were often experienced Englishmen, for example William Felton in Poitou and the Limousin and Richard of Totesham in Saintonge and the Angoumois, but they also included such trusted Gascons as Elie de Pommiers, once more made seneschal of Périgord and the Cahorsin, and Amanieu du Fossat, seneschal of Rouergue. These men had a long record of service to the English king-duke and certainly their support was essential to the maintenance of the duchy. They usually served on the king's council which had functioned actively in the duchy during the early part of the century. It is less certain that the prince made much use of it, or to what extent it was diluted by his English entourage. The core of important Gascon support, and the team which had worked together over a number of years, began to dissipate in the early 1360s. Elie de Pommiers, for example, after thirty years of service appears to have retired in 1365 with a settlement of 1,000 marks as well as an annual rent of £100 and a cup of gilded silver and a ewer.[21] He had already had a great financial success, both in generous grants and in his share in the settlement for the capture of the count of Eu at Poitiers which brought him 30,000 florins. Fossat was replaced in 1365 by Thomas Wetenhale, a friend of the prince and a cousin of Sir Hugh Calveley, one of the best known and most aggressive of the mercenary leaders. The new seneschal of the Rouergue was disliked locally for his cupidity and insensitivity and did little to improve the image of the English.[22]

What appears very clearly from even the most cursory look at the administration of the greatly extended Aquitaine of the principality is that it had, of necessity, been extended too quickly. The original structures designed for the duchy had been reinforced by a tradition of local involvement and by the development of a class of administrators and clerks from well-respected local families who served the king-duke loyally. The prosperity gained in this service buttressed their loyalty but did not totally account for it. The new *senéchaussées* had no such spirit of attachment to the English government and no such pool of personnel on which to draw. The local men in the new territories who retained their subordinate positions under an English or Gascon superior were accustomed to look to the king of France, not to the duke of Aquitaine. Inevitably the extended structures were fragile and the administration never received the necessary overhaul to enable it to deal with the new conditions. The prince's lack of interest in such matters and his fatal absorption in the Spanish campaign provide both an explanation and an excuse for the rapid breakdown of the principality between 1368 and 1370.

The weakness and sketchiness of the organization is illustrated by the situation of the court of Gascony during these years and its inability to deal with the new problems. The old court of Gascony had simply been the court of the seneschal and was never very carefully delineated. Delays in its procedures were complained of constantly. When King Edward granted the principality to his son he had retained sovereignty and *ressort* in his own hands, thus allowing Gascons to bring appeals to him if they were dissatisfied with the judgments of the prince's great council when it sat as the *Cour des Grands Jours* in Bordeaux. This situation proved totally unsatisfactory and by 1370 the king had decided to set up a Court of Sovereignty in Aquitaine to hear appeals from the prince's court. This proved to be an exercise in futility. No appointments seem to have been made until 1372 when the abbot of Saint-Maixent in Poitou was named royal chancellor in charge of the court. The court was to have been set up at Saintes, but that town was captured by French troops in 1372 and the proposed chancellor had transferred himself to the French allegiance by January 1373. As well, the duplicate of the great seal sent to the new chancellor seems to have been lost in the English naval disaster off La Rochelle in 1372. The court was transferred to Bordeaux and remained there till the end of English rule, but its prestige was weakened by the willingness of the English kings to continue to hear appeals from it.[23]

Most descriptions of the Black Prince's rule in Gascony devote a major share of their attention to his involvement in the affairs of Spain.[24] Such interest in Spain was not new. Both England and France had spent much time and effort seeking an alliance with Castile, primarily because of the importance of its navy. Its permanent service of fighting galleys used fast, manoeuvrable and light ships, commanded by professionals. Its large merchant marine with home ports all along the northern coast, bordering the Bay of Biscay, could serve as useful reinforcement. In the early fourteenth century Edward III had hoped to counteract France's success, in establishing a preponderant influence in Castile, by marrying his daughter to Pedro, heir to the throne of Castile. Joan's death of the plague at Bordeaux on her way to Castile ended this possibility. King John of France, with the active assistance of Innocent VI, had more success, for Blanche of Bourbon was married in 1352 to Pedro, now king.

Pedro, nicknamed the Cruel, had inherited a situation of violence and intrigue, to which he added his own full measure. His queen was abandoned immediately in favour of his mistress and was later imprisoned. Such behaviour encouraged the French to look with some favour on the pretensions of Enrique of Trastamara, Pedro's bastard half-brother. When the Aragonese began negotiations with the French in 1365 over an invasion of Castile in support of Trastamara, King Charles had several reasons to lend his support. In June 1362 a political and military alliance had been signed in London between England and Castile, probably encouraged by the Black Prince himself, as his possession of Aquitaine would be strengthened by an ally in the neighbouring Spanish kingdom. Charles was naturally happy to support the opposite side as part of his struggle against the English. In addition, it suggested a way of ridding the kingdom of France from the tyranny of the mercenary Companies, who looted and terrorized so much of the French countryside, by providing them with military employment safely beyond the Pyrenees. The pope was equally enthusiastic since the Companies also threatened Avignon. Bertrand Du Guesclin was named commander and proceeded to round up his forces, which ultimately included even Anglo-Gascon contingents under Hugh Calveley and Matthew Gournay. When the Black Prince did nothing to prevent such a use of Anglo-Gascon troops he acted in contradiction to the terms of the alliance of 1362, a matter of which he was reminded by a vigorous letter of Edward III in December 1365 threatening punishment for any of his subjects who joined such an attack.[25] The order was too late, the soldiers had departed and, by the end of March 1366, Pedro had been forced to flee and Enrique was crowned king of Castile at Burgos.

Pedro turned for help to the Black Prince, who invited him to Aquitaine, going to meet him at Capbreton. During the summer of 1366 negotiations went on between them, Charles the Bad, king of Navarre, who controlled the essential pass of Roncesvalles, and the Gascon lords who would necessarily form a major part of the army if an expedition to Spain was made. The Gascons were willing to fight but made it clear that they must be paid, and this obligation the Black Prince assumed. Pedro swore that he would repay him 550,000 florins within two years for the cost of the troops, but for the present merely agreed on the sale of his jewels and the grant of a number of Spanish lordships to the Prince and Chandos when Castile was reconquered. King Edward gave his approval to the expedition and John of Gaunt, the prince's younger brother, agreed to bring an English contingent to the force. The final agreements were signed at the Franciscan house at Libourne in September 1366.[26] The raising of forces and the preparation of equipment were rapidly put on foot. From the description given by Chandos Herald the arrangements were lavish: 'Then might you see swords and daggers forged at Bordeaux, coats of mail, and bassinets, lances, axes and gauntlets. Exceeding noble would the equipment have been, had there been thirty kings.'[27] It was to be an impressive army which gathered at Dax in December and January, probably about 10,000 men.

Chandos, who as constable of Aquitaine served as the prince's chief of staff and his chief adviser, was not in favour of the expedition, Froissart claimed, but once it had been decided upon, bent every effort to make it successful. He saw to the recall of the Companies who had been fighting with Du Guesclin in Spain and advised the prince to melt down a great part of his gold and silver plate to make coinage with which to pay the Companies so that, as Froissart realistically says, 'he would be better and more willingly served'.[28] Chandos Herald calls the roll of the most important barons who had joined the prince and mentions among the Gascons, the count of Armagnac, the Sire d'Albret and two of his relations, the Captal de Buch, all the Pommier brothers, and the lord of Mussidan.[29] The Company had not been achieved without unfortunate conflict. At the beginning of December the prince had begun to realize the great financial liability he had accepted and attempted to cut the number of men-at-arms under his wages. The Sire d'Albret had contracted for 1,000 men but the prince notified him to bring only 200. Albret, avaricious and beset with debts including the ransom owed to the count of Foix, had made an alliance with Charles the Bad of Navarre as well as swearing fealty to the prince for his Gascon lands. He had also begun to flirt with the possible profits to be made in a French connection. A violent quarrel broke out between him and the prince over such a major cut in his expected revenue. Armagnac, warned of the dispute, approached Edward and with the help of Chandos and Felton smoothed matters over temporarily. Albret joined the expedition with the requested 200 men, but the ill-feeling remained.[30] The always touchy pride of the Gascons and the unbending arrogance of the prince made this encounter a harbinger of the difficulties to come.

Chandos advised the prince that if the expedition failed his prestige would suffer and his enemies would be delighted to swarm against him, while if he was victorious he would be indebted to so many men that war might result in his lands. His warning proved only too accurate.[31] The prince's victory at Najera was to cost him very dear although it certainly reinforced his reputation as a general and a strategist. He led his army up through the mountainous pass of Roncesvalles in appalling February weather, marched his men safely through difficult countryside and forced Trastamara and his French supporters into battle when Edward himself had picked the better position for his army and its style of fighting. Najera, fought on 3 April 1367, was the third of the Black Prince's great victories but it had less permanent results than Crécy or Poitiers. Trastamara fled, while Du Guesclin, Marshal Audrehem and the Count Denia were merely the most distinguished among a large number of prisoners. However, although the Anglo-Gascon army went on to Burgos, which the prince entered with great solemnity with Don Pedro, the cracks in the alliance appeared almost at once. Pedro neither could nor would pay the debts he had incurred to the prince, nor would he hand over the lands he had promised. The prince's army was without pay and without food in the heat of a Spanish summer. In August the prince turned back to Aquitaine, disillusioned by Pedro's perfidy, with his coffers empty and no way to restrain the Companies who had fought in his service from oppressing Aquitaine until he could manage to pay them off. As well, he himself had been attacked by the disease that was to incapacitate him and lead to his death eight years later at the age of forty-six.

The prince needed money desperately on his return to his principality and it was natural to call a meeting of the estates and to request their agreement to a *fouage*. This was not a new tax. Well known in France, where it was frequently imposed by the French king, it had already been levied by the prince several times in the principality, although at a low rate. The assembly at Angoulême in January 1368 voted a *fouage* of 10 *sous* a year for five years. In return for this grant the prince made a series of concessions. The value of money was pegged for the next five years—the gold mark was to be worth 61 *livres bordelais* and the mark 5 *livres 5 sous bordelais*. A host of privileges were granted which amounted almost to a charter of reform, correcting infringements on the rights of lords and towns as well as promising greater control of erring or over-zealous officials.[32] Their nature suggests that Froissart's rhetoric against the oppressive officials of the prince and their lack of care for justice had its foundation in actual happenings. In addition, the fact that so many of the offending officials were English caused a double grievance for the native felt aggrieved by his inability to gain such lucrative employment and resented the exploitation of his lands and revenues by foreigners.

The major discontent was among the feudal lords who had

found that peace—and therefore unemployment—had cut drastically into their revenues. This was particularly true for those lords, especially Armagnac and Albret, who owed sizeable ransoms to Gaston Fébus. In addition they resented the commercial privileges granted the towns, which had made them generally content with the prince's rule. Unfortunately the prince was no diplomat and no conciliator. An English chronicler mentions his arrogance and disdain towards the important barons of the country, making them wait four or five days before he would speak to them and, when they were admitted into his presence, requiring them 'to kneel and change knees for a quarter of an hour before he ordered them to stand'. Froissart compares the poor reception given to any knight or baron of the duchy at the prince's court with the gracious welcome they were offered at the court of the French king, 'and that is the thing that men-at-arms require, and especially those of the marches of Gascony'.[33] King Charles' policy was wholly bent to the rupture of the humiliating treaty of 1360 but, unlike the prince, he was willing to wait, to move cautiously behind the scenes until he could find a situation in which he would have, or appear to have, legal right on his side. The French king took advantage of the years of peace to stabilize his government and to put on a solid footing the structure of taxation which would provide the resources to maintain adequate military forces and also to pay generous pensions and grants to Gascon lords who could be persuaded to turn to his side.

Although the *fouage* was accepted by most of the prince's lands the count of Armagnac and his closest supporters stood out against it. This was not a new departure on the part of Armagnac. He had also refused the *fouage* of 1364, claiming that his lands were free of such an imposition, and that the prince had sworn to maintain him in his rightful estate. He was also angry at the non-payment of his costs in the Spanish expedition and the devastation in his lands caused by the Companies. Armagnac had never been a wholehearted supporter of the prince, although he had been glad to borrow money from him to pay off his ransom, nor had he ever fully accepted the transfer of allegiance required by the treaty of 1360 since it separated him from Languedoc where he had been French lieutenant. His lands in Rouergue adjoined French lands and were extremely remote from the core of English Aquitaine around Bordeaux. Both Armagnac and his nephew

Albret were involved in a double game. Albret was headstrong and probably the most avaricious of the Gascon lords.[34] His links with Charles V went back to his attendance at his coronation and on 4 May 1368 he married Marguerite de Bourbon, the king's young sister-in-law. At the beginning of June he received 10,000 *livres* from the royal treasury and became a vassal of Charles V, only excluding his Gascon fiefs. Meanwhile, Armagnac, as his uncle, was naturally in Paris for the wedding celebrations. Messengers had been sent to England complaining of the prince and demanding justice from King Edward, but Armagnac and Albret were simultaneously engaged in secret negotiations with King Charles. These concluded in the secret treaty of 30 June by which they, along with the count of Périgord and Bérard d'Albret, were assured by King Charles that he would receive their appeal against the prince by virtue of his right of sovereignty and *ressort* which they recognized, denying any such right to the king of England or his son. In turn, they were to receive from Charles subsidies to enable them to sustain any war which might be waged against them.[35] The fatal consequences of the misunderstanding between the king in England and the headstrong prince in Bordeaux and the slowness of their communication added fuel to the fire for the discontented Gascons.[36] English ambassadors, including the experienced John Streatley, were in Paris from mid-September to the end of October but by 8 September Albret had officially launched his appeal to the French king, though he gave the ambassadors another brief of complaints against the prince to take back to England. The ambassadors do not seem to have realized that, unlike King Edward who still hoped to negotiate and smooth over the breach, King Charles was merely slowing the rupture of the treaty until his diplomatic and military preparations were complete. His vaunted hesitation in accepting the Gascon appeal was a clever and successful tactical device.

Before the end of the year King Charles had taken the appellants under his protection, provided a huge pension for Albret, used circular letters to the 'good towns' of Aquitaine and elsewhere to show the correctness and loyalty of his own attitude, and summoned the prince to answer before his court in Paris. To put crudely what the king continued to elaborate in more and more complex legalistic terms, the French contention was that the treaty of Calais had only suspended the French use of sovereignty and *ressort* for one year unless the final renunciations had been made by both kings within this time. The renunciations were never made and therefore King Charles was at full liberty to resume the exercise of merely suspended powers. It was not the best of arguments for even the king's devoted biographer describes Charles' argumentation as 'fundamentally more subtle and perhaps specious than fully convincing'.[37]

According to Froissart, when King Charles' summons was brought to the prince at Bordeaux in January 1369 the prince reacted violently. Confined to his bed, he resented bitterly the French discounting him as already dead and unable to do them any harm. With more bravado than diplomacy he sent back word that he would gladly obey the French king's summons but with his helmet on his head and 60,000 men at his back.[38] These were bold words but they could not be followed up with strong deeds and his imprisonment of the messengers, in contradiction to the accepted code, caused further annoyance in France. Despite the prince's recall of Chandos, who had retired to his lands in Normandy, the duchy was in military disarray. King Charles' careful preparations and the appearance of the duke of Anjou at Toulouse to lead the French forces quickly led to a large number joining the original appellants. By March 1369, before any official renewal of the war 921 castles, towns and strongholds in the duchy had recognized King Charles' sovereignty and joined the appeal.[39] As an anonymous but well-informed correspondent in Gascony wrote to his friend in England on the multitude of their misfortunes:

> I would know how to write you for a whole day on this matter before I could reach the end, but for the great haste I have at present for all the other needs with which I am occupied, I cannot write as much as I would wish on this matter.[40]

Early in May 1369 the appeal was heard in Paris and the Parlement declared the prince at fault. During the summer the local prelates of Languedoc—all French in sympathy—preached against the English occupation in the centres of Rouergue and Quercy. However, it was not until 30 November that Charles announced the confiscation of Guyenne because of the disloyalty of his vassal—a condemnation formally renewed in May 1370.[41] While the complex legal manoeuvres unrolled in Paris fighting continued all through Aquitaine with an almost unbroken succession of major losses for the English and only occasional and temporary successes. The prince, incapable of leading his troops himself because of his health, suffered the loss of his closest companions and trusted commanders. Sir James Audley died in the autumn of 1369 and the universally respected Chandos died as the result of a skirmish at Lussac at the beginning of 1370. His death was regretted by both English and French as the loss of a great captain and a wise and valiant knight. Froissart suggests that the French were particularly sorry that he had not been captured instead of killed because 'he was indeed so wise and so imaginative that he might have found some way by which there might have been peace between France and England'.[42] There was no one of equal calibre on the English side to fill his place.

Some of the most devoted Gascons, including the Captal de Buch and Elie and Jean de Pommiers (their brother Amanieu had prudently departed on crusade to avoid any problems of allegiance) rallied to the prince's cause but the principality shrank day by day. The *fouage* had been withdrawn by order of the King Edward in November 1369, but such action seemed irrelevant to the campaign in progress. French forces had got as far as Bazas by the end of 1369 and by 1370 much of the Agenais had again turned French. English loyalty was stronger in the north and fighting continued in Poitou, but the obvious incapacity of the prince prompted King Edward to send John of Gaunt at the head of a force to strengthen the principality. The surrender of Limoges to the French troops under the duke of Berry was the final goad to the prince's wounded pride and sense of honour, for the city's gates had been opened to the French by the bishop of Limoges, a one-time councillor of the prince and godfather to his son Richard. Edward swore to punish the traitors and, carried to the siege in a litter, supervised a vigorous attack which on 19 September breached part of the city's walls, allowing the English troops to enter and to pillage and murder indiscriminately. It should be remembered that the sack and massacre at Limoges were not contrary to the medieval code. This allowed the total destruction of a besieged place which refused to surrender, and Chandos Herald, while admittedly a propagandist for the prince, found nothing out of the ordinary in his hero's behaviour.[43] Other chroniclers, most notably Froissart, claimed that the inhabitants of the city had regretted their decision and had sought an agreement which the furious prince denied them. When entry had been made and the inhabitants sought mercy the prince's troops 'without pity and without mercy killed all they could find and encounter'.[44] Limoges undoubtedly ended the military career of the Black Prince on an unhappy note, which has blackened his reputation down the centuries.

In January 1371 the prince and princess set sail for England with young Richard. Just before their departure they had suffered a final blow in the death of their much loved elder son Edward, a boy of six. In a final meeting the prince called together some sixty loyal Gascon lords. He bade them farewell, begged them to obey John of Gaunt as they had obeyed him and urged them to keep faith loyally and to defend their heritage from French encroachments.[45] Unfortunately, the principality of Aquitaine was dead in all but name—the prince would formally surrender it in 1372—and the dreams of glory and military fame, which had seemed so near and enticing in 1355 had vanished in a morass of misjudgment, malice and physical weakness. At forty-one the prince should have been in his prime, instead he was a fatally sick man—suffering from dropsy and probably amoebic dysentery —who had seen all his triumphs turn to ashes. Illness and the loss of such friends and advisers as Chandos and Audley had undermined his sense of equity and his ability to make the suitable military and administrative decisions. Gascony's hour of glory had vanished too. With its forces and finances in disarray, and with only sporadic support from England, the diminished duchy found itself fighting a rearguard action to maintain its very existence.

CHAPTER XIII

The Ebb of English Power

The history of English rule in Gascony during the last years of
Edward III's reign is one of weakness and continued defeats, a
reflection of the changed atmosphere in England. The ageing
king and ailing prince could no longer provide encouragement
and leadership for ambitious campaigns, while the ardent young
nobles who had fought with skill and zest in France and brought
glory to Edward's Order of the Garter had grown old or died.
The war with France became much less popular in England when
there were no longer showy military triumphs. The cutting off
of the massive inflow of ransoms created new problems in war
financing for the royal treasury, while further down the scale the
lesser nobles and military captains felt aggrieved by the scarcity
of prisoners and booty. The weight of taxation required to mount
even the necessary defence operations roused bitter complaints
among all classes in the realm. Available funds had to be divided
among the various theatres of the war and Aquitaine always
received the least. In a comparison of the amounts applied to
the various theatres of the English war effort between 1368 and
1381 (i.e. northern France, the war at sea, the 'barbican' of Calais
and its march, and Aquitaine) northern France and Calais received 63 per cent, the war at sea (including transport) 23 per cent
and Aquitaine only 14 per cent.[1] Once the war in Gascony became
a holding operation, it no longer appealed to military adventurers,
for destructive and profitable raids were not a suitable technique
for holding the loyalty of newly acquired districts. The rapid
decline of English interest in providing adequate defences for
the duchy is obvious in the almost total lack of financial assistance after 1372, when 90 per cent of all the money allotted to
Aquitaine between 1368 and 1381 had already been spent.[2] The
history of these years in Gascony is one of pessimism and concern
in which the diminished duchy began to look to its own survival

and the maintenance of the English connection, despite English disinterest.

Early English military strategy had relied on rapid raids into enemy territory, sowing fear and devastation among the population, reaping rich rewards in booty but few permanent conquests. During the first period of the war the English had shown superior strategic and tactical sense in the few pitched battles and, at Poitiers especially, had achieved diplomatic results out of all proportion to their real military importance. By the late 1360s the tide had begun to turn, as Charles V's policies became effective. His military strategy, so ably carried out by Du Guesclin, was to harass and wear down his opponent, to capture selected tactical locations but never to offer pitched battle. The French, with a far larger population and greater basic revenues, had the advantage of land lines of communication as they rebuilt their military strength. The taxes first imposed to pay King John's ransom became part of a coherent and continuing tax structure which financed their military forces.[3] Alliance with Castile, and the beginnings of a French navy, challenged the English control of the Channel established after Sluys: the French and Castilians not only attacked English shipping, they brought the war to the English coastal towns. The long and difficult trip to Gascony became more dangerous and subject to attack, encouraging England to concentrate its efforts in northern France, so much more easily reached.

Discouragement had been heightened by the fruitless English efforts in Gascony in 1372–73. In April 1372 the earl of Pembroke was named lieutenant of Aquitaine with a small personal retinue but the power to recruit extensively in the duchy. A king's clerk was appointed to accompany the expedition, carrying £12,000 to pay the soldiers' wages. Unfortunately, when Pembroke, his retinue and his war-chest left Plymouth in mid-June they sailed in a small fleet, neither manned nor prepared for a major battle. As they approached La Rochelle they were attacked by a fleet of at least twelve Castilian galleys. The Franco-Castilian alliance of 1368 proved its worth in this valuable assistance by the Castilian fleet, whose fighting galleys were far more manoeuvrable at close quarters and in shallow waters than the English sailing ships. The battle raged for two days and on the second day the Spaniards succeeded in spraying oil on the decks and rigging of some of the English ships and then firing them with burning arrows. The result was total disaster, for all the English ships were burnt or captured with a great loss of life. The earl himself was taken as a prisoner to Spain where he was forced to remain for nearly three years, dying on his return journey home. His treasure was seized and the duplicate of the Great Seal, which he was bringing for the use of the Court of Sovereignty, was lost.[4] The defeat was a terrible blow to the English cause in the south-west, wasting scarce resources and discouraging the local adherents. The English government came under criticism for sending such a small and unprotected force to Poitou, although one monastic chronicler was happy to blame the misfortune on Pembroke's notoriously evil life and his speech in a previous parliament against the rights and liberties of the Church.[5]

One defeat led to another as the remaining English strongholds in Poitou and Saintonge slipped from their grasp during the summer. La Rochelle was under siege, Poitiers was taken and the Captal de Buch was captured in a battle at Soubise at the end of August. This was a major blow, since Jean III de Grailly, Captal de Buch, was not only the constable of Aquitaine in succession to Chandos, but was known as 'the most famous knight of Gascony and the one whom the French feared the most'.[6] He was certainly one of the legendary figures of his time. A descendant of the Jean de Grailly who had served Edward I as seneschal in Gascony the Captal's family had established itself in the duchy and grown in riches, prestige and power so that the head of the house was recognized as one of the leading barons of the duchy. The Captal's mother, Blanche of Foix, was descended from the royal house of France and Jean numbered among his cousins Charles the Bad of Navarre, Gaston Fébus and Cardinal Talleyrand de Périgord. An early member of the Order of the Garter, the Captal was active in the forces of the Black Prince in 1355–56, and played a crucial role at Poitiers. During the period of peace in Aquitaine he fought for Charles the Bad and was captured at the battle of Cocherel (1364). Charles V was so anxious to win the Captal to the French side at that time that he freed him without ransom and offered him the castle of Nemours in return for his homage. Grailly had agreed to this but when he was taxed with infidelity by the Black Prince on his return to Aquitaine he at once renounced his homage to Charles and his new acquisitions. From 1367 the Captal was closely linked with the prince as the leader of the local Gascon lords and received such profitable favours as the grant of 15*d.* on each tun of wine passing his town of Cadillac on the Garonne.[7] His capture at Soubise was most discouraging to English morale. When Grailly refused King Charles' offers to turn French the king then refused to ransom or exchange him and kept him closely guarded. His policy was not popular with the French knights who found it contrary to their ideas of military honour and was particularly resented by the squire who had actually captured the Captal and had seen his dreams of financial gain from the ransom dwindle into a mere royal grant of 1,200 francs. King Charles was often described disparagingly by his more warlike contemporaries as a mere lawyer, but his prudence and reliance on reasons of state had helped to consolidate French successes. The French king was only too aware of Grailly's prowess and organizing ability and distrusted his ability to raise a vigorous opposition in the south-west. Both sides remained stubborn. The Captal refused to turn French despite all inducements and he was kept in captivity in Paris until he died in 1376.[8]

The disasters of the summer of 1372 galvanized King Edward into one final burst of activity to save the remnants of Aquitaine. He gathered a mighty naval force at Sandwich at the end of the summer. The expedition included the king and prince in person as well as some 6,000 men-at-arms and archers. Such a force required a very large transport fleet, probably 175 to 200 ships and 5,000 sailors, and could have made a major military impact but once more the weather took a decisive hand. Despite the fleet's attempt to leave England at the beginning of September it was buffeted by the equinoctial gales and had got no further than Winchelsea by early October. The king was forced to admit his inability to proceed and the great expedition returned to harbour having achieved nothing.[9] The prince formally resigned his principality before the assembled lords in November.[10]

With this gesture Aquitaine receded once more into the background of English concerns, while the loss of Poitou and Saintonge to the French continued without further English intervention. In the summer of 1373 John of Gaunt attempted a great *chevauchée,* hoping for the glory and success which his brother had gained in such an expedition. This would both aid Gascony and open the way to Castile, now Gaunt's greatest concern after his marriage to Constance of Castile, heiress of the murdered King Pedro. The duke and his force started out from Calais in

June, following the general south-eastward direction of King Edward's army of 1359, but Gaunt's failure was even more severe. Du Guesclin continually harried the force, picking off strays, destroying possible forage, but never giving battle. The duke was finally forced to continue through the harsh upland country of the Auvergne as his only route to the safety of Bordeaux. When he finally arrived there at Christmas he had lost some half of his troops through cold, hunger and attrition and had achieved no real successes.

Meanwhile, the efforts of a series of papal legates vainly pursuing peace between England and France sound as a constant obbligato until the death of Edward III. Frequently such efforts were merely the unheeded accompaniment to military campaigns which neither side was really willing to terminate. In addition the English had a profound and often justified distrust of the later Avignonese popes as tools and spokesmen of the French interests, a reality particularly obvious in the activities of both Innocent VI (1352–62) and Urban V (1362–70). Innocent had served the French king as a judge in the *senéchaussée* of Toulouse before his election and, just before his death, had loaned money to the French treasurer to aid in carrying out the first treaty with Enrique of Trastamara. Urban, the Benedictine abbot of Saint-Victor, Marseilles before his election, was a conscientious reformer anxious to return the papacy to Rome, but his sensible reforms were refused in England because of his blatant interference in the marriage of the heiress of Flanders in order to protect the French northern frontier. The pope withheld the normal dispensation for marriage within the forbidden degrees of relationship from the marriage arranged between Edward III's son Edmund and Margaret, heiress of Louis Mâle, count of Flanders, Artois and Nevers, but granted exactly the same dispensation to Duke Philip of Burgundy, Charles V's brother, who married Margaret and succeeded his father-in-law in 1384. However, Urban was not always totally subservient to French wishes. When the pope had determined to return to Rome King Charles tried every persuasion to keep Urban at Avignon. In March 1367 a prestigious French embassy made an impassioned emotional appeal to the pope. They reminded Urban that Rome was not as Christian as France, that the holiest relics were in France which was predestined for the development of the Christian religion. According to the geographers, they claimed,

Marseilles was the centre of Europe and the Vicar of Christ should sit at the centre of Christianity. As well, the pope had been born in France and should imitate Christ who had remained in his own country.[11] These ingenuous and self-serving protestations did not deter Urban who left for Rome the following month, returning to Avignon only a few months before his death.

As the fighting between the French and English flared up again Pope Gregory XI (1370–78) struggled to bring the warring sides together. Gregory was himself a Limousin, the nephew of Clement VI, and was especially concerned as the new campaigns devastated so much of his native district. Nevertheless it was not till after Gaunt's ill-fated *chevauchée* that the English wished even to discuss peace. Lancaster managed to arrange a short truce with Du Guesclin after his arrival in Bordeaux and immediately returned to England, but the French were unwilling to extend the truce beyond its original term of May 1374, having decided on a three-pronged offensive for the summer. The duke of Bourbon campaigned in the Limousin where he had little difficulty reversing the surrenders made to Gaunt during his *chevauchée* of the previous year. By August the duke of Anjou was ready to begin a further attack on central Guyenne and moved to attack La Réole. Before his departure Lancaster had named Florimond, Sire de Lesparre, a loyal noble from the Médoc, to share the government of Gascony with Thomas Felton, the seneschal. Lesparre attempted to reinforce La Réole with munitions and a force commanded by Hugh Calveley but, despite this help, the town opened its gates to the French without a fight and was rewarded by French confirmation of all its privileges. The castle refused to surrender at once, but was finally forced to capitulate on 8 September after a week's siege and pounding by a French bombard. After thirty years the French were once more established in La Réole, thereby threatening Bordeaux and the smaller towns dependent on it. Enrique of Trastamara, now king of Castile, had planned to concert his forces with those of Anjou, but the Spanish attack on Bayonne was ineffective. Enrique withdrew, leaving Bayonne still in English hands.[12]

Negotiations for peace finally got under way at Bruges in the summer of 1374. The proposals put forward at this conference have come down to us in a collection of the more important documents passing through the hands of the two papal nuncios who were trying to bring the French and English to some agreement.[13] They provide an interesting glimpse of the vigorous efforts of the presiding cardinals and the various initiatives put forward by the embassies but all were doomed to failure. The French and English were quite unable to arrive at a compromise on the possession and sovereignty of Aquitaine even if the disputes over its territorial extent were settled. Real peace was unattainable even without the quibbles over the involvement of Castile and Brittany. However, it finally proved possible to arrange a truce which was proclaimed in June 1375 and lasted till 1377.

Meanwhile, within the sadly truncated duchy of Guyenne the city of Bordeaux faced internal problems.[14] In 1375 the mayor and jurats passed an ordinance reducing the number of jurats from twenty-four to twelve and denying the right of nobles to be elected to the jurade. Since the purpose of the measure was obviously to limit the power of the nobles within the city it is possible that the merchant bourgeois, concerned with the city's economic life, mistrusted the easy infidelity of so many Gascon nobles since 1368 and wanted to ensure the city's loyalty to the English connection. The number of nobles involved was not very great. A few, like the Captal de Buch and Pierre de Landiras, inherited their rights to the bourgeoisie from the fiefs they held within the city; others could only be granted the privilege by royal decree. Because membership in the bourgeoisie carried with it the valuable exemption from the custom on wine, it was a profitable and sought-after privilege. Jean Colom, who carried Bordeaux's petition to England for the king's confirmation argued that this restriction and the lowering of the number of the jurats would actually reinforce the royal power within the city. The king agreed, adding a further clause denying to the nobles even the right to become bourgeois. This, in turn, much upset the nobles and petitions flowed back to England protesting their loyalty and long-established rights, as well as deploring the reduction in the jurade as likely to lead to the city's 'great peril and perdition', because twelve could more easily plot evil than twenty-four.[15] Disputes continued to rage on this matter until Gaunt finally abrogated the ordinance in 1392, so that nobles were again made eligible for the jurade, although that body remained at twelve.[16]

The problem of loyalty surfaced even more dramatically in the case of Guilhem-Sanche de Pommiers, viscount of Fronsac, who was arrested at Libourne in March 1377 on the charge of high treason. Arnaud-Amanieu d'Albret had been busy trying to raise adherents for the French cause in the duchy, even close to Bordeaux. The gaining of Pommiers to the French allegiance would have been a glittering prize as he came from a noble family which had loyally supported the English crown for a century and his relatives had been active in the forces of the Black Prince. Even more important for French plans, the castle of Fronsac which he held was one of the most crucial fortresses near Bordeaux since it controlled the Dordogne at its meeting with the Isle. Albret had invited Pommiers to Tartas in mid-winter and laid bare to him the French campaign plan for the summer of 1377. The proposal was for a triple-pronged attack on Bordeaux: the French and Castilian fleets blockading the city from the sea, while land forces attacked from both the north-east and the south-east. Albret tempted Pommiers with an invitation to turn French immediately since in that way he could make enormous profits while if he waited till he was made French by force he would gain nothing. The prospect was too tempting and Pommiers agreed to Albret's offers of French money and men, but before he could put his treachery into effect he was seized. On 11 April 1377 he was brought before the Court of Gascony presided over by Felton as seneschal. Probably because of the key location of Fronsac and the threat which its surrender held for Bordeaux the sentence of the court was harsh and immediate. Pommiers and Jean Colom, who had acted as his clerk, were to be beheaded in the Ombrière as false and traitorous. All their lands and goods were to be confiscated, but Pommiers' body was to have religious burial 'because of the loyal service of his father and other relatives'.[17] Pommiers had merely followed the example of a large number of Gascon nobles who had cheer-fully sold their allegiance to the French and been untouched by English reprisals. Fronsac was too essential to the very existence of the duchy and the Pommiers had for so long been loyal ad-herents of the English cause that Felton appears to have felt it necessary, in view of the coming French campaign, to make an example of the perils of disloyalty even at the cost of alienating Guilhem-Sanche's relatives.

The summer campaign of 1377 was crucial for the duchy. It marked the culmination of Charles V's efforts to drive the English from France at a time when England was preoccupied with the death of Edward III and the accession of the nine-year-old Richard II, as well as plagued by internal dissension and power struggles. Little attention could be paid to Guyenne. Anjou again led the French forces and achieved a remarkable series of successes. His army, reinforced by Du Guesclin and his troops, massed on the frontier of Périgord at the beginning of August. Their first major objective was Bergerac, the intensely valuable strongpoint on the middle Dordogne at the intersection of the borders of Gascony, the Limousin, Rouergue and Quercy. The town which Henry, earl of Lancaster, had regained for the English in 1344 was now held by John of Gaunt. Its captain was Berducat d'Albret, a bastard half-brother of Arnaud-Amanieu. Thomas Felton, the seneschal, was rightfully concerned over the fate of Bergerac, while his previous pleas to England for help had been disregarded. He called together the remaining loyal Gascon lords to aid in a relieving expedition, for siege had been set at Bergerac on 22 August. The French quickly decided to shorten the siege by reinforcing their fire power with the 'engines' they had stored at La Réole and dispatched a force to bring them back. Felton, hearing of this, laid an ambush at Eymet on the river Dropt, which was on their line of march. Anjou's spies provided early information on English moves, permitting the duke to send off a strong French advance party which surprised and defeated the English force on 1 September. Felton himself was captured, as were several of the most faithful Gascons, including the lords of Mussidan, Duras, Rauzan and Langoiran. The following day Bergerac itself surrendered and Berducat d'Albret, sharply characterized as 'a typical routier with no scruples or moral sense', turned French.[18]

The way was open to the very heart of the duchy and the fortresses and towns along the Dordogne—Sainte-Foy, Castillon, Libourne, and Saint-Emilion—capitulated more or less rapidly, but there was considerable fighting around Blaye. During the siege of Castillon the four captured Gascon lords were under considerable pressure to 'turn French' and finally agreed. The lord of Langoiran, Bérard d'Albret (cousin of Arnaud-Amanieu), was rewarded with an annual rent of 2,000 francs and the commission to force the surrender of Entre-deux-Mers from Rions to Bec d'Ambès with permission to grant the captured places as he saw fit. Créon and Sauveterre were taken and Saint-Macaire captured after a siege, while a part of the French army crossed the Garonne to capture Langon and Landiras on the left bank.[19] The French were firmly in command within twenty miles of Bordeaux, while the government of the duchy was in considerable disarray after Felton's capture. The unfortunate Felton remained a prisoner till 1380, since he had great difficulty in raising his ransom. Partial financing was provided by Gaston Fébus, obviously as a purely business transaction; Fébus urged the French to set the ransom as high as possible, since his profit would be greater if a higher sum was required. King Richard finally turned over to Felton a French prisoner whose ransom he was allowed to set so as to pay off his own amount due and get some return on the money owed him for service in Aquitaine.[20] The government of the duchy was carried on temporarily by the king's council in Bordeaux, which assumed the responsibility in the absence of any seneschal and worked vigorously with Richard Rotour, the constable of Bordeaux.

Saint-Macaire had fallen the first week in October and the threat of an immediate siege of Bordeaux was very great. The city was saved by the change of heart of the lords of Duras and Rauzan, who had been allowed to return to their lands to rally support for the French. They began to regret their oath to turn French and philosophized that it was better to forswear the recent oath to the French king than the long-standing one to the king of England, 'our natural lord who has done so many good things for us'.[21] Therefore, instead of returning to their lands they went to Bordeaux, explained the situation and reaffirmed their fealty to the English king. When Anjou heard of their move he was infuriated and swore to attack and destroy Duras and Rauzan. However, such a change in strategy required the abandonment of the siege at Cadillac and the return of the French army to Duras, some fifteen miles north-east of La Réole. Its siege took three weeks in October and its brisk defence made the French fall back on cannon as well as the more usual stone-throwers to break its resistance. By the time Duras capitulated the campaigning season was almost ended. Anjou himself was anxious to return to Toulouse, the men needed to spend the winter in garrison and the horses had been dying off, unable to stand the strain of the bad weather after a strenuous three-month campaign. Bordeaux was saved again.

The campaign of 1377 had won 134 towns and castles, mostly of major rank, and had been a personal triumph for Anjou.

Nevertheless, it was fundamentally a failure, for Anjou had let himself be distracted from his best opportunity to capture Bordeaux and thus drive the English from the duchy. By 1378 English strength had been rebuilt. John Neville, baron of Raby and an able and experienced soldier, had been dispatched to Gascony as seneschal to organize the local opposition. The Anglo-Gascons retrieved some of the losses of the previous year and their morale rose as some strongpoints were retained and the inhabitants turned English again. Of the two remaining Gascon lords who had been captured by the French at Eymet, the lord of Mussidan became very unhappy in Paris and returned to the duchy. He sought out Neville, renewed his English fealty and remained loyal until his death. The lord of Langoiran, who remained French, rashly attempted a single combat with the captain of the English garrison at Cadillac and was defeated and killed.[22] The French forward movement had been halted. Bordeaux developed a network of surrounding towns, its *filleules*, which it encouraged with military support. The duchy was much diminished, but England had maintained its control of the vital centres of Bordeaux and Bayonne and the narrow coastline strip connecting them.

By the end of 1380 the great protagonists of the middle of the century had all vanished from the scene. The Black Prince had died in 1376, King Edward in 1377 and Charles V in 1380. Both France and England were ruled by minors with all the internal quarrelling this inevitably entailed. Charles V had brought France back from the disgrace of Poitiers and the bitter terms of Brétigny and Calais. His legal manoeuvrings had given him, with the assistance of some disgruntled Gascon lords, the necessary loophole to reopen the struggle, while his strategy of containment, of selective conquests and the avoidance of pitched battles had greatly improved France's military position. Nevertheless, this cautious stance had denied him the major crushing victory he needed to put an end to the war. In the 1380s England still held important ports in France: Calais, Bordeaux and Bayonne as well as Brest and Cherbourg. In the phraseology of the time, these served as 'barbicans', outer defences of the realm, which helped protect the Channel and the Bay of Biscay despite the attacks of French and Castilian fleets. Such centres also served as valuable entry points to France, easily available to English troops, from which they could sally forth to raid and terrorize the countryside. The internal upheavals in both countries and the pressing problems of government meant that serious negotiations for peace were unlikely during the minorities of either Richard II or Charles VI. In addition, the papacy was no longer interested in seeking peace after 1378. The outbreak of the Great Schism with two competing popes—one in Rome, one in Avignon—meant a corresponding political split in their supporters. The reality that there was an Avignonese pope, supported by France and its allies, and a Roman pope, recognized by England and its supporters, hardened the determination of each pope to support the political position of his adherents in order to save his own power. Peace might have resulted in the dismissal of one of them.

Both France and England were financially exhausted, their peasants angry and even their magnates unenthusiastic. The duke of Lancaster, who might have been expected to show interest in Gascony, pursued his obsessive dreams of a kingdom in the Iberian peninsula and channelled England's military expenditures towards his own ends. As well, the amputation of so much of the duchy provided financial problems for the government at Westminster. Gascon revenues had always been based on the custom collected on wine, but the volume of the wine trade had plummeted under the successive blows of war, devastation of the vineyards, recurrent years of plague and the flocking of the peasants to the relative safety of the towns, leaving their lands and vines unworked. The figures on the export of wine from Gascon ports illustrate the catastrophic slide. The most successful year, 1308–09, saw the export of 102,724 tuns. During the peaceful years of the principality from 1363–67, when Aquitaine was at its greatest extent, the average export was close to 34,000 tuns. By 1377–78 the total had dropped to 12,456 tuns, of which more than half was from Bordeaux itself.[23] The wines of the Haut Pays, such a large factor in the exports of the early fourteenth century, had now almost completely disappeared, victims of the political changes and the devastation caused by the raiding of troops and ever-present mercenaries. The history of the 1380s in Gascony is unremarkable, for it was a period of truce when Aquitaine no longer seemed important in English policy. The machinery of administration ground on and Englishmen were appointed to fill the offices of seneschal and constable, though they were given little support besides what the duchy itself could provide.

The career of John Stratton, constable from 1381 to 1387, proves of particular interest as he was one of the small number of Englishmen who settled permanently in Gascony. His career and relationships can be followed, showing the occasional interweaving of English and Gascon. Stratton had come to Gascony with the Black Prince in 1355 and in 1358 he married Isabel de Saint-Symphorien, one of the great heiresses of the Bordelais, who was related to the lords of Langon and Roquetaillade. Her lands included the lordship of Landiras, near Podensac on the threshold of the Landes. Stratton settled permanently in Gascony. During the years of the principality he benefited from grants of goods and lands confiscated from rebels and had begun to expand his vineyards and his warehouses. He fought against Anjou at Landiras in 1377 and was highly regarded by Richard II and John Neville whom he served with a retinue of fifteen men recruited in England.[24] Appointed constable of Bordeaux in August 1381, he also carried out the seneschal's duties in the interval between the departure of Neville and the arrival of Scrope in 1383.

Stratton's network of English contacts was obviously good. In January 1382 John Fordham, keeper of the privy seal and recently chosen bishop of Durham, who had also served in Aquitaine with Prince Edward, gave to Stratton, 'his most dear friend', the house in the Ombrière which Fordham had received from the prince.[25] Meanwhile, Stratton's daughter Marguerite had married Bernard Arnaud de Preissac, Soudan de La Trau, who had fought with the prince at Poitiers, Najera and Limoges, had acted as captain of La Rochelle for the English in 1372 and served as a banneret in the Portuguese expedition of the earl of Cambridge. The Soudan's fine military record had been recognized in his election to the Order of the Garter in 1377.[26] His daughter again married into the Gascon nobility. By 1397 Stratton was obviously nearing the end of a long and satisfactory life in Gascony and was making suitable arrangements for his burial. In April of that year he was allowed to take back to Gascony from London, without custom or subsidy, two marble stones for his tomb and that of his wife marked with his arms, as well as a hogshead filled with harness and implements.[27] Gascony had become home and would be his final resting-place.

During these years ecclesiastical affairs in the duchy reflected the practical effects of the schism in the church, while the acrimonious struggles between the supporters of the rival popes demonstrate its political nature. As might be expected, districts under French control generally followed the French line and acknowledged Clement VII of Avignon as pope, while those loyally English accepted Pope Urban VI of Rome. The situation was complicated by the fact that all the bishoprics of one ecclesiastical province did not necessarily share the same papal allegiance. In the province of Bordeaux, for example, the Urbanist appointment as archbishop established himself within his own diocese, but practically all of his suffragan bishops were Clementine and dealt with an archbishop appointed by Clement. Dax and Bayonne in the ecclesiastical province of Auch, which was strongly Clementine, nevertheless had Urbanist bishops. The awkward criss-crossing of allegiances particularly affected clerks holding benefices in opposing jurisdictions. The case of Arnauld de Cavreroche, the Urbanist abbot of La Sauve-Majeure in Entre-deux-Mers, suggests the difficulties. He was deprived of his priory of Saint-Antoine d'Agen by Clement VII but, when he switched allegiance to Clement in order to maintain his hold on the priory, he was rapidly deprived of his abbey by Urban.[28] It would appear that he was replaced with an Englishman whose Urbanist loyalties were more certain, for Edmund Bromfield, master in theology, was named bishop of Llandaff in 1389 after being abbot of La Sauve. Less important Gascon clerks who picked the wrong side found that outspoken adherence to Pope Clement was likely to land them in the Tower of London if they rashly came to England. They remained imprisoned until they admitted their error.[29]

A new controversy arose in the duchy when King Richard in 1390 granted Aquitaine to the duke of Lancaster for his lifetime, giving him full powers there and only reserving sovereignty.[30] This was a peculiar document in two ways. First of all, King Richard made the grant with the advice of his parliament and 'in his position as king of France', although the duchy of Aquitaine was a territory held by hereditary right by the king of England. Secondly, the king recognized that his subjects in the duchy had received the privilege of never being detached from the English crown but claimed that the privilege was not being revoked, but merely suspended for the lifetime of the duke of Lancaster. It was unprecedented for the king to grant the duchy to anyone but the heir to the throne. Apparently, Richard wished to reward his uncle for his support and to encourage him in pursuing the policy of peace with France which had assumed growing importance for the king.[31] The terms of the grant lent colour to the Gascon suspicion that Gaunt's expressed desire for friendship between England and France—as proclaimed in his settlement with the king of Castile in 1388—was a prelude to a change in the status of Aquitaine. They were willing to accept Lancaster as their duke, if allegiance and sovereignty to the king were maintained, but they were certainly aware of the rumours that circulated as to King Richard's real intentions— his desire to achieve peace with France even if it meant detaching Aquitaine to a junior member of the royal family who could more easily pay homage to the French king and would set up his own lineage within the duchy. They were not interested in turning French, for the English connection had served them well and they considered France a foreign country and French a foreign tongue. Nor were they enthusiastic about a permanently resident over-lord who would curtail their cherished privileges. These sentiments were not felt only in English Gascony. The counts of Armagnac and Foix, with such supporters as Albret, looked askance at the likelihood that their lands would be included in a newly constituted duchy of Aquitaine, since such a move would seriously affect the almost complete freedom of action which they had pursued so diligently and successfully.

For the time being Gaunt did not go to the duchy personally, but sent William le Scrope as his seneschal, while devoting most of his own time to the peace negotiations. Richard's original grant of 1390 was confirmed in 1392 and 1394 with the intriguing explanation that this was done to dispel rumours brought to England by Bordeaux representatives that the gift was against the king's own wishes.[32] When the mayor and jurats of Bordeaux wrote to the duke, probably in 1392, they insisted on their loyalty and obedience to his seneschal, but emphasized their fear of continuing French aggression. They underlined their poverty, weakness and shortage of men-at-arms and reported that the French on their borders claimed the only campaign they would spend money on in Guyenne was an attack on Bordeaux 'because that conquered all could be conquered'. They wished to make their mistrust of the French abundantly clear.[33]

In the autumn of 1394, when the negotiations at Leulinghen had achieved a truce, and perhaps even a secret treaty, the duke of Lancaster finally set sail for Gascony. He was forced by contrary winds to land in Brittany in early November and did not arrive at Libourne until the beginning of December.[34] It soon became apparent that he would have difficulty in formally taking possession of the duchy. The mayor and jurats of Bordeaux insisted that they were happy to welcome the duke as son of King Edward, but not as sovereign lord. As a form of passive resistance they insisted on the need of consultation with Dax and Bayonne and the Three Estates of Gascony, further delaying the duke's ceremonial acceptance. Gaunt had moved from Libourne to Lormont, hoping to negotiate a speedy entry. At first he was only given the right to pass through the city on the way to Saint-Seurin where he was allowed to stay as a more convenient locale for continued negotiations. It was not until March that Lancaster succeeded in coming to agreements with the jurats of Bordeaux and the representatives of the Three Estates of Guyenne. The duke had been forced to make very considerable concessions and, in many ways, the documents read as a charter of reforms, of controls on the arbitrary power of the duke and his officials. Emphasis was put on the necessity of choosing officials from honest and capable men knowing the country, while the clergy ranked the importance of the duchy's benefices being given to men from Guyenne above any need for their being in the English king's obedience. No new taxes were to be levied without the consent of the Estates: only in the matter of coinage did the duke refuse to modify his rights.[35] The far-reaching nature of these charters gives ample proof of the determined insistence of the Gascons on their privileges and practical autonomy. Both sides agreed to submit these agreements to the approval of the king and, in the meantime, Lancaster was allowed to take up residence at the archbishop's palace at Saint-André with the right to govern 'justly and legally'.

Froissart's very detailed account of the council meeting when the Gascon representatives of the towns and estates came to plead their case in the summer of 1395 makes it clear that the Gascon opposition to the duke of Lancaster was primarily based on the apparent decision to make the duchy a possession of Lancaster and his heirs. Froissart was formidably well informed on this occasion as he rode to Eltham with his old friend Jean de Grailly, bastard of the great Captal de Buch and captain of Bouteville for the English. There he met Richard de Stury, his companion in the days when they both served in King Edward's household, who was present at the four-hour council meeting on 22 July and told Froissart all about it as they walked the pleasant vine-shaded alleys of the king's palace garden. The Gascons emphasized the inalienability of the king's heritage and his coronation oath to uphold the rights of the crown and its inheritance. They further argued that if Lancaster was accepted by the men of Guyenne, who would then be quit of homage and obedience to England, there was the possibility of his heirs losing their devotion to the crown or falling into alliances with the king's enemies through their marriages. This could put the land of Guyenne in jeopardy for their ambitions and they emphasized that the whole country wanted to remain in the demesne of the crown of England.

After the arguments had been put forward the Gascons and Gaunt's representatives were asked to withdraw while the argument raged within the council.[36] The political considerations put forward by the Gascon representatives, emphasizing the danger of Aquitaine being absorbed into the kingdom of France if the grant to Lancaster was maintained, were reinforced by the legal officers of the Crown who reported that Bordeaux's privilege of attachment to the Crown could not be reconciled with the terms of the king's grant to his uncle. Although no final decision was taken at this council meeting, the Gascons were generously treated and no further serious attempt was made to enforce the terms of Lancaster's grant.

Meanwhile in Gascony the duke had been attempting to conciliate his unwilling subjects and maintain the truce with the French along his borders. In a meeting with Marshal Boucicaut at Bergerac Lancaster reassured the French leader that he was a good friend and neighbour and would certainly keep the truces since he had helped to bring them about.[37] However, Lancaster was recalled to England before the end of 1395. When Richard married the six-year-old Princess Isabel of France in 1396, he also concluded a twenty-eight-year truce with France. It was not a peace, and its provisions did not settle either the vexed question of sovereignty or the territorial extent of English power.[38] Once more all the problems were put into abeyance, as the truce called for a continuation of the *status quo* with no mention of sovereignty or of Richard's continued use of the title of king of France. It was sweetened for the English king by a large dowry of 800,000 francs for his child-bride and by the knowledge that for a long period he would not have to find cash for military expeditions.[39]

The Gascons by their outright refusal to accept Lancaster as their duke had hobbled the idea of achieving peace by creating a separate Aquitaine under a Lancastrian dynasty thus by-passing the problem of sovereignty between the two kings. The war paused, but a final peace was as far off as ever, blocked by the insolubility of the problem of Aquitaine. The men of Guyenne had succeeded in dislodging John, duke of Lancaster, as their duke; they were to find themselves in a few years with his son as their king as well as duke.

CHAPTER XIV

Lancastrian Policy in Guyenne

The deposition of Richard II in 1399 and the accession to the throne of Henry of Derby, son and heir of the duke of Lancaster, was bound to raise questions of loyalty in Guyenne. Despite Richard's birth in Bordeaux there seems to have been little sentimental allegiance to his person in the duchy, which he had left permanently at the age of four. Richard's grants show that he was devoted to his Gascon nurse,[1] but politically Guyenne's affairs seemed of little concern to him. The long-drawn-out arguments over the duchy's sovereignty and its intransigence in the face of his appointment of Lancaster as its duke impeded Richard's overmastering desire for peace with France. The exactions of Gaunt's officials had also given rise to vigorous opposition. For the men of Guyenne the Lancastrian nature of the new dynasty was likely to be of more concern than the disappearance of Richard II.

Froissart reports that the duke of Burgundy was sure that the men of the duchy would be upset by the news and that immediate negotiations might win them over to France 'because we ought to have them now or never'.[2] In pursuit of this strategy the duke of Bourbon was sent to Agen to encourage defections to the French cause and the representatives of Bordeaux, Bayonne and Dax went to parley with him there. They were greeted with rhetorical flourishes and extraordinary promises of privileges in perpetuity, but the caution of the bourgeois is evident in their reaction when they returned home for consultation. The weight of French taxes was well known and they realistically feared that they would soon be treated in the same way. 'If the Londoners have deposed King Richard and crowned King Henry, how does that touch us? We will always have a king. . . . We have more trade . . . with the English than with the French and we lean more in that direction naturally. Let us be careful not to make a treaty which we might regret'.[3] The decision did not satisfy everyone as factions favouring the French also existed in the towns, but the supporters of the English were encouraged by Henry IV's first moves.

As a diplomatic gesture Gaillard de Durfort, lord of Duras and Blanquefort and one of the most loyal of the Gascon nobility, was named seneschal, a remarkable appointment for a native Gascon. In April 1400 Durfort and Nompar de Caumont, appointed seneschal for the Agenais, returned to Gascony from England, supported by small retinues of men-at-arms and archers. They were accompanied by Hugh Despenser and followed by Henry Bowet and John Trailly, both reappointed to their previous positions as constable and mayor. Bowet, who was soon to be promoted to the see of Bath, and Despenser were appointed royal proctors with François Uguccione, the archbishop of Bordeaux. The archbishop was a native of Urbino who had held the see since 1384 and was recognized as a learned lawyer devoted to the English cause. The proctors were given generous powers, suggesting the king's recognition of the fact that conditions in the duchy were precarious and its inhabitants dubious at the reappearance of officials identified with Gaunt. King Henry was inevitably regarded with suspicion by those who had opposed his father. There was serious factional struggle in Bayonne and similar but less serious problems in Bordeaux and Dax. The royal proctors generally succeeded in calming the disturbances and reassuring the men of the duchy of Henry IV's pacific and politic proposals for Guyenne and its support.[4] Bordeaux's loyalty was further encouraged in February 1401 by Henry's extensive grant, which confirmed all the privileges granted the city under Edward III and Richard II (some of which were reissues of still earlier privileges). These included the right of remaining united to the throne and never being alienated to anyone except the heir to the throne (the great point at issue against Lancaster), the many privileges to Bordeaux merchants and the rights Bordeaux was allowed to exercise in its *banlieue*. All these were then proudly recorded in the great *Livre des Bouillons*, the precious register on vellum of the ancient privileges of the city. It was commissioned by the jurade after this grant of Henry IV's and was kept chained and triple-locked in the municipal archives.[5]

Durfort's position as seneschal bristled with difficulties. Inevitably enmeshed in the complex network of relationships and alliances spread like a spider web across Guyenne and south-western France, he found it difficult to detach himself completely from his own concerns in local politics. The most striking example of this was in his relations with the new count of Foix. When Gaston Fébus died in 1391 leaving no direct heirs he was succeeded by Matthieu de Castelbon, grandson of Fébus' uncle. Castelbon ruled only seven years and on his death the county of Foix and the viscounty of Béarn passed to his sister Isabelle, wife of Archambaud de Grailly. Not only was Archambaud a member of one of the greatest local families of the duchy, he had also inherited the lands and title of Captal de Buch from Jean de Grailly, the great warrior and friend of the Black Prince. Thus, Archambaud's accession in 1398 to the county of Foix and the viscounty of Béarn in right of his wife inevitably provoked a tussle between French and English for his allegiance.

The Graillys had always been loyal supporters of the English and their lands in Entre-deux-Mers and the Médoc were strategically important for the existence of the duchy and the safety of Bordeaux. The county of Foix, because of its proximity to Languedoc and the lands of Armagnac was important to the French, while Béarn looked westward to Bayonne and the English trade. A skilful acrobatic performance, balancing opposing claims, was required to maintain an independent equilibrium and Gaston Fébus had dexterously played one side against the other with enthusiasm and skill. Archambaud, faced with the further complication of the Grailly lands, continued to assert the freedom of Béarn from the sovereignty of either France or England. In return for French recognition of this claim and to ensure his hold on the rich county of Foix, he abandoned the English cause in March 1401, swore to be a faithful and loyal vassal of France and was pardoned for his adherence to the English.[6] The rumours of the count of Foix's oath to the French king was naturally of great concern in the Bordelais and prompted a flurry of correspondence with London. Archambaud had close relations with many of the Gascon lords and clergy, including Durfort, who had concluded an alliance with him in 1394.[7] Such English officials as John Morhay, writing to Henry Bowet, felt that Durfort would find it difficult to oppose Foix with the necessary wholehearted enthusiasm.[8]

The seneschal was also faced with demands for military action which neither he nor the king's council in Bordeaux could finance. Troops should have gone to the Landes to put down the endemic local warfare there but there was no money to pay them. This situation was improved in July 1401 with the reappointment of Matthew Gournay as seneschal to the Landes. A tough experienced soldier, who had fought with the Black Prince and the Free Companies, he had already filled the position in 1378 and knew the country. Such particular problems, as well as the king's recognition of the need to send a man of prestige to deal with the delicate situation, accounted for the appointment in July 1401 of the earl of Rutland, the king's cousin, as lieutenant of Guyenne for three years. The earl was very much in the pattern of previous lieutenants of the duchy—important magnates, usually related to the king, who were sent out at times of great stress. The lieutenant outranked the seneschal and provided a closer connection at a higher level with the government in England. It is obvious that there was continued concern in England over the suitability of Durfort even as seneschal, for council declared in May 1402 that they felt it expedient that Rutland should be seneschal of Guyenne, as no native Gascon had filled that office up to now.[9] Since Rutland only remained in the duchy for a year, the suggestion was not acted upon.

The defection of the count of Foix to the French brought in its wake the loss of the castle of Bouteville in southern Saintonge, captured by the count for the French. The castle of Chalais, some thirty miles south of Angoulême, was also under French pressure, though it was forcefully held by its captain, Peyroat de Puch, who refused to surrender it to the French. The English found it a valuable outpost in enemy territory but Peyroat was more confirmed in his vigorous attachment to the English by the valuable *appatis*, or impositions, he could levy on the surrounding French countryside so long as he remained English. Henry IV granted possession of the castle to Peyroat and his son Jean for their lifetime in July 1402 with extravagant praise for their devotion to the English crown.[10] Although the truces between France and England officially continued there were a number of warlike skirmishes and aggressive approaches. In January 1402 Charles VI made the provocative move of naming his eldest son, six-year-old Louis, duke of Guyenne and in October 1403 a large army which included such nobles as the count of Clermont and Charles d'Albret (son of Arnaud-Amanieu and now constable of France) moved south from Orléans. Although it captured several castles in the Limousin it returned at the onset of winter with no major successes. The French continued their policy of nibbling away at Guyenne from the north and east, while the forces of Foix, Armagnac and Albret waged desultory war in the south and menaced Bayonne. The situation remained precarious, but King Henry had at least established his authority in his shrunken duchy and won over some of those suspicious of the Lancastrian connection. The king's troubles in Wales and the rebellion led by the Percies prevented him from devoting much money or time to affairs in Gascony during the early years of his reign. The French exploited his difficulties by aiding the Welsh rebels at the same time as they stepped up their attacks in Guyenne.

The affairs of Gascony and its desperate need for reinforcement were on Henry IV's mind when he wrote to Archbishop Arundel in September 1404 for help in raising a loan, as money was desperately needed in Wales and Gascony, and by the end of November the king was summoning outsiders—probably those well informed about the duchy—to meet with his council to deliberate on its 'estate and salvation'.[11] It had become apparent by the spring of 1405 that the piecemeal provision of arms and some assistance to the beset officers of the duchy was not sufficient and that the French threat to Bordeaux was ever more menacing. The general deterioration of economic conditions in the duchy is suggested by a statute of 1400 in the cartulary of Saint-Seurin reducing the cost of canons' funerals because the prebends had been so eroded by death, war, frosts and storms that 'a simple canon can scarcely live of his prebend'.[12] Bad harvests meant deterioration in the wine trade and an ever greater need for imported grain, with a corresponding decline of money available for defence. In March 1405 Thomas Swynbourne was appointed mayor of Bordeaux and given a sizeable retinue of fifty men-at-arms and 100 archers. A man of military experience who had previously captained one of the outlying fortresses near Calais, he was an excellent choice to provide useful military leadership as well as reassurance to the threatened citizens.

Piecemeal French campaigns continued during 1405, primarily in the Agenais, but the storm broke over Bordeaux and its surrounding towns in 1406. Archbishop Uguccione, now a cardinal, wrote anxious letters to the king throughout the spring and summer, informing him of the desperate state of the duchy and its need for help.[13] The cardinal deplored the death of the lord of Mussidan, who held the important stronghold of Blaye and who had been one of the most faithful of the Gascon lords. His heir was his daughter and the matter of her marriage was of grave concern lest her husband incline towards the French, despite her father's deathbed injunction that she should live and die in true obedience to the king and take no husband outside that obedience. The cardinal's letters are inevitably gloomy and apprehensive and the discouraged prelate obviously felt his efforts were disregarded. A cry from the heart on 30 June suggests much of the tone: 'I have written to you so many times and so lengthily concerning the state of your land, and I have cried so much that my voice has become hoarse.' He went on to underline the likelihood of the loss or destruction of all the duchy if the French made war 'because one cannot defend one's own only by words'.[14] His gloomy forebodings were well based. The autumn of 1406 brought news of the imminent descent of a large army led by the duke of Orléans to add to the force which Albret had been commanding in the Charente. The news of this danger galvanized the jurade of Bordeaux, the governing group of the city, into continued activity. They proved their loyalty to the English connection and their concern for the surrounding towns, their *filleules*, by defensive preparations in the city itself and a strenuous programme of aid and military assistance to the outlying districts. This proud episode in Bordeaux's history has often been disregarded, especially by earlier more chauvinistic French historians, who could not comprehend the strong particularism of the Gascons and could not believe that the fifteenth-century men of Guyenne regarded the French as even more foreign than the English.

The registers of the meetings of the jurade of Bordeaux from September 1406 to January 1407 provide a compelling first-hand account of the alarms that swept the city, the countless discussions on possible strategy and the practical initiatives adopted to deal with the enemy attacks.[15] News came of the French army in the Charente as early as September and by mid-October the duke of Orléans had summoned the Gascon towns to surrender. Blaye, Bourg, Fronsac, Libourne and Saint-Emilion were all threatened and apprehensive, though Libourne wrote bravely to Bordeaux that they were not disheartened by Orléans' threats, for 'by the grace of God, the Virgin Mary and Monsieur Saint George'—

G*

and aid from the city including an expert to take charge of their 'engines'—they would defend themselves.[16] Meanwhile the jurats had put Bordeaux's own defence in readiness. They had enrolled Gascons and English to guard the river banks and the towers on the walls. The ditches outside the walls had been repaired, the gates which led to the river were to be barred, and careful watch was to be kept. Any French in Bordeaux who had safe-conducts were to be segregated in the Rue Saint-Jacques.

Concern for Blaye, as the most likely point of attack, was very much to the forefront. A French chronicler admits that Orléans' more experienced military leaders had suggested that the time was not ideal for a siege, since there was no forage or grain available and the weather might be poor. They felt it would be wiser to establish the army in good winter quarters and begin the attack with the onset of better weather in the spring. Those closest to the duke regarded inaction as dishonourable and recommended an immediate attack on Blaye if it could not be bought or cajoled into surrendering. The chronicler ruefully adds: 'as often, the less wise party prevailed'.[17] Bordeaux was at first suspicious of the trustworthiness of the abbot of Saint-Romains, whose abbey lay just outside the walls of Blaye, and then discovered that he had indeed sold out to the duke of Orléans for a payment of 2,000 crowns and other concessions in France, allowing the duke to use the abbey as his headquarters. As well, the control of the town of Blaye was dubious. The daughter of the deceased lord of Mussidan was castellan and the captain of the town was Jean de Grailly, the Captal's bastard son. He was an able and vigorous knight who had fought consistently for the English, but was apparently active in encouraging a marriage between the lady of Mussidan and one of the sons of Archambaud de Grailly, count of Foix and Jean's step-uncle. Because of the count of Foix's allegiance to the king of France and the fact that one of his sons was currently fighting with the French forces the marriage was regarded in Bordeaux with much suspicion. Even if the young Grailly agreed to take the oath to the English king, would he be trustworthy? However, an agreement was reached which left that question in abeyance, spared Blaye from hostilities by either side and tied its fate to the result of the siege of Bourg, a few miles up the Gironde from Blaye and at the very mouth of the Dordogne.

Orléans' forces set a major siege at Bourg at the beginning of

November. The catapults of the French were countered by Bordeaux's dispatch of one large cannon and four small ones complete with a quintal of powder and the services of a competent gunner. Efforts were put on foot to provide naval support—important for Bourg itself, and to prevent the French from blockading the river. The English wine ships currently in the harbour of Bordeaux were prevailed to stay and help in this effort. The jurats also took the decision to dismantle the castle of Lormont, on the right bank of the Garonne just downstream from the city. The castle belonged to the archbishop but the jurade decided that it might be too dangerous, both for the city and the surrounding district, if it fell into enemy hands. As well, the two cannons in its towers could menace shipping in the river. The reproaches of the cardinal-archbishop at this destruction of his property had no effect on the determined citizens. By the beginning of December Bourg was running low on provisions and armed ships were sent to guard the river so that the city's little ships could safely provision the besieged town every day. The river banks were completely closed off with the requirement that all gates and warehouses had to be walled up under the pain of heavy penalties. The extraordinary exertions of the people of Bordeaux convinced the duke that the siege might be long and that he would need further supplies.

A flotilla from La Rochelle bearing provisions was intercepted by ships from Bordeaux in the Gironde below Blaye. A violent battle ensued, apparently made more difficult by heavy fog, in which the Gascons and their English allies finally forced the French fleet to flee and even took a number of prisoners. According to the Saint Albans' chronicler the victorious Gascons sent upstream one of the fire ships used against the French, so that it would burn 'in the eyes of the proud duke'.[18] Besides this success, the defenders had the weather on their side. A Gascon source piously imputes Orléans' problems to the fact that 'God fought him with rain, strong winds and heavy mud'. The French were more specific, if less convinced of divine intervention. The winter was a very rainy one. The tents leaked, the supplies began to rot, the soldiers went in mud to their knees, while many died of dysentery and others of hunger. The duke's soldiers were understandably anxious to abandon the siege and urged him to withdraw. It was a blow to his pride, but by mid-January he was forced to raise the siege and return north, having accomplished nothing.[19] On the advice of Durfort and the consent of the jurade the abbey of Saint-Romains was to be mined and destroyed so that the duke could not make use of it again.

By the end of January the strain had dissipated and life had begun to return to normal. When the jurade met on 29 January they could discuss such pleasant topics as the sale of the castle and lordship of Ornon to the city by Henry Bowet, once constable of Bordeaux, now bishop of Bath and soon to be promoted to the see of York, and the grant to Brother Thomas Alkarld, 'English hermit' of the hermitage of the Porte-Dijeaux with its profit.[20] Without help from England Bordeaux had proved its ability to withstand a major attack and to organize its own defence. The removal of the threatening French army gave Bordeaux a breathing space. The assassination of the duke of Orléans in November 1407 by the retainers of the duke of Burgundy not only spared Guyenne from further immediate attack, it opened a period of civil warfare in France. The opposing factions struggled to control the person of Charles VI, so frequently incapacitated by madness after 1392, in order to rule France in their own interest. As the danger of invasion of the duchy lessened, English contributions to its finances grew less. Bordeaux, freed from continuous campaigning, became even more confident of its own political and economic strength. It concentrated power in the hands of the jurats, all representatives of the rich bourgeois of the town, and treated the English officials rather more as diplomatic representatives and channels of communication to London than as active administrators. Although such important castles as Fronsac continued to be commanded by an Englishman, usually the mayor or constable of Bordeaux, and its garrison officially paid by the English exchequer, Bordeaux itself helped to raise forces and send reinforcements to those frontiers which seemed to its jurats of special importance for their own safety. For the time being the political force of the duchy was in the hands of Bordeaux because of its economic strength. Although proud of its English connection the city basked in its prestige, its exercise of power and its practical autonomy.

Meanwhile in England thoughts of Guyenne continued to concern King Henry, despite his more immediate problems with the Scots, the Welsh and the general peace of the realm. The king was not primarily interested in the claim to the French throne, although the title was kept alive in the royal documents. What

Henry IV worked to obtain, whenever conditions seemed favourable, was a return to the provisions of the Treaty of Brétigny and the recognition of his sovereignty over Aquitaine. His opportunity lay in the exploitation of the factional strife between Burgundians and Orléanists after the murder of the duke of Orléans. Many of the southern nobility, including the count of Armagnac and the Sire d'Albret had been ardent followers of Orléans and continued to support his young son Charles in his struggles for revenge against Burgundy. Unfortunately, the king and Prince Henry favoured opposing sides in France. During the period January 1410 to November 1411 when the prince presided over council because of his father's illness he favoured the Burgundian faction. In March 1411 the minutes of a council meeting at Lambeth, dealing with the allotment of the moneys raised by the current subsidy on wool, clearly demonstrate Prince Henry's priorities. Three-quarters of the subsidy had already been allotted to the safeguard of Calais while the duchy of Aquitaine, which needed £11,000 for the wages of a small force for its protection, the garrisoning and provisioning of the castle of Fronsac, as well as other necessary expenses, was cut to 4,000 marks (£2,666).[21] When Prince Henry received pleas for help against the young duke of Orléans from the Burgundian ambassadors he was happy to send off an expedition, led by the earl of Arundel, which successfully attacked the Orléanist forces at the bridge of Saint-Cloud south-west of Paris. It returned home loaded with the gifts and gratitude of the duke of Burgundy.

When Henry IV recovered from his illness at the end of 1411 and resumed his control of the council, he removed the prince and his party bringing back his own supporter, Archbishop Arundel, as chancellor. Almost immediately English policy towards France was revised in favour of the Orléanists who also made overtures for English help. A secret treaty of alliance was made at Bourges on 18 May 1412 between King Henry and the dukes of Berry, Orléans, Bourbon and the count of Alençon which concentrated on the restitution of the duchy of Aquitaine in full sovereignty to the English king as its rightful duke. The French lords went so far as to agree to hand over certain castles and towns which they now held in the duchy, or to help regain them for King Henry at their own cost. The duke of Berry was to hold the county of Poitou for his lifetime from King Henry, and Orléans that of Angoulême, with certain important castles held by Henry as security. In return the king promised to aid them in their quarrels with the duke of Burgundy and to send an expedition of 1,000 men-at-arms and 3,000 archers to their assistance, although these were to be paid by the French after the first two months.[22]

The Orléanist nobles regarded their alliance, whose secrecy had been compromised even before it was ratified, as merely another bargaining counter in their struggle with Burgundy for the control of Charles VI and seem to have had no real intention of assisting the English in Guyenne. When they were accused of disloyalty to France they soon denounced the treaty (22 July 1412) and participated in a touching, if momentary, reconciliation with Duke John of Burgundy.[23] However, the English had already embarked on their preparations for the expedition and, despite the change in climate, the promised force sailed for France in August. It was under the leadership of the king's second son, Thomas, newly created duke of Clarence and lieutenant of Guyenne, supported by a number of magnates, including the duke of York and Thomas Beaufort, earl of Dorset and half-brother of Henry IV. The force landed at Cherbourg and marched across country towards Blois, the original rendezvous. From there Clarence wrote a high-handed letter to the duke of Berry refusing to accept the cancellation of the alliance. He insisted that as the English were carrying out their share of the agreement Berry's party must also fulfil their obligations.[24] No response came from the erstwhile allies, but it soon became evident that the English troops would have to be bought off before they overran the countryside and fairly generous payments to the leaders were arrived at in settlement. The ease with which Clarence's forces marched from Cherbourg to Bordeaux revived memories of the successful *chevauchées* of the days of English domination in France, but achieved nothing substantial. Clarence arrived in Bordeaux early in December and settled into the archbishop's palace for the winter.

Because the southern nobles, especially Armagnac and Albret, were such strong supporters of the Orléanist cause, Clarence devoted much of his time in Bordeaux to encouraging those who had signed the treaty of the previous May into returning to the English allegiance. As so often in the affairs of south-west France the knowledge of the marriage alliances is the guiding thread through the maze of political manoeuvres and explains the sudden rise to power of lords who had previously been of second rank. The case of the counts of Armagnac is a striking example of what marital links with royal relatives could achieve in enhanced status. Jean I of Armagnac had put his family on the road to more than local influence when he married his daughter to the future duke of Berry in 1360. Twenty-five years later, Jean III was captain-general for the duke when Berry was lieutenant-general in Languedoc. His son Bernard married the duke's daughter in 1395. In her turn, their daughter married the young Charles d'Orléans, a political marriage which nevertheless developed into a close bond of affection. It was natural for Count Bernard VII of Armagnac to be at the centre of the coalition against Burgundy, especially after the murder of Louis of Orléans when young Charles naturally turned to his father-in-law as his most experienced and probably most able relative. The preponderance of the count's Gascon troops in the coalition resulted in the party being called the Armagnacs.

Despite Count Bernard's growing success and influence he was still locked in the traditional rivalry with the count of Foix, as both struggled to hold the balance in Languedoc and to make good their rival claims to Bigorre. Jean, the heir of Count Archambaud of Foix, had been serving in the French forces, and his father had concluded an alliance with Burgundy, once more in control of the government. When Jean succeeded his father in 1412 he continued his policy and was named royal lieutenant-general in Languedoc and Guyenne with the express duty of seizing Armagnac's lordships.[25] The opposition of Armagnac and Foix in these strictly local issues helps to explain their manoeuvres in constantly changing sides in the French-English conflict in Guyenne. As well, the counts of Foix early developed a scheme which became very popular in the south-west. When families had lordships and territories in both French and English areas they often so arranged inheritances that different members of the family could have different allegiances. This both served as insurance against total disaster by confiscation from either side and contributed to the maintenance of the family fortune during the fluctuations of war. Thus, Count Archambaud obviously divided his possessions on French and English lines. Jean as the oldest son received the county of Foix, the viscounty of Béarn and Marsan and Gabardan, which bordered on it, as well as the viscounty of Castelbon. Gaston, the second son, was given the title of Captal de Buch, the viscounties of Benauges and Castillon and the original lordships in Savoy including Grailly. The recognition of the value of family solidarity was underlined in February 1412 when Jean and Gaston swore a treaty of alliance at Orthez, promising mutual support, only excepting their sovereign lords.[26]

An agreement was arrived at in Bordeaux on 14 February 1413 between Clarence, Charles d'Albret and Armagnac. Compared to the expansive terms of alliance at Bourges this document reveals a far more cautious approach. Although Armagnac and Albret agreed to do homage for their lands and lordships in Guyenne to the English king as its duke, they specifically reserved the sovereignty to the king of France and insisted on their right of appeal to him. In return for this rather grudging concession to the ducal rights they were to receive their lands now in the king's hands and also those which had been granted to others. If they suffered attack from the French they were to be aided as quickly as possible by the royal officers in the duchy and if this proved insufficient, by the dispatch of a special force led by a royal lord.[27] All of this rather reluctant reconciliation was obviously designed to strengthen their hands against Jean I of Foix in his post as the French king's representative in Languedoc and Guyenne. Any gains from this arrangement were dependent on Clarence's ability to score successes against Burgundian-held territories in the duchy. Clarence had no time to put his various initiatives into action. When the news of Henry IV's death reached Bordeaux the duke prepared to return to England. Responsibility for Guyenne was delegated to the earl of Dorset while William Clifford was dispatched from England to serve as constable and castellan of Fronsac, and John of Saint John as mayor of Bordeaux.[28]

Although Dorset continued for a few months the aggressive military policy of Clarence and had limited success in raising money locally to pay his troops, the turn of political events elsewhere affected the situation in Guyenne. The Cabochien uprising in Paris culminated in an Armagnac victory over the insurgents and the discrediting of the duke of Burgundy. As the Armagnac faction regained their earlier positions of importance and power English support in the south became less necessary. In addition, the accession of Henry V, able and eager to press his claims to France, implied the reversal of his father's policy. Even as prince, Henry had favoured the Burgundian side, as had been obvious in 1411. Perhaps he was influenced by his position as captain of Calais and by his recognition of the importance of English trade with Burgundian Flanders, but his interest in Guyenne appears to have been minimal. He only looked for any practical or legal aid it could give him in the continuing diplomatic manoeuvres of the first years of his reign. Henry continued to exploit England's rights and claims in the duchy to buttress his growing demands in the north and as propaganda justifying his warlike moves. For example, on his way to embark on his first invasion of France in 1415 he had all the treaties which his father had made with the Orléans party in 1412 copied and the transcripts sent to the dignitaries at the Council of Constance 'so that all Christendom might know how French duplicity had injured him and how he was almost unwillingly forced to raise his standard against the rebels'.[29] In planning this first expedition Henry had carefully maintained his freedom of choice. Even when the invasion of France had been settled on, the indentures provided that service might be either in Guyenne or in France. As late as the time of embarkation there seems to have been no public knowledge of Henry's own decision to attack Normandy through Harfleur.

It may have taken some time for Henry to arrive at this decision since the appointment of Sir John Tiptoft as seneschal of Gascony in May 1415 appears to have implied that other knights with their retinues would accompany him. In the end Tiptoft arrived at Bordeaux in August 1415 with only his own retinue of 140 men-at-arms and 700 archers, a small force for anything but a holding operation. Although Tiptoft retained the appointment as seneschal until 1423 much of his time was spent outside Guyenne, either in military service in Normandy or on diplomatic missions for the king. Tiptoft has been likened to John Stratton as an Englishman in Gascony, but in reality they represent two different types. Both held lands and offices in the duchy but Stratton made his home as well as his career there; Tiptoft merely extracted the profits. He was also of higher rank and importance than Stratton as he had already served with Henry of Derby in 1397 and held important offices during his reign as well as that of his son and grandson. Speaker of the House of Commons in 1406, then treasurer of the household and appointed treasurer of

England in the summer of 1408, he seems to have used his positions to his own advantage. Early in 1408 the king named him seneschal of the Landes and castellan of Dax in succession to Matthew Gournay. Tiptoft had married Matthew's widow, Philippa, and she had made over to him all the extensive rights and lands she had inherited in Gascony. Six months after his first appointment Tiptoft was further rewarded with a lifetime grant of the prévôté of Entre-deux-Mers and the profits of the markets of Bordeaux and of the *issac*, its petty custom.[30]

Despite these territorial grants, which appear to have been exercised through a lieutenant, and even his nomination as seneschal of Gascony, it is obvious that Tiptoft's main concern with Gascony was the receipt of the assigned revenues. He had no personal interest in the duchy. His wife, unlike Stratton's, was originally English and they had no children to put down roots there. When Philippa died Tiptoft married a daughter of the Charlton family in the Welsh Marches and acquired through her the title of Lord Powys. His later interests, both territorial and political, were rooted in England and Wales though he used his position on the king's council to claim repayment of over £11,000 for his expenses as seneschal in Gascony. In 1426 he was granted an interim payment of 7,000 marks to be drawn from the lordship of Lesparre in the Médoc, worth 3,000 *francs bordelais* a year.[31] Although he never returned to Gascony he continued to hold office in the Landes and Entre-deux-Mers until his death in 1443. Tiptoft's rewards in Guyenne illustrate only too clearly the fatal English weakness in the fifteenth century, for a general policy developed of dispersing Gascon revenues to non-resident English grantees who showed little interest in anything but their financial returns. They had no personal stake in improving the military or political situation within the duchy.

Guyenne remained relatively unconcerned with happenings in the north. There had been earlier royal requests for siege engines and guns but as the siege of Harfleur dragged on Henry wrote to Bordeaux asking for wine and victuals for his army. The citizens agreed to the dispatch of 200 tuns to the king and 100 tuns to other lords with him, while Bayonne also provided supplies.[32] Henry's victory of Agincourt was properly celebrated when the news arrived in Bordeaux, but for the next few years it was painfully obvious that Aquitaine was of no immediate importance to the king. Royal policy began to change in 1419.

With much of Normandy in his power, Henry again turned his thoughts to the duchy and sent to Bordeaux for all possible information on the status of Aquitaine to buttress his diplomatic negotiations. On 4 April Archbishop David Montferrand wrote to the king that he was sending copies of all the acts which established the sovereignty of the king of England over Aquitaine, including a full copy of the report of the homages rendered to the Black Prince in 1363.[33] By autumn Henry had obviously decided to pursue his interests in Aquitaine more vigorously. In September–October a number of royal letters were sent from Gisors and Mantes to the people of Guyenne explaining the charge given John Radcliffe, the newly appointed constable of Bordeaux, and John Saint John, the city's mayor, to explain the king's wishes and 'our great desire to defend and conserve our land, as to resist and grieve our enemies'. The royal emphasis on high costs and excessive expenses was the inevitable prelude of a commission to his officials to seek a *fouage* from the clerks as well as the laity. The problem of dealing with the touchy Gascons was to be made easier by the presence of Gaston de Grailly, Captal de Buch and earl of Longueville.[34]

By the spring of 1420 Bordeaux had been galvanized into action, encouraged by the hope of at least some military if not financial assistance. A meeting of the Estates was held at Dax on 17 May—just before the official proclamation of the Treaty of Troyes—and John Radcliffe expressed Henry's regrets for not undertaking military operations in Aquitaine personally and gave his promise to continue the war until the duchy was recovered. A *fouage* of 1 gold noble was requested, to be spent entirely within Guyenne. The deputies indulged in a series of delaying tactics to avoid giving definite answers. The city authorities in Bordeaux agreed to raise 100 men-at-arms to fight the French and to pay them for three months. The citizens were anxious to move against those French strongholds which endangered the city's security and commerce. Rions, in the hands of the French since 1378, was captured in July and Saint-Macaire capitulated on 15 August after a vigorous siege which was reinforced by the loan of Bordeaux's big bombard. Tiptoft returned to Gascony a week later with a force of men-at-arms and archers and a supply of grain. Tiptoft, besides commanding the military efforts, had also been empowered to arbitrate between the archbishop and the city authorities. The line between the ecclesiastical and secular jurisdiction was a hotly contested one all during the middle ages.[35]

The Treaty of Troyes naming King Henry as heir and regent of France had little effect in the duchy for it was irrelevant to his Gascon subjects whom he ruled in his right as king of England. In the treaty Henry had committed himself to conquering the territories held by the dauphin, but in practice this obligation held him north of the Loire.[36] The king attempted to encourage the great lords of the French south-west to take on themselves the task of recovering lands held by the dauphin in their sphere of interest for their own profit. The most important noble with whom he had to deal was the count of Foix, for death had recently removed Foix's leading opponents. Count Bernard of Armagnac had been killed in Paris in 1418 and had been succeeded by his son Jean IV, aged twenty-two. Jean, through a second marriage to the niece of the king of Navarre, encouraged new relationships to the south and an eventual treaty of alliance with Navarre. The county of Armagnac was so suspended between the poles of French and English power that the counts found it necessary to play one side against the other. Jean IV was primarily interested in protecting his own domains, but allowed his son, the viscount of Lomagne, to fight openly on the side of Charles VI. In 1415 Charles d'Albret, constable of France, had been killed at Agincourt and was succeeded by his son, Charles II, who carried on desultory negotiations with the English.

Neither Armagnac nor Albret were at this time powerful enough to challenge Foix's superiority. Henry V embarked on a long, complex, and ultimately futile series of negotiations with Foix to encourage him to take on the military responsibility for conquering the lands in the south in the name of Charles VI and Henry. The count was aided in this high-level haggling by the mediation of his brother Gaston, Captal de Buch and a strong supporter of the English. Certainly the count's terms for his support were high, and continually got higher. He was to be named governor of Languedoc and Bigorre, with the duty of regaining these territories. Bigorre had been a bone of contention between Armagnac and Foix since the end of the thirteenth century and had sparked the war between Gaston Fébus and Jean I in the 1360s. Béarn was to be recognized as a free allod, owing no homage, and the English king committed himself to the payment of large sums of money for the payment of the soldiers to make these conquests. Negotiations and agreements abounded while the count procrastinated and manoeuvred to avoid any real action. After Henry V's death the regents for the infant king were unable either to induce or to force the count to keep his promises. Despite all the diplomatic effort and the expenditure on advance payments no action was taken by Foix and nothing was achieved for the English cause in the south. By 1425 Charles VII had bought back Foix's loyalty by naming him lieutenant of Languedoc and Guyenne—with no burden of military effort on his part—and granting him the possession of Bigorre.[37]

Bordeaux had continued its leading role assisted by the aggressive action of John Radcliffe. In the summer of 1421 Budos, near Podensac, was besieged and captured and by 1423 Puynormand, Sauveterre, Rauzan and Pujols had all been regained and garrisoned while Bazas at last surrendered in 1425. Radcliffe had been named seneschal in 1423, replacing Tiptoft, and had also been made captain of the castle of Fronsac. However, like Tiptoft, his presence was required elsewhere as well. He served in Normandy and was one of the ambassadors to the Congress of Arras in 1435 while he was still seneschal, but his many services to two kings resulted in debts rather than riches. He had borrowed 7,500 *francs bordelais* from the citizens of Bordeaux for military activities and was owed over £7,000 by the exchequer for his wages and the wages of his men when he died.[38] The order to pay off this debt to his executors exemplifies the difficulties of so many royal officials in the duchy:

> As he rendered long service to the king in war and otherwise in times past, and by continuance thereof sold a large part of his revenues and was deeply in debt to a number of his friends which, as in his lifetime he informed the king, would redound to his utter ruin but for the king's special favour.[39]

Final satisfaction does seem to have been made to his heirs.

In the duchy life proceeded more or less normally. Certain military successes were achieved. Marmande was recaptured in 1428 and Bergerac in 1431. Appointments were made to the Court of Sovereignty, now sitting as a court of appeals in Bordeaux. Its personnel in 1423 included Bernard de La Planche, prior of Soulac, who became bishop of Dax and represented the English king at the Council of Basle, and Pey Berland, canon of Bordeaux destined to become the city's most famous archbishop.[40]

Some rebuilding was done during this period of peace. Dax, for example, got certain concessions including the right to charge tolls on their bridge, so that they could rebuild the towers, walls, and bridge of the city, which were in a deplorable state and beyond their own resources to repair. Certain merchants were attempting to avoid all custom duties on their wines by putting them in small barrels. The king's letter to his council in Guyenne threatens that anyone who loads wine in this fashion may suffer the confiscation of his vessel as well as the wine.[41] The chapter of Saint-André was reproached for appointing to canonries and other offices those who were not loyal subjects, for such a hidden enemy 'nourished serpent-like' was more dangerous than those who showed themselves openly. Bayonne in 1432 petitioned for its own mint, citing the difficulties in disturbed times of carrying silver or plate to Bordeaux for coinage. The request was granted with profits to be used for the city's defence, but all the costs to be at the expense of the inhabitants.[42]

The problem of ensuring the loyalty of the king's councillors and officials in Guyenne was obviously a vital one, for in March 1433 the bishop of Dax and Bernard Angevin, the king's chancellor in the duchy, brought some of the requests of the Gascon council to England. The king strictly forbade that any councillor or official in Guyenne should accept wages or pensions from local lords or take any oath to them. Such action was to be punished by deprivation of office.[43] The problem of factions within the duchy was never an easy one to eradicate. The king also promised, in response to the council's request, that a seneschal would soon be sent, for without a resident seneschal the work of the council was difficult to achieve.

The years of relative normality were not to continue much longer. The Congress of Arras in 1435 represented still another inconclusive attempt to conclude a peace. When that attempt failed the duke of Burgundy took advantage of the changing political situation to return to friendship with Charles VII. The problem which had prompted the beginning of the war between France and England continued to bedevil its final phase. It had become glaringly apparent that no settlement could ever be reached between the two countries on the vexed question of sovereignty in Guyenne, even if the English king should agree to renounce his claim to the throne of France. Both sides assumed equally antagonistic and entrenched positions and each fell back on any available argument. One of the few light moments in all the repetitive history of tortuous negotiations and inconclusive conferences came at Oye in the summer of 1439 when the English buttressed their claim to the rightful possession of the kingdom of France with the popular prophecy of Saint Bridget. The French immediately countered with the prophecy of Jean, 'a holy hermit', who had said that 'the English, as the scourge of God, would waste and destroy the kingdom of France and finally they would be destroyed'. At which Cardinal Beaufort, one of the English negotiators, replied that a marriage between Saint Bridget and the hermit would be a good thing.[44] Certainly it would have been in the best tradition of royal marriages to extinguish opposition. In any case, both at Arras and at Oye it was truce, but not peace. France had almost recovered from the disaster of Agincourt and the Treaty of Troyes, as it had sixty years before from Poitiers and the Treaty of Brétigny. It was becoming obvious that the final answer could only be provided by military success and that the defection of the duke of Burgundy once again weighted the scales in favour of the French.

CHAPTER XV

Looming Defeat: Pey Berland and the Resistance of Bordeaux

The final period of the history of English Gascony illustrates more clearly than ever the duchy's basic ambivalence and insularity. Detached from the main current of military and political activity in either England or France it reacted to the major happenings outside its boundaries only as they impinged on its particular concerns and requirements. Thus, both French and English national sentiment and internal squabbles seemed equally foreign to the Gascons. Joan of Arc, despite the Gascon parentage of such of her companions as Poton de Xaintrailles or La Hire, raised no ripples of enthusiasm in Aquitaine and is totally overlooked in Gascon sources of the time. The growing political cleavage in England between the peace party headed by Cardinal Beaufort and the military enthusiasm of Gloucester, anxious to retain by force every crumbling fragment of his brother's conquests, concerned the Gascons only in the effects such policies had on English support for Guyenne. The English had for some time regarded Gascony, with its valuable ports of Bordeaux and Bayonne, primarily as a useful barbican which protected the sea for English ships and safeguarded the integrity of English territory. As the financial strain of the war began to weigh more heavily on England in the form of taxation, while its results provided neither glory nor profits, the costs inherent in maintaining Gascony became less acceptable.

The Gascons were characterized by Froissart as notorious for their instability and their eye for the main chance, but the chronicler, who wrote with such gusto about the surface panoply of chivalry, never bothered to look below the surface for some of the reasons for their changeableness. There were many fairly substantial explanations.[1] The laws of inheritance varied far more widely in the south of France than in England or even northern France, and frequently called for division among the various heirs. Often small seignories might have to be divided among a number of sons, and even daughters, creating a natural tension between the individual's ambitions and the solidarity required to maintain the family in its wider form in the midst of a fluid political situation. In the more important families, such as Foix and Albret, it is relatively easy to uncover the careful balancing of political risks by the splitting of allegiances among family members, but the extent of their lands frequently disguised their very real financial weakness and their desperate need for the profits of war and military command. A recent study of Montaillou in upper Foix shows how strong this sentiment for the maintenance of the *domus*, or extended family, was among even poor peasants.[2] The constant fluctuations in French and English military pressure from the mid-fourteenth to the mid-fifteenth centuries, which brought corresponding shifts in the loyalties of the affected fortresses and towns, meant that the ravages of war also destroyed the territorial base of many seignorial revenues.

As the campaigns were sporadic the destructions were capricious and sometimes inexplicable. Certain districts—Béarn, for example—were almost completely spared, while others suffered recurrent devastation from planned military campaigns or the freebooting pillage and forced contributions effected by bands of *routiers*. Because fire was such a convenient weapon and most buildings made of wood, destruction was extensive and discouraging. In the duchy of Aquitaine the Agenais and Quercy suffered heavily. Near the end of the fourteenth century a priest in Cahors exclaimed that 'throughout his lifetime he had seen nothing in his diocese but war'.[3] The Bordelais was reasonably sheltered from attack until the end of the fourteenth century, but its vineyards once destroyed were slow to re-establish and the English market hard to hold. Since vineyards required much agricultural labour throughout the year the depopulation of the country affected the wine harvest especially. The peasants fled to the towns, for safety behind the town walls and because they could no longer make a living from their devastated lands. In some sections, such as around the Charente, such departures meant that the once drained and fertile marshes were again flooded. Everywhere food crops decreased as marginal agricultural land was quickly abandoned with the dwindling of the population. Conditions were equally harsh in the frontier towns and in such key fortresses as Bourg or La Réole, which changed hands between English and French eight times in less than a hundred years. They were so often captured and recaptured, frequently after hard sieges, that their walls were ruined and their people fled.

War as well as famine and plague—not only the single catastrophe known as the Black Death, but the recurrent attacks which afflicted much of Europe during the fourteenth and fifteenth centuries and which were particularly lethal in the crowded conditions of medieval towns—caused a dramatic decline in population. It has been estimated that the total population of English Guyenne in 1414, based on the calculation of hearths for the tax of that year, was around 150,000. This compares to a population of about 600,000 a century before, at a time when the duchy was about the same size. By 1414 much more of the population was concentrated in Bordeaux and the Bordelais, probably even one-third of the whole.[4] These changes in the pattern of life necessarily had profound social ramifications. The labourer, benefiting from reduced numbers, improved his relative position enormously. By 1500 his average daily wage had tripled from that of 1300. Peasants whose lands had not suffered too heavily from the ravages of war profited from the need of their lords for money, and many bought themselves free from serfdom and their more oppressive obligations. Merchant fortunes also increased as towns became more dominant in the social pattern. The lords were the main sufferers, for their revenues declined as their costs went up. Profits from justice went down as the population of their lands diminished; rents and other rights were more difficult to collect. For this class, particularly in south-west France, war seemed the best way of improving their financial position, and royal pensions or grants from French or English were eagerly sought to fill the gaps in their eroding revenues.

The English regime in Guyenne had relied on two main currents of support. One flowed from the commercial classes, especially of Bordeaux and Bayonne, who found a steady market for their wines and dye-stuffs in England and who imported grain and English cloth in large quantities. Bordeaux's prosperity was particularly dependent on trade with England and the structure of that trade involved the small workman and casual labourer on the riverside as well as the wealthy wine merchant or shipowner. In addition Bordeaux profited from its position as the centre of government and from the traffic and commerce initiated by the presence of officials, courts of justice, and distinguished visitors and their retinues. It was in the group of second-rank Gascon nobility who had a share in these official appointments that the English had also managed to create links to the English crown cemented by practical advantages and an increase in prestige. Allegiance was repaid by grants of office, pensions and rents, but these Anglo-Gascons should not be characterized as totally grasping. In a number of cases fifty years of service to the English connection was not lightly thrown over. Nevertheless it would seem unreasonable to expect that such territorial lords as the Montferrands, the Lamothes, and the lower branches of the Graillys would not be singularly conscious of the importance of maintaining their hold on their own lands and safeguarding their future. English officials, after all, came to Gascony and served more or less faithfully, frequently feathering their own nests and working their way to the next rung on the ladder, but when their term of office was over they left the duchy. Given the feeble English support for Guyenne in the first half of the fifteenth century, as well as the growing strength of the French and the developing determination in their attacks on the English strongholds, it is surprising that so much loyalty remained in the duchy.

The fidelity and vigour of Bordeaux in upholding the English cause, and coincidentally its own independence, were quite remarkable in the last years before the final collapse. They are perhaps best typified in the career of Pey Berland, the most remarkable of Bordeaux's medieval archbishops.[5] The Tour Pey Berland, the bell tower of Saint-André, is still a landmark of modern Bordeaux and keeps alive his name and some suggestion of his importance in his day. Thanks to the inquest carried on for his canonization, which was eagerly encouraged by Louis XI anxious to gain goodwill from his reluctant and newly French subjects of Bordeaux, we know a great deal more about the archbishop as a human being than is usual in the middle ages.[6] Even with the necessary allowances made for its pious purpose and for an excess of zeal among the witnesses in testifying to the saintliness of their beloved archbishop, some flavour of the personality of the man, as well as an account of his varied activities, breaks through the ecclesiastical formalities. Pey Berland was born *c.* 1380 at the small settlement of Saint-Raphael in the parish of Avensan in the middle of the Médoc. He came from a comfortable peasant family and must have shown early signs of intellectual curiosity as he received his first lessons from a retired notary of the district. From this beginning he went on to Bordeaux for further study and a career in the Church. The young peasant boy obviously exhibited considerable promise for he managed to go to the University of Toulouse where he received a bachelor's degree in canon law. By this time he had attracted the attention of Cardinal Uguccione, archbishop of Bordeaux for some twenty years, and soon after his ordination he was appointed his secretary. It was perhaps an early sign of his unusual piety or the influence of the cardinal, that he became a priest at a time when so many clerks were happy to remain in minor orders until they had achieved a benefice which required them to be ordained.

The training for a young cleric in serving as the secretary of an old and experienced archbishop, who had been legate at Barcelona before his appointment to Bordeaux, was to prove invaluable and to give Berland considerable knowledge of the world beyond Gascony. In the autumn of 1408 he accompanied the cardinal to England on his mission to encourage the English acceptance of the cardinals' summons to a council at Pisa to attempt to settle the Great Schism. Uguccione was a convincing advocate and ensured the presence of an English delegation at the council, which unfortunately did not end the schism but merely added a third pope to the two current rivals. The cardinal returned to Italy, accompanied by Berland whom he rewarded in 1410 with one of the canonries of Saint-André. On Uguccione's death at Florence in 1412 Berland, having seen to his patron's burial, went on pilgrimage to the Holy Land and then returned to Bordeaux where he began to establish himself in the chapter of Saint-André. Given the charge of Bouliac on the right bank of the Garonne opposite Bordeaux, with the associated parishes of Quinsac and Lormont, he devoted himself to his new duties. In 1413 Berland was given a prebend by Pope John XXIII, who had been requested by Cardinal Uguccione not to forget 'his beloved servant'. Berland climbed the ecclesiastical ladder rapidly, for by 1423 he had been appointed to the Court of Sovereignty of the duchy and figured on the council. When Archbishop David de Montferrand died in 1430 the chapter of the cathedral speedily elected their canon, experienced in both ecclesiastical and secular matters, archbishop, and Pope Martin V was happy to confirm the election.

The new archbishop was to serve Bordeaux for over a quarter century at the most troubled time in its history. Berland's personal holiness of life, genuine pastoral concern for the people of his diocese and love of scholarship were much to the fore in the minds of the witnesses at the inquest for his canonization. Certain accepted elements of medieval piety and asceticism fall discordantly on modern ears—the constant wearing of a hair shirt, for instance, and so rigorous an insistence on chastity that the archbishop would no longer sleep in his bedroom after it had been occupied by the earl of Huntingdon and his wife. It is easier to accept and admire his devotion to prayer, his extensive charity to the inhabitants of the city in times of famine and his building of the new hospital of Saint-Pierre near Saint-Seurin. Unlike so many grasping clerics of the time he was never accused of avarice, simony or undue exaction but, in the words of one witness, 'was held most highly among his fellow citizens in good fame and esteem'. A forgiving man, when one of his servants made off with some of his plate he sent him away secretly without requiring repayment, so as not to expose him to contempt.[7]

The archbishop's constructive activities showed his practical concern for the good of his diocese. The famous bell-tower, decided on by the chapter of the cathedral in 1429, was begun in 1440, not only to add to the dignity of Saint-André, but to provide work for the peasants who had fled to the city from the depredations of the *routiers* in the surrounding districts. The long-felt need for Bordeaux to have a university of its own was pursued at the Curia until in 1441 the pope granted the city its own *studium generale*. It provided a centre within the duchy for higher education, which up till now had had to be pursued at Toulouse, Paris, Orléans or one of the Italian universities. Even closer to Berland's heart was his foundation of the college of Saint-Raphael in 1442. This early prototype of a diocesan seminary was to educate twelve poor young men destined for the priesthood. It bore witness to the archbishop's recognition of the desperate need for an educated clergy and his practical method of attempting to provide it. His will illustrated his continuing fondness for his foundation for he left it all his books with the stern proviso that no one was to take them away from the college under pain of excommunication. If a future archbishop needed to consult any of them he might be allowed to borrow them for a short time, but only if he left as a pledge books of equal value. A very real concern for books and education also appears in other legacies which provided funds for poor students to continue their education or to buy books.[8] Unfortunately, the years of Berland's archiepiscopacy did not allow him much leisure for his beloved books, for the concerns of the duchy and the serious threats to Bordeaux weighed heavily on him.

Pey Berland became the embodiment of the Bordeaux spirit of resistance to the French conquest. His leadership in an active political role was particularly essential since Gadifer Shorthose, mayor of the city 1434–51, was extremely weak and had rather poor judgment. The archbishop worked within the duchy, sending a subordinate to the Council of Basle, and, as a faithful subject of the English, totally rejected for his diocese ecclesiastical control by the French king claimed in the Pragmatic Sanction of Bourges. War came closer to Bordeaux in 1438 when a French force, headed by Albret and Poton de Xaintrailles and reinforced by the troops of the notorious *routier*, Rodrigo de Villandrando, converged on the Bordelais and the Médoc. In essence this was merely a *chevauchée* of unusual strength which did great damage and pillaged the countryside. The suburb of Saint-Seurin was sacked and the neighbouring vineyards destroyed, but the city itself was too strong behind its walls to be attacked by an army unprepared for a siege. The French withdrew after having ambushed and killed some 800 unwary Anglo-Bordelais.

The ease with which the French force overran the countryside was a warning to the authorities in the city as well as a signal to Charles VII that it would be easy to mount an all-out attack. In the summer of 1439, while discussing peace at Oye, the English sent the earl of Huntingdon to Guyenne with the largest force despatched since 1412. Huntingdon was named lieutenant of the duchy, to serve for six years, and his indenture specified a force of 300 men-at-arms and 2,000 archers. The earl—supported by Sir Thomas Rampston as seneschal and Sir Robert Clifton as constable—arrived at Bordeaux at the beginning of August. During the next year he reconquered Bazas, began campaigns in the Landes and gave promise of some English successes, only to be recalled without explanation at the end of 1440.[9]

Huntingdon's recall was unfortunate, but perhaps even more damaging to the English cause in Guyenne was his pursuit of the policy which was obvious earlier in the career of Sir John Tiptoft. During his brief stay in the duchy the earl acquired the lordship of Lesparre for himself and his heirs as well as distributing Gascon lands and offices among his supporters and members of his household.[10] This expedient had been adopted earlier by the duke of Gloucester and Huntingdon had been given specific permission to alienate lands worth 1,000 *salus* in annual value. After Gloucester's fall from power the only change was that the rewards went to the followers and servants of Suffolk. At a crucial moment in the history of the duchy the royal prerogative of encouraging Gascon loyalty by grants of lands, offices or pensions to them was much reduced by the creation of absentee officers and landholders. The result was further discouragement among Gascons who saw no hope of rewards from the English, while they were being wooed with generous offers from the French. This policy fanned dislike of the English who monopolized such Gascon rewards to the disadvantage of the natives, eroding still further the duchy's already meagre revenues.

In 1442 war was again initiated by the French while the possibility of a marriage between Henry VI and a daughter of the count of Armagnac was discussed at the English court. Such a marriage would flatter Armagnac and, the English hoped, might serve to tighten the links with other disaffected Gascon lords. By the end of May the king had empowered his secretary, Bishop Bekynton, Sir Robert Roos, and Edward Hull, a squire of the king's household, to negotiate for the marriage. Before Bekynton and Roos left England hostilities had flared again around Tartas. The journal of their mission not only describes the ins and outs of their abortive marriage negotiations with Armagnac, but also gives a vivid and personal account of the leading men of Gascony and the tenor of life in Bordeaux as it reacted to the depressing rumours and genuine bad news that poured in over the months. The journal covers the period from 5 June 1442 to 20 February 1443 and is supplemented by an unusual and fragmentary account of Bordeaux's treasurer from February to August 1442.[11]

The French army of 1442 was commanded by the king himself and included several lords of the south-west, among whom were the count of Foix and viscount of Lomagne, oldest son of the count of Armagnac. As the army moved south it crossed Armagnac and the valley of the Adour to come to the aid of Tartas, the only stronghold in the district remaining in French hands after the campaign of 1438. Sir Thomas Rampston, seneschal of Guyenne, had continued the military pressure initiated by the earl of Huntingdon in 1439–40, and had been actively besieging the French forces at Tartas. After a long siege the defenders had finally agreed to surrender if a major French force did not arrive by 24 June. Charles and his army appeared on the 23rd, and the fortress was saved for the French. From there Charles' army went on to Saint-Sever, the commanding position for English power south-east of the Landes, which they took in three days, capturing Rampston himself. From Saint-Sever they again moved westward to Dax, the final obstacle before Bayonne. This depressing news was brought to Roos and Bekynton as their ship arrived in the Garonne on 14 July.

When they disembarked in the city two days later they found, as they wrote to the king, 'as sorowful a town and as gretly dismayed and discoraged as any might be in th'erth'.[12] Roos and Bekynton were particularly alarmed by the rumours spread by one John Goer, who had landed at Castillon and ridden overland to Bordeaux, thus arriving before the ambassadors. He had spread the news that the king's letters implied that no aid would be given by England, so that the inhabitants felt totally abandoned. The ambassadors wasted no time in trying to improve the situation. They landed on Monday, met the council on Tuesday, showed them Henry's letters, had them translated and given to Archbishop Berland. On Wednesday the archbishop made a stirring speech and read the letters from the pulpit of the cathedral, reassuring the citizens of the king's zeal and exhorting them to further efforts of their own. This report by Roos and Bekynton to the king, written at the beginning of August, reminds Henry that his promises of aid had not been fulfilled and the people were beginning to despair. They exhort him to remember 'how this your Duchie of Guienne is oon th'oldest lordship longing to your coroune of Englande'. They urge him to send aid as hastily as possible so that 'by negligence or delaies it comme not to late, and inconvenients irrecuperable be growen the meene tyme'.[13]

The king's ambassadors had been accompanied on their voyage by Armagnac's negotiator, Master Jean de Batut, who only parted from them on 21 July when bad news had already accumulated. No doubt he returned to the count at Lectoure with a description of the weakness of the duchy which would throw into question the advisability of the marriage. The marriage negotiations, which had been the primary reason for the journey, became bogged down in an exchange of meaningless civilities, strategic delays over the provision of the necessary safe-conducts, and the availability of the artist required by King Henry to paint the Armagnac daughters in their kirtles so that he could choose his favourite from the portraits. By the end of August when the English had been fully informed of the activity of Armagnac's son in the attacking French army, Roos wrote a very stiff letter to Batut. He informed him, for the count's benefit, that the king was no longer interested in the marriage, given the activities of the viscount de Lomagne. The arrival of an English army was expected shortly and Armagnac would be in danger of attack.[14] From this time on Roos, who had been named regent by the Three Estates of Gascony on 15 August, and Bekynton devoted themselves to the reinforcement of the duchy and continuing attempts to awake the council in England to its desperate situation although desultory and useless letters were exchanged with Batut.

The progress of the French campaign is mirrored in these letters, while the city's own efforts to encourage the resistance of the surrounding towns can be seen from the entries in the treasurer's report which tell of the dispatch of packages of bowstrings to Saint-Macaire and of such materials as cords for scaling-ladders for a planned attack on Bazas.[15] They also turned their efforts to improving the defences of Bordeaux itself. Walls and towers were repaired; entrenchments were made around the barbicans to provide defence against artillery fire; and the artillery of the city was put in order, both guns and the older missile-throwers. Gunpowder was stored in the main town gates and cannon balls were brought to the city from outside quarries. When Archbishop Berland sailed for England on 26 July carrying letters from the ambassadors on the state of affairs, a considerable amount had already been done for the defence of the city.

Nevertheless, both Bekynton and Roos were very dubious of the local loyalty. In terms reminiscent of the letters to the Despensers more than a century before, they laid the blame for the unrest and division in the duchy on misgovernment by council and the lack of English people. In a separate letter to the lord treasurer they suggested that he talk extensively with the archbishop, whom they characterized as a truthful and simple man, to learn more about the activities of the ducal council, for they thought he might be prevailed upon to go beyond his instructions.[16] Despite their continued negotiations with such distinguished members of council as Bernard Angevin, the Captal de Buch and Bertrand de Montferrand, Bekynton was convinced that the council did not care for the king's interests. He quoted the dean of Saint-André who had openly insisted that Bordeaux must bow to whoever came there with superior force. The news was indeed discouraging, but reliance on the English was also fraught with problems. The English mayor, Gadifer Shorthose, was openly contemptuous of the orders of Roos while the constable, Sir Robert Clifton, was on the point of death.[17] It was in this disturbed atmosphere that a letter was sent to the king in the utmost secrecy bearing the worst news. It was written on a long narrow piece of vellum and then sewed up in the border of an old pilgrim's garment.[18] Despite their worries and the desperate nature of the summer it is pleasant to read in the journal that there were occasionally lighter interludes. The ambassadors were frequently invited out to dine with such worthies as the bishop of Bazas, the mayor and Bernard Angevin. Bekynton rode to Saint-Seurin to see the process of winemaking in September, sailed to Lormont and explored some of the Entre-deux-Mers.[19]

By 8 October, however, despite vigorous efforts at reinforcement, the town of La Réole was stormed and taken, though the castle continued its resistance for another two months. A number of other important points along the Garonne also fell, including Marmande, Tonneins, Sainte-Bazeille, and even Langon. Equally discouraging was the lack of news from England. No ships had arrived since the departure of the archbishop in July—not even a balinger, the ambassadors noted bitterly—until on 21 October a ship finally arrived with letters from England.[20] Among its passengers were the archbishop's doctor, a servant of the regent, and Edward Hull, a strong Lancastrian and trusted member of the king's household, who was to be appointed constable to replace Clifton. Pey Berland himself had stayed in England to sustain English interest in Bordeaux's plight. The king's letter to the citizens of Bordeaux, dated 21 September, recognized their suffering from the war and their need for help, as well as paying tribute to their loyalty as described by the archbishop.

Henry assured them that he would certainly send sufficient help under an important leader.[21] In reality the indenture for John Beaufort, earl of Somerset, the leader of the expedition referred to by the king, was not even drawn up until April 1443 and ultimately went to Normandy instead of to Guyenne. The weak state of the Lancastrian finances contributed in no small way to the difficulty of mustering sufficient troops when war was being waged on two fronts in France. Guyenne, further away and often less attractive to those in power, tended to lose out.

King Charles' army of 1442 had won some notable successes along the Garonne. The castle of La Réole finally capitulated on 7 December, as did Monségur nearby, but these were the last victories. With a return of confidence the Gascons had regained Langon and Saint-Loubès, while a fire in La Réole drove King Charles from his lodging in his shirt. Gascon efforts were aided by the coldest winter in many years. The rivers froze and food supplies were difficult for the French army which withdrew to Montauban and then north, providing another respite for the beleaguered men of the duchy. Bekynton returned to England, leaving Bordeaux in January 1443, and the marriage project with Armagnac was totally abandoned.[22]

Further negotiations for peace and for Henry's marriage to a French princess continued throughout 1443. A marriage was arranged at Tours in May 1444 between Henry and Margaret of Anjou and was accompanied by a two-year truce.[23] Margaret was the daughter of René of Anjou, King Charles' brother-in-law and fondly known in Provence as 'Good King René' for his introduction of the muscat grape. He was a patron of culture and chivalry, but a profligate and incompetent ruler, and his daughter unfortunately proved to be an autocratic and ruthless queen. The two-year truce was subsequently extended for another two years, though the negotiating party had obviously found it impossible to grapple with, much less settle, any of the main issues. In the old familiar pattern a royal marriage was once more expected to aid peace between the two countries and once more the queen from France helped to foment civil war in England.

Nevertheless the years of the truce meant a vital respite for Guyenne. It could make a start on repairing its losses, rebuilding its revenues and putting its fortresses in order. The citizens of Bordeaux even indulged in a running controversy with the Captal de Buch and his son over disputed rights of pasturage in the

Palus, the riverside meadows to the north of the city.[24] As an omen for the future there was an acceleration in the process of shifting allegiance among the lords of the region. Such important Gascon lords as Bérard de Lamothe, lord of Roquetaillade, and François de Gramont from the Chalosse weighed the French successes in 1442 and decided to turn to Charles VII to safeguard their lands. Other members of the nobility of the Landes followed their example. Their lands, pensions and rents held from the English king were officially confiscated and reassigned, often to Englishmen, but such grants frequently could not be enforced because the districts were under French control.[25] King Charles also used the lull to his own advantage and clipped the wings of his most troublesome and double-dealing vassal, the count of Armagnac. Jean IV had angered both the French and English kings with his insolence and totally egotistical policy. King Charles was now strong enough to crush him. He sent an army against Jean at the end of 1443, captured his town of Rodez and attacked the count in his castle at L'Isle-Jourdain. Jean was forced to surrender, was arrested, the town was pillaged and his domains confiscated for his evil behaviour to the crown. The count was finally released in 1446 but he had been rendered politically impotent and died in 1450, leaving his son an unfortunate legacy.[26] One more obstacle had been cleared from King Charles' path when, after his success in Normandy, he turned to an all-out attack on the duchy in 1450.

CHAPTER XVI

Final Collapse

Charles VII denounced the treaty of Tours in 1449 and launched an offensive against English strength in Normandy. The French king's efforts were aided by the division and disaffection in England where by 1450 both the impeachment of Suffolk and Jack Cade's rebellion precluded much help to the English lands in France. By the summer of 1450 French attention had turned to the south-west where the king encouraged the count of Foix, his lieutenant in the south, to improve his own situation in Béarn by an attack on Mauléon. This fortress had always had a notorious reputation for preying on the surrounding countryside and it was now under the rather half-hearted protection of the king of Navarre, though with a strongly English garrison. It soon capitulated and Foix's troops also occupied Guiche, thus menacing Bayonne, but instead of pushing on to attack the port the count of Foix was satisfied to make a triumphal entry into Orthez, the capital of his viscounty of Béarn.

An autumn campaign approached Guyenne from the borders of Périgord. One force under Xaintrailles, with artillery directed by Jean Bureau, besieged Bergerac which surrendered in October and then moved down the Dordogne as far as Sainte-Foy-La-Grande. A second contingent under the command of Amanieu d'Albret, lord of Orval, approached from the south-east, capturing Bazas and then swinging west to attack Bordeaux from Blanque-fort. Albret had a disciplined force of about 500 fighting men and when he approached the city the impetuous Shorthose hurriedly gathered a miscellaneous troop of English men-at-arms, municipal militia and Gascon knights who sallied forth to the attack. The result was disastrous since there was neither proper leadership nor any coherence in the helter-skelter attack on d'Albret's well-organized troops.[1] The skirmish on 1 November lives in Bordeaux's history as *La Male Journade* because so many citizens were killed, wounded, or had to flee. Archbishop Berland, seeing the bodies brought back on carts amid the lamentations of the city, was so overwhelmed that he retreated into private prayer for two days.[2] It was only too obvious that Bordeaux was ripe for conquest. The prospects of English support were minimal and the city itself had finally begun to lose heart. However, November was considered too late to begin a siege. The French command may have remembered the overly optimistic efforts of the duke of Orléans in 1406–07 when the appalling winter weather contributed heavily to his embarrassing retreat. It was wiser and more certain to wait till spring.

Preparations were carefully made, not only to achieve military success, but to attempt to gain the sympathy of the Gascon population. The king promulgated strict regulations requiring soldiers to pay the inhabitants for all supplies taken and enjoining heavy penalties for theft and other misbehaviour. It would appear that every effort was made to achieve negotiated surrenders without the total destruction of fortresses and towns and to win the allegiance of the Gascons whom the chronicler Thomas Basin described 'as attached to the English and their rule by a singular affection'.[3] The French army which attacked Guyenne and the Bordelais from the north in the spring of 1451 was led by Dunois, the Bastard of Orléans. A highly regarded military commander, he had been a supporter and comrade-in-arms of Joan of Arc and a valiant upholder of the interests of the Orléans family. By the beginning of May his army had moved to besiege Blaye, that essential fortress on the Gironde, which shared with Bourg the reputation of being 'the keys to open Bordeaux'.[4] A strong fleet of eighty to a hundred ships, mainly from La Rochelle, but including Spanish ships, reinforced the army by blockading the Gironde against help from England, while Dunois' own army was strengthened by the artillery of Jean Bureau. Blaye had recently had its garrison reinforced and was well provisioned so refused haughtily when first summoned to surrender. After a few days of siege Dunois held a council to debate the possibilities of an all-out attack. The counsels of the bold prevailed and, after a day of vigorous fighting, Dunois' men had managed to enter the town while its defenders withdrew to the castle. One source suggests that those in charge of the garrison, including the incompetent Shorthose, were personally responsible for a shortage of men-at-arms because they had taken wages for eighty but only brought twenty-five because of their pride and greed.[5] By 23 May the castle had also surrendered.

The conditions of the treaty were reasonably generous and held out inducements to those of the duchy who would swear allegiance to King Charles promising that they would have all their inheritance returned. From Blaye Dunois went on upstream to Bourg which capitulated within a week. The next major fortress above Bourg was Fronsac, a strong and easily defensible castle, but by this time the defenders were losing heart before the weight of the French attack and their string of successes. Within three days (5 June) Fronsac had promised to surrender if they had not received sufficient English aid in ten days to drive Dunois and his company out by force of arms. While Dunois waited in the lines outside Fronsac some of his men were sent to take Libourne and Saint-Emilion while Xaintrailles and the young count of Armagnac, Jean V, captured Rions and menaced all of Entre-deux-Mers.

Bordeaux's spirit of resistance was crushed and the practical desire of its citizens to obtain the best possible terms, to safeguard their goods and their vineyards, urged them towards a settlement before a siege even began.[6] The Captal de Buch, uncle of the count of Foix, made the initial approach to the French while the Estates of Bordeaux were represented by Pey Berland, the lord of La Brède, and Bernard Angevin, chancellor of the duchy and long-time civil servant. The treaty arrived at by 12 June with Xaintrailles, Jean Bureau, and Augen de Bréquit, the judge of Marsan, who had been empowered by Dunois, was ratified by Charles VII at Saint-Jean-d'Angely on 20 June.[7] The terms were remarkably generous and testify to Charles VII's political good sense in attempting to conciliate these new and reluctant subjects. The inhabitants of Guyenne were to take the oath of fidelity to the king of France, but the king, or his lieutenant, would swear on the day of their entry into Bordeaux to respect the privileges of the city and its surrounding lands. Those inhabitants who did not wish to take the oath were to have six months to quit the duchy with all their moveables while their other goods would pass to their heirs. Those absent on business who were uncertain as to whether to take the oath would have a year to make up their mind without losing any of their rights. Safe-conducts to leave were to be given easily at the cost of one gold crown. A general amnesty for the inhabitants of Guyenne and Gascony was to be proclaimed so that inhabitants might keep their goods and ecclesiastics their dignities and benefices. Most grants of land, castles and lordships made by the English king were to be confirmed. The inhabitants were not to be submitted to new—that is, French—taxes, to pay new duties on imported merchandise, nor were they subject to military service outside Guyenne. Not only was money to continue to be coined at Bordeaux, but the king agreed to abandon some of the profits from the coining to improve the new money and to allow the old money to run for two years. A court of sovereignty (like the English model already set up) was to be established at Bordeaux and the French king's officers of justice were to respect the local privileges and customs. Bordeaux's negotiating skills and its previous independence of the French crown had provided it with a remarkably generous document; what remained to be seen was how it would be carried out in practice.

Immediately after the settlement had been reached plans were put on foot for the formal and ceremonious entry of Dunois into Bordeaux. The various French officials gathered at Blaye and proceeded upriver on Tuesday 29 June. That night they spent on board the fleet, while the men-at-arms were lodged at Lormont and the other small villages close by. Early on Wednesday morning they disembarked and sent the heralds to summon the men of the town. The jurats with the lords of Montferrand, Duras and Lesparre presented the keys of the city to Jean Bureau who had been appointed mayor by the French and the procession moved off towards the cathedral. It consisted of picked groups of archers and men-at-arms leading the French officials and captains with all the ceremonial so dear to the medieval mind. The heralds and trumpeters preceded a richly caparisoned horse bearing the king's seal in a casket and two fleur-de-lis banners were carried before Dunois, dressed in white, riding a horse with blue trappings. It was a very hot day and a long walk from the riverside to Saint-André so that one of the French lords had placed a tun of wine outside the cathedral to refresh his companions. At the front of the church Dunois, followed by the other French officials, took the oath to observe Bordeaux's privileges and then the archbishop and the more important men of Bordeaux swore fealty to King Charles. Dunois then took possession of the Ombrière and lodged there for a few days while the last details of the city's new government were worked out.[8] Bayonne remained to be captured so there was little time to relax.

Dunois led his army south and siege was set before Bayonne by 6 August. It soon appeared that the citizens had no heart for a long siege nor did they wish to be taken by force of arms and thus subject to total destruction. Negotiations were begun and an agreement arrived at. The treaty was not as generous as Bordeaux's as the French insisted on compensation for bringing the army south and formally setting up the siege. The citizens of Bayonne were required to pay an indemnity of 20,000 crowns, surrender the captain of the city as a prisoner to the king as well as a gunner whose culverin had killed a French knight during a truce. All the artillery, from cannons and bombards to crossbows, was to become the property of King Charles and the gunners prisoners. The privileges and franchises of the city were to be at the pleasure of the king. However, the English in the town were allowed to go free, primarily because the citizens dreaded the confiscation of their own property in England unless this was granted, but their goods were to be surrendered to the French commissioners. French prisoners currently held in the town were to be released free of all obligations except their own debts for loans or merchandise. The requirement of the oath of fealty and the subsequent confirmation of goods, offices and benefices was on much the same terms as Bordeaux, though only six months was allowed for those currently away to make up their minds to return. Meanwhile all their goods were to be under the control of their wives.[9]

The formal handing-over of the keys to the city on 20 August was signalized by an extraordinary cloud formation, a white cross in a black cloud which rested above the town for about an hour. Some, perhaps more imaginative, even suggested that the cross was headed by a crown which changed into a fleur-de-lis. One devout chronicler was convinced that it signified that 'God wished this land should be surrendered to him who wore the white cross, who had the right and justification, since God sent the banner of France there'.[10] In any case, it speeded the removal of the red crosses of England from Bayonne's towers and gates and their replacement by the banners of France.

The conquest of Guyenne was complete but not yet final. To ensure its stability Bordeaux—by far the most important centre politically and commercially—needed to be convinced of the reality of French goodwill and its implementation of the terms of the treaty. It required sensitivity on the part of the newly imposed French officials to conciliate the commercial and religious interests, both strongly English. The French seneschal in Bordeaux, Olivier de Coetivy, was a young and aggressive Breton who had already served King Charles, commanding La Réole after its capture in 1442. Both he and the mayor, Jean Bureau, were primarily king's men who surrounded themselves with French councillors and allowed the local interests no influence. The chapters of Saint-André and Saint-Seurin were consistently anti-French, for both the archbishop and the dean of Saint-Seurin, Pey du Tasta, were vigorous upholders of the English cause. Berland, having once sworn the oath, refrained from pro-English action, but Pey du Tasta had left for England in 1449 and continued to serve Bordeaux interests and to encourage revolt from his privileged position on Henry VI's council in England. It is not too surprising that the chapters were subjected to an immediate attack by the new French officials who insisted that the provisions of the Pragmatic Sanction (which insisted on recognition of the requests of the lay power) must be extended to any elections to fill empty places arising in the chapters. They seem to have put particularly heavy pressure on the archbishop since on 7 July 1452 Berland took the unusual step of swearing an oath before the high altar of Saint-André that he would neither abandon nor renounce his archbishopric but wished to live and die archbishop.[11]

The unrest of the Gascons, determined to maintain their rights and concerned about the market for their wines under their new ruler, was brought to the boiling-point by the insistence of the French receivers of finances on imposing a *taille* on the population to pay troops to protect them. This was clearly in contradiction to the terms of the treaty and embassies were sent to the king at Bourges protesting such an invasion on the immunities promised them. They were, they claimed, more capable of defending their own country than any garrison and had no need for remedies which were worse than the dangers. The king refused to listen and the unsatisfied delegates returned to Bordeaux. Their report to the inhabitants opened the gates of disaffection for the fiercely independent Bordelais who feared that they would be reduced to servitude.[12]

The spirit of rebellion inspired by French heavy-handedness, for the Gascons did not perceive themselves as 'French', was encouraged by an active pro-English faction within the city which King Henry tried to encourage by a flow of donations to Gascons, dependent on English recapture of territories. Pey du Tasta was the anchor in England of this policy. Already called to the king's council in 1450 he had begun to garner English prebends in 1451 and was described as a king's clerk. Particularly active on the council during 1454-55, he remained a constant member until well on into the reign of Edward IV.[13] This ardent supporter of the Gascon cause was probably the correspondent in England for Pierre de Montferrand and other rebellious Gascon nobles who laid a conspiracy to overthrow French rule. The delegation left Bordeaux for London in August 1452. This time their message that Bordeaux would welcome the English if they returned with a fleet and a good army coincided with a temporary settlement in the looming civil war. The efforts of Tasta on the council reached sympathetic ears and the king agreed to the dispatch of an army headed by John Talbot, earl of Shrewsbury.

Talbot was the last survivor of the military captains who had fought in the victorious days in France. He was certainly elderly for command, probably between sixty-five and seventy, but his age has been exaggerated along with his exploits. Given command of a force of some 4,000 men, he and his army left England in mid-October. According to one chronicler, on his way to Bordeaux, Talbot encountered the count of Clermont, the French captain of the city, returning from the Médoc and pursued him and his company so vigorously that Clermont had to abandon ship and flee to safety at Bourg, stripped to his doublet for greater agility. The English made a rich haul when they captured the ship which held Clermont's baggage, jewels and seal.[14] Perhaps it was this skirmish which helped to enshrine Talbot's name in popular folklore for in the Médoc a century ago a quarrelsome child who threatened or beat up his friends was characterized as 'like King Talbot'.[15] By the evening of 22 October Talbot had arrived outside Bordeaux where the city gates were quickly opened to him. The unpopular Coetivy was betrayed by a Bordeaux bourgeois, had to surrender to Louis de Brutails, a leader of the insurrection, and was sent off at once to England where he remained till 1454.[16] Encouraged by the appearance of an English army most of the smaller towns of the surrounding

223

territory returned to the English allegiance. Only Fronsac, Bourg and Blaye, with reinforced garrisons, ensured a continuing French presence.

King Charles was angry, insistent on regaining Bordeaux and Guyenne and punishing the guilty rebels. However, it was decided that it was again wise to wait till spring before launching a general campaign which the king himself would lead. Meanwhile the English also put the winter to good use by sending reinforcements to Bordeaux, including extra troops under the command of Viscount Lisle, Talbot's son, and Lord Camoys, the last English seneschal of Gascony. The attacking French army was divided into four sections, two in the south, operating from Saint-Sever, and two in the north, proceeding along the Dordogne. The revolt against the French had not spread to the south and Bayonne remained docile so that some of the southern troops came up through the Landes to attack Bordeaux from the west. A skirmish at Martignas in May between Talbot and the French troops resulted in a defeat for the English who scurried back to the safety of Bordeaux. Meanwhile the French forces along the Dordogne had had to besiege Chalais in Saintonge, which held out against them until taken by assault. Its Gascon defenders were beheaded and the English put to ransom. Gensac and Montravel in the river valley swiftly surrendered and discussion arose among the French leaders concerning the next objective. In the judgment of Jean Bureau the most strategic move was to besiege Castillon. The importance of this man and his skill with the royal artillery cannot be over-estimated. Jean Bureau was a bold and valiant peasant who had previously served the English as master of their artillery.[17] The small man's cunning in handling his primitive guns and his skill in arranging their emplacements was an important factor in reassuring the French troops and in destroying English morale. His ability gave him an important place in the French military councils. He argued that the capture of Castillon would put the whole of the Dordogne in French control and allow them to descend on Bordeaux and Entre-deux-Mers with full force and his judgment was accepted.

The siege was set at the beginning of July and Bureau arranged a strong French emplacement to the east of Castillon. This park was surrounded with a deep ditch, had high walls of earth strengthened with tree trunks and was armed with a large number of serpentines and culverins. The possibility of storming it successfully was very small. Other French troops, primarily archers, were placed in the abbey of Saint-Florent slightly to the north of the park. When the news of the siege of Castillon came to Bordeaux the inhabitants urged Talbot to keep his promise to combat the French and to go and raise the siege. Talbot was not enthusiastic about this since he felt the French could be more easily fought on territory more accessible to Bordeaux, but the mutterings within the city decided him to make the effort. He gathered both English and Gascon troops—the contemporary chroniclers as always disagree on numbers, but probably around 6,000—and marched out of Bordeaux on 16 July. Arriving at Libourne in the evening he paused and sent out spies towards Castillon, both to bring encouragement to the defenders and to find out the disposition of the French troops. The defenders sent back a message to attack the troops in the abbey first so without further pause Talbot and his army marched through the night, arriving at Castillon at dawn on 17 July. With a great shout they rushed on the unsuspecting French in the abbey and a violent mêlée ensued in which a number of French soldiers were killed though many fought their way to safety in the fortified park.

Talbot returned to the abbey to refresh himself and his men. Finding ample provisions and five or six pipes of wine they made short work of all the supplies. Nevertheless, it was still early in the morning and Talbot was preparing to hear mass when an unsubstantiated report was brought to him that the French were abandoning their camp and fleeing. This rumour was inspired by the sight of a great cloud of dust—for it was a hot, dry day—which was actually caused by the French grooms taking the horses off to forage. Talbot, without stopping to check the truth of the information or to finish hearing mass, set off in hot pursuit. He did not take the time to properly arrange his force or to wait for the arrival of his footsoldiers and artillery which had not yet caught up with him after the all-night march. Impatient with more cautious subordinates who tried to dissuade him from attacking such a well-fortified camp without all his forces, Talbot reproached them for their timidity, raised his standard and pressed the attack towards the park. Foolhardy rashness brought its own punishment. The French artillery was deployed to good effect and the French soldiers then sallied out to pursue the discomfited English. The battle became a rout as the troops with Talbot took flight, the footsoldiers coming up were so overcome by the disaster that they ran away. Talbot himself, riding a hackney because of his age, though he had dismounted his other men, and wearing a brigantine covered with scarlet velvet, appears to have been wounded in the leg by a gunshot but killed by a dagger stroke. In any case the body was so mutilated that the French could not identify it and were not sure whether Talbot had really been killed or had escaped. The terrified Anglo-Gascon troops fled for safety to the surrounding woods or across the fields to the river where many were drowned trying to escape the pursuing French.[18]

Today a monument to Talbot stands near the river bank where he is reputed to have met his death. Until the French Revolution there was a chapel there, but now a large cross and a monument commemorating the 500th anniversary of the battle look out over the quiet fields and vineyards where bloody fighting once raged. Nevertheless it is possible to form an idea of the scene of death and despair that greeted the English heralds on the day after the battle as they took up their duty of identifying the dead. Talbot's herald was asked by the French if he would recognize his master and agreed happily, thinking he was a prisoner. Instead he was shown the body of an old man whose facial wounds defied identification but whom the herald could recognize by a broken tooth. Weeping, he fell on his knees by his master, praying God to forgive his misdeeds, and covering the body with Talbot's coat-of-arms which he had worn as his herald for forty years.[19]

Castillon has been described as 'the Waterloo of Gascon nationality'[20] and the Anglo-Gascon defeat there must be laid primarily at Talbot's door. In a battle reminiscent of the tragic impetuosity of John Chandos at Lussac in 1369 or the fool-hardiness of Clarence at Baugé in 1421, an impatient commander threw away caution and good generalship in favour of panache and a reckless attack. The French showed in their disciplined control of their troops and their inspired use of the new military technology that they had finally learned the lessons of Crécy, Poitiers and Agincourt. In this case it was the English who clung to an old and now outdated strategy of battle. At Castillon this weakness resulted in a heavy loss of life, from the commanders down, but more seriously it destroyed the last

English effort to maintain their hold on a duchy which had been part of their king's inheritance for two and a half centuries.

The defenders of Castillon, deprived of all hope of reinforcement by Talbot's defeat, surrendered in two days and the noose around Bordeaux was steadily tightened. Libourne and Saint-Emilion collapsed. Xaintrailles captured Saint-Macaire and Albret Villandraut, while a French force ravaged the Médoc. By 13 August King Charles himself had arrived at the castle of Montferrand, near Ambès, to supervise the final struggle for Bordeaux. This time the city's inhabitants had resolved to continue the fight despite the defeat at Castillon, the death of Talbot and the loss of so many troops. Lord Camoys was re-elected leader of the city's forces, was voted money to strengthen the fortifications and to pay archers and garrisons. What could be done to reinforce the nearby towns was set on foot, but the French strength was overwhelming. Blanquefort on the north-west and Cadillac, some seventeen miles upstream, were put under siege. On 19 September Cadillac was subjected to an unprecedented artillery barrage. Frequently, primitive artillery produced more terror by its noise and unselective damage than tactical results. In this case, the artillery was well controlled, aimed first against a wooden bulwark erected outside the city gate for its protection and, when that had been destroyed, at the tower of the city gate. The bombardment was so effective and dislodged so many stones from both the tower and the nearby wall that they practically filled up the moat. The French easily crossed to wage hand-to-hand combat with the defenders of the town. During the ensuing heavy battle the English were gradually forced back and had to retire to the castle, abandoning the town. Their effort to achieve a treaty by surrendering the castle and paying a fine of 10,000 crowns if allowed to go free was contemptuously refused by King Charles. More artillery was brought up and the castle was finally bombarded into submission. The final treaty put the English to ransom, but the Gascons were to be held at the king's pleasure. Cadillac capitulated on 27 September and its Gascon captain had his head cut off. Soon after Blanquefort also surrendered and besieged Bordeaux stood alone.[21]

King Charles relied on the proved success of his artillery, redeploying around Bordeaux all the guns which had been successful at Cadillac and Blanquefort. Bureau promised the king that he had positioned the artillery in such a way that he could in a short time render the city so totally destroyed and devastated by the flight of artillery that those within would not know where to stand. In a brave last-ditch effort the city's own navy of little ships had been active between the city and the Médoc and had done considerable damage to the besieging French. To shut off this last loophole the king had to bring a fleet from La Rochelle, well equipped with men-at-arms, to stop their attack. It had become obvious that surrender would soon be necessary and that it might be possible to improve its conditions by negotiation. By 5 October Camoys, supported by some twenty-five citizens of Bordeaux, went to Lormont to discuss terms with the chancellor. The first demands were impossibly harsh but Charles' desire to punish the Bordelais severely for their rebellion had to face the reality of the development of plague within his army and the wisdom of arriving at a rapid settlement. By 9 October Camoys, accompanied by eight to ten of the most important English and citizens of Bordeaux, went to Montferrand to meet the king.[22] The subsequent treaty, though very much harsher than the settlement of 1451, provided a full pardon to all the inhabitants of Bordeaux and restored them their goods. However, the city lost all its privileges which were to remain at the king's pleasure, and the inhabitants were to pay a fine of 100,000 gold crowns. The English were to be allowed to leave freely while twenty leaders of the rebellion—including the Montferrands, Gaillard de Durfort, the Captal de Buch and his son—who had invited the English back and opened the city to them, were to be banished from the kingdom. Camoys had at least succeeded in having their lives spared. French prisoners in Bordeaux were to be let go, free of all ransom.[23]

The conditions were harsh but acceptable and the city was finally rendered to the French on Friday 19 October. Charles himself had already left for the north when the king of France's banners were placed on the gates which had for three centuries known the English arms. Rions and Benauges, which had refused to accept Cadillac's inclusion of them in its treaty, were the last holdouts and were soon forced to surrender.[24] English resistance in Guyenne had come to an end and the links forged during the long period of English rule had finally snapped.

Gascony was irretrievably lost and 1453 has always been

considered the closing date of the Hundred Years War. Nevertheless no truce, much less peace, marked the loss of the duchy
or the failure of the last English expedition in the south. England's
slide into the War of the Roses and the struggles of King Charles
and Philip of Burgundy, often supported by the dauphin,
continued the familiar pattern of various factions angling across
the Channel for help against a domestic enemy. When Louis XI
became king of France in 1461 and Charles the Bold succeeded
Philip the Good in Burgundy in 1467 one last flicker of the old
Anglo-Burgundian alliance of the days of Henry V encouraged
Edward IV to invade France in 1475. The attempt was an
ignominious failure but the treaty arranged at Picquigny in
August 1475 between Louis and Edward was a final milestone.
It made a seven-year truce and submitted the English claim to
the throne of France to four arbiters: the archbishops of Canterbury and Lyons, the dukes of Clarence and Dunois. Their sentence
was to be binding. In the interests of trade the requirements for
safe-conducts for English and French merchants trading in the
two countries were abolished. Most importantly, it made Edward
IV a pensioner of the French king. The English army was to be
removed when Louis paid Edward 75,000 crowns and in addition
the English king was to receive 25,000 gold crowns every year
for the life of both kings.[25] On this less than heroic note hostilities
between the two kingdoms finally ground to a halt. Louis de
Brutails, an important Gascon emigré who continued to urge
war against France, gained notoriety for his refusal to share
the pious belief of the enthusiasts for the treaty who were convinced that the white pigeon which obstinately perched on
Edward's tent at Picquigny was an apparition of the Holy Spirit.
Brutails unromantically insisted that the bird had chosen the
king's tent because it was the tallest and the bird wanted to dry
itself.[26]

The treaty at Picquigny was to make little difference to Bordeaux and the south. The original bitterness of the inhabitants
had been inflamed by the French captains who wanted to destroy
the city's walls because of the perfidy of the inhabitants. King
Charles had ruled against this but instead had begun the building
of two large new castles as a means of controlling the city and
its citizens. The Château Trompette, at the north-east corner
of the river (where the Place de Quinconces now stretches)
and the Fort de Ha at the city's south-west extremity were 'to

serve as a yoke from which they could not extricate their necks' if they ever wanted to welcome an enemy.[27] The fortresses were even more resented since they were to be constructed at the cost of the citizens themselves. However, passions abated and the rigours of the treaty of capitulation in 1453 were slightly mitigated in 1454 when Charles reduced the city's fine to 30,000 crowns. He also reconstituted a limited form of municipal government, although he retained the right to name the mayor and five of the jurats.[28] Pierre de Montferrand's attempt to spark another rebellion in 1454 was totally unsuccessful and Montferrand himself was caught and executed. Pey Berland resigned his archbishopric in September 1456 and retired to his beloved college of Saint-Raphael where he died in January 1458. Since he must have been at least seventy-six when he resigned it is not necessary to presume a major plot to oust him. He was succeeded by Blaise de Greelle, French and a friend of King Charles, who was encouraged by the pope to pursue certain ecclesiastics involved in conspiracies intended to deliver the city to Charles' enemies.[29] Whether this refers to actual sedition or to the continued opposition of the Bordeaux chapters to the new archbishop and French influence is an open question.

In any case, the accession of Louis XI in 1461 signalled a more conciliatory policy towards Bordeaux and its important commercial interests. In March 1462 Louis, in a remarkably generous document, confirmed Philip IV's privileges of 1295 to the city and recognized the jurisdiction of the mayor and jurats over all of the town, its *banlieue* and the river within those boundaries. He removed the new taxes imposed by Charles VII and returned the wine duties to the levels applied under English rule. The Bordelais were to be exempt from other taxes but were to contribute in time of war to the equipment of the free archers. No one, even accompanying the king, was to be lodged in Bordeaux except at his own expense and by the arrangement of the mayor and jurats. The city was also to have two fairs a year to increase its good reputation, presumably as a commercial centre.[30] This new policy, which encouraged a period of greater prosperity, was bolstered by the disappearance through emigration of the most Anglophile of the Gascons and their replacement by French immigrants, as well as by the rise of a new generation which had no nostalgic links to the English. Nevertheless, the particularism of the Gascons, and especially those of Bordeaux, their sense of being alien to the French, died hard. As late as 1585 the jurats of Bordeaux could proclaim bitterly: 'Nous sommes dans un pays de conqueste'.[31]

CHAPTER XVII

The Balance Sheet

No sketch of the history of the duchy of Aquitaine under English rule can be complete without some attempt to estimate the results for both sides. For 250 years after the death of Eleanor of Aquitaine, English kings and their officials had ruled Gascony as an overseas province of the realm. For 160 years France and England had waged episodic war, negotiated flimsy truces and the occasional impermanent 'final peace and concord', in all of which the problems of Aquitaine had played a leading part. The capitulation of Bordeaux in 1453 marked the end of English rule and of an era. What were the effects in Gascony itself of this long period of English control? What were England's gains and losses from this first, almost accidental experiment in overseas rule?

The English influence in the duchy, particularly in Bordeaux and its neighbouring region, helped to reinforce the very strong Gascon sense of identity, of local particularism. Even in modern centralized France some vestige of this remains in such slogans as '*Occitanie pour les Occitans*'. Those ardent nineteenth-century Gascon historians, Ribadieu and Troplong, emphasize this point most forcibly. They remind us that for the majority of medieval Gascons the French were the invader and the enemy, whose language was quite as foreign as the Anglo-Norman used by the English, and whose policies, as they saw them enforced by French officials along their borders, were far more repressive and onerous in their financial demands than the less centralized system under which they lived and flourished. Bordeaux still regards the fourteenth century as its first golden age, only equalled by the great period of expansion in the eighteenth century which left its architectural imprint on the modern city. The wine lovers of the world owe a special debt of gratitude to the English because it was the assured English market and the protected shipping provided for the wine fleets which encouraged the concentration of viticulture in Bordeaux and the surrounding territories. The wine trade very early became a highly specialized and profitable commerce. Secondary products, such as salt and pastel for dyeing cloth, were also ideal for export to England where the climate was too damp and cold for their successful production. In return Gascony received grain from England, even in times of shortage, wool, cloth and hides. This commercial nexus brought prosperity to the towns of the duchy which flourished under the municipal charters of liberties so freely granted by successive English kings. The towns, particularly Bordeaux, became rich and politically formidable under the protection of English rule. These municipal liberties and commercial gains were spread over a wide range of the duchy by the creation of so many bastides in the thirteenth and early fourteenth centuries.

After the middle of the fourteenth century the effects of constant warfare bore most heavily on the peasants, least protected from pillage and destruction. The rural districts became depopulated and such smaller towns as Saint-Macaire and La Réole, which were so frequently besieged, shared their fate. Such experiences did not encourage the development of a French national sentiment in Gascony, which was of reluctant and tardy growth among all classes. The Gascon nobles most devoted to the English had been banished or left voluntarily at the time of Bordeaux's capitulation. Others, who had zigzagged between French and English allegiance to achieve their own immediate ends, found their independence of action and political importance greatly curtailed with their subjection to an unopposed French sovereignty. Gradually the balance changed. Louis XI's policy of appeasement, the disappearance by emigration of the Gascons most loyal to the English connection, the arrival of new immigrants from the French provinces to work the abandoned fields and vineyards blunted the antagonisms and were reinforced by the rise of a generation that had never known English rule. By the end of the sixteenth century a Gascon and an Albret, Henri IV, was to sit on the throne of France.

Although it seems impossible to trace accurately the actual numbers of English immigrants to Gascony or Gascons to England during the period of English rule, the constant trade and the flow of officials, soldiers, merchants, sailors and messengers created a large group of men who moved easily between Bayonne, the Gironde, English ports and the king's court. A spirit of independence, of familiarity with the English pattern of administration and commerce, was bred in Gascony during those years. Even today a certain Anglophile sentiment and interchange, especially in the wine trade, recalls the medieval past. It left its mark in French literature as well. Two great French authors, Montaigne and Montesquieu, were both men of the old duchy and knew and loved Bordeaux and its medieval traditions. Montaigne's great-grandfather was one of the early Gascon emigrés in 1451, and both Montaigne and Montesquieu reflect in their writings the influence of the English connection and pattern of thought. Montesquieu in particular brought into the mainstream of French political thought an understanding and appreciation of the English parliamentary system and the rule of law. Such enthusiasm for English precedents came most naturally to a native of the Bordelais who had even served as president of the Parlement de Bordeaux and who is apostrophized by a modern Gascon as 'the spiritual heir of the Gascon emigrés of post-1453'.[1]

While the effect on England of its prolonged involvement in Gascony is less obvious it had far-reaching consequences. The contact with the strong urban centres of south-west France, many of them dating from Roman days, taught both Simon de Montfort and Edward I the importance of obtaining political support from the towns and commercial element as well as the feudal lords. The English possession of a rich and important territory overseas, neighbour to so many competing powers, made isolation impossible and led to English involvement in continental politics where her importance was out of all proportion to her size, population or resources. English conquests in France during the early years of Edward III astonished most of Europe, as men as dissimilar as Froissart and Petrarch report. The exploits of the king himself, the Black Prince and such leading nobles as Henry of Lancaster and John Chandos were enhanced by chivalric folklore. The English became convinced that war on the continent brought them success and wealth so that it was not difficult for Henry V, particularly after Agincourt, to revive the dream of French conquest. However, the average Englishman was not ready to face the frustrations and financial burden when the tide finally turned and defeat loomed. The cost was too great, the returns too small but this very issue of involvement on the continent exacerbated the civil wars of the fifteenth century. The Gascon emigrés, the most diehard in their opposition to France, helped to keep the war going as long as possible. Several of them were active at Calais or served as diplomats to Italy or Spain. For thirty years they hoped for a reconquest of Guyenne and tended to support the Yorkists as the war party. When Louis XI showed himself conciliatory and it became obvious that English abandonment of Guyenne was a final reality, some of the more important Gascon lords returned to their own province, but most of the others remained and were assimilated to English life.[2]

English political and diplomatic involvement at the court of France and the Papal Curia, combined with the pursuit of alliances among the lesser princes of Europe, required the utilization of trained diplomats with adequate documentation to deal with the almost continuous pattern of negotiation and conference. The needs and problems inherent in the possession of Gascony kept England's eyes focused on the mainland of Europe and encouraged an early specialization among her officials. The duchy was a training-ground for administrators as well as diplomats. Separated from the centre of authority by some 500 miles and slow communications, the men in charge in the duchy had to show initiative and the ability to deal with the very different conditions, customs, temperament and manners characteristic of Gascony. If they succeeded there it usually meant promotion; if they failed they were likely to summary recall. Long before the Hundred Years War the running controversy between England and France over Gascony created among these administrators and their retinue of clerks, jurists and other experts a dislike and distrust for their French equivalents whom they perceived as manipulating treaties and laws to ensure unquestioned power for the French king over a more centralized and submissive kingdom. This bad feeling had taken root before the end of the thirteenth century, as Edward I's summons to the archbishop of Canterbury in 1295 so eloquently demonstrates,[3] and was fuelled by every protracted and inconclusive encounter. The calibre of royal officials was particularly high during the reign of Edward I and their feelings and experience had more importance than might be suspected. Like later civil servants, the clerks and administrators in the royal service, though often unremarked, were important and influential. They not only tended to pass on their prejudices to their successors but also served as the crucial hinge where policy was transmuted into practice and thus had an ideal opportunity to affect both.[4] Anti-foreign sentiment was easy to arouse in the middle ages, and the English experience in Gascony reinforced their natural tendency to xenophobia and fuelled a specifically anti-French feeling.

More concrete and positive results also derived from England's long association with Aquitaine. Frequent ships and travellers from Gascony quickly spread the news of new technical developments and refinements on the continent. The highly civilized court of the duke of Aquitaine at Poitiers, so influential in the twelfth century, was reincarnated far less successfully under the Black Prince but many of the ideas and patterns common to the duchy, as well as those developments brought to it by its continuous relations with Italy and Spain, helped to fertilize a more isolated English culture. Gold coins were minted in Aquitaine before they were in England. Paper, a Spanish import, was used in the duchy in the thirteenth century and found its way to England some years later. The idea of an admiral in charge of a fleet came to England from Sicily, via Castile and Bayonne, to be adopted for the first time at the end of the thirteenth century.[5]

Indeed, England's future as a maritime nation with supremacy on the sea was forged from the struggles over Gascony and the consequent need for continuing use of ships for transport and fighting. Medieval English seamen learned their seafaring skills in the troubled waters of the Bay of Biscay and the difficult passage up and down the Channel, excellent practice for the move into the Atlantic which exploration and improved technology encouraged in the fifteenth century. Some of the Gascon emigrés were in the forefront of early trade to Iceland, while ports such as Bristol, which had built much of its prosperity on the Gascon trade, were forced to look for other outlets for their merchants and sailors once Gascony was lost. These practical developments were reinforced by a new theoretical approach as well. England might be forced to accept French claims to sovereignty in Gascony, but in return it formulated its own claim to sovereignty over the seas up to the very coastline of France. It maintained its 'barbicans' —Calais, Bordeaux, Bayonne, and, for a time, Brest and Cherbourg—to make what Garrett Mattingly has perceptively described as 'a fortress with a wide moat', for those outposts safeguarded its supremacy in the Channel and the first reaches of the Atlantic.[6]

236

As the link to Gascony and the continent was broken the great age of exploration was developing. Portugal, inspired by Prince Henry the Navigator, grandson of John of Gaunt, was adventuring into the southern Atlantic and along the coast of Africa. Interest in the north Atlantic was also quickening and England found herself no longer on the edge of civilization but lying across a new main route of sea traffic. She had the technology, the trained sailors and a theory of supremacy on the seas to enable her to play a major role in the age of discovery. The loss of Gascony meant loss of prestige and the dreams of continental conquest, but in return it provided a new and valuable freedom of diplomatic manoeuvre and release from a continuing financial drain. England was no longer forced by her continental commitments to join any war. It had no irrevocable alliances and her friendship or neutrality had to be continuously solicited and paid for. The experiment in overseas government which failed in Gascony helped to lay the foundations for the far-flung empire based on sea-power which England was to develop over the next three centuries.

Note on Money

The question of medieval moneys and coinage is bedevilled with complexities and any effort to simplify it, especially over a period of two and a half centuries, courts inaccuracy and confusion. To deal with the matter properly requires a historian who is also a numismatist, as well as a profusion of detail unsuitable for a general survey. Some of the available studies are listed in the bibliography. A few elementary explanations may help the general reader.

Medieval sums of money divide into two categories: moneys of account and actual coinage. *Moneys of account* in England, France and Aquitaine were all based on the *livre* or pound, which was made up of twenty *sous* or shillings, each worth twelve *deniers* or pennies. The pound sterling in England, the *livre tournois* or *parisis* in France and the *livre bordelais* in Gascony were all made up of 240 pennies but fluctuated in exchange values depending on the monetary policy and manipulation of the two kings. The *livre bordelais* during this period ranged in value from four to five shillings sterling and the *livre tournois* from five to six shillings sterling. The *livre parisis* was fractionally stronger than the *livre tournois*, but was commonly used only in French royal accounts. The mark, worth thirteen shillings six pence sterling, was a common English money of account. In English Aquitaine, especially during the thirteenth century, some local moneys such as the *livre chipotin* of Bigorre and the *livre morlaas* of Béarn also appeared on accounts.

Coinage. The profitable right to mint money had originally been a feudal privilege, but was progressively developed into a royal monopoly. This process was considerably slower in France than in England because of the greater power of the feudal lords and princes. The French king, for example, was never able to enforce the circulation of French moneys in Guyenne until after the final conquest. The basic unit of actual currency was the silver penny, which was also a money of account. The king of England as duke of Aquitaine jealously maintained his right to coin and shared his profits from the mint at Bordeaux with the archbishop. The Black Prince, in line with his ambitious policy in Gascony, struck a gold and silver *léopard*, and a less valuable gold and silver *guyennois*. Florins were originally Florentine coins but, by the fourteenth century, were also minted elsewhere. The florins used in papal accounts and revenues were usually worth a little more than half the value of a *livre tournois*. In the mid-fourteenth century the French king first minted the *écu* or crown and the franc, both originally in gold and later in silver.

Notes

Printed sources and important secondary works are identified in abbreviated fashion in the notes and listed in full in the bibliography. Highly specialized material of limited application quoted in the text is completely identified bibliographically in the notes only.

ABBREVIATIONS

AHG	*Archives Historiques de la Gironde*
AM	*Annales du Midi*
AMB	*Archives Municipales de Bordeaux*
BEC	*Bibliothèque de l'École des Chartes*
BIHR	*Bulletin of the Institute of Historical Research*
Bordeaux	*Bordeaux sous les rois d'Angleterre*
BPH	*Bulletin philologique et historique (jusqu'à 1715) du comité des travaux historiques et scientifiques*
CCR	*Calendar of Close Rolls*
CChR	*Calendar of Charter Rolls*
CPR	*Calendar of Patent Rolls*
EHR	*English Historical Review*
MA	*Le Moyen Age*
PPC	*Proceedings and Ordinances of the Privy Council of England*
RBP	*Register of the Black Prince*
RG	*Rôles Gascons*
RHB	*Revue historique de Bordeaux et département de Gironde*
Rot Parl	*Rotuli Parliamentorum*
RS	*Rolls Series*
SHF	Société de l'histoire de France
TRHS	*Transactions of the Royal Historical Society*

PROLOGUE

1 F. M. Powicke, *King Henry III*, 209.
2 M. Burrows, *The Family of Brocas and Beaurepaire and Roche Court* (London, 1886), 18, 27.

Chapter I The Duchy of Aquitaine: The Inheritance

1 Severus, Dialogue I, quoted in E. M. Pickman, *The Mind of Latin Christendom* (London, New York, 1937) I, 232.
2 Eleanor of Aquitaine is a popular subject for biography; both R. Pernoud, *Éleanor of Aquitaine* (London, 1967) and A. Kelly, *Eleanor of Aquitaine and the Four Kings* (Cambridge, Mass., 1950) are useful. W. L. Warren, *King John* (New York, 1961) gives a convenient survey of John's troubles in France.
3 F. M. Powicke, *The Loss of Normandy (1189–1204)* (Manchester, 1913), 200–205; Rymer I, i, 38.
4 Vielliard, *Le guide du pèlerin*, 18–19.
5 *Ibid.*, 18–19, 80–81.
6 *Ibid.*, 19.
7 *Ibid.*, 21.
8 F. B. Marsh, *English Rule in Gascony 1199–1259* (Ann Arbor, 1912), 151–55.
9 C. L. Kingsford, 'John Benstede and his Mission for Edward I', *Essays in History presented to R. Lane Poole* (ed. H. W. C. Davis, Oxford, 1927), 352–53.
10 Knighton I, 334.
11 Vielliard, *op. cit.*, 20–21.
12 Trabut-Cussac, *L'Administration anglaise*, xvii. This detailed study is the fundamental work on Gascony in the thirteenth century.
13 *Royal Letters* I, 37–38.
14 Renouard, *Études* I, 86–91.

Chapter II The Restless Duchy: Simon De Montfort

1 Powicke, *King Henry III*, 156–206; *The Thirteenth Century*, 270–318.
2 C. Bemont, *Simon de Montfort*: M. W. Labarge, *Simon de Montfort*, (London, 1962; reprint, 1972).
3 Bemont, *Simon*, 264–65.
4 *Calendar of Liberate Rolls 1245–51*, 288–89, 309, 239.
5 Bemont, *Simon*, 267.
6 Vielliard, *Guide*, 22–23: Guinodie, *Histoire de Libourne* III, 179–81.
7 *Royal Letters* II, 76–81.
8 *Ibid.*, 70–76.
9 *Papal Letters* I, 285.
10 Bemont, *Simon*, 279–321.
11 *Ibid.*, 298.
12 *Monumenta Franciscana* (ed. J. S. Brewer. RS, 1858) I, 123; Matthew Paris, *Chronica Majora* (ed. H. R. Luard. RS, 1883) V, 287–96.
13 Rymer I, i, 160.
14 Bemont, *Simon*, 321–24.
15 *Ibid.*, 267.
16 Powicke, *Thirteenth Century*, 117.
17 *Lettres des rois* I, 122–23.
18 *Close Rolls 1253–54*, 247–48.

19 M. Gouron, 'Aliénor de Castille en Guienne (1286–1289)', *MA* 28 (1927), 14–15.
20 *RG* I, no. 2111.
21 *RG* I, nos. 2076, 2077, 2958.
22 Rymer I, i, 186–7.
23 *Close Rolls 1254–56*, 389.
24 Tout, *Chapters* I, 270–72.

CHAPTER III THE PEACE TREATY THAT BROUGHT WAR

1 M. Gavrilovitch, *Étude sur le Traité de Paris de 1259* (Paris, 1899); P. Chaplais, 'Le Traité de Paris de 1259 et l'Inféodation de la Gascogne Allodiale', *MA* 61 (1955) 121–37.
2 Rymer I, ii, 50–51.
3 Joinville, *Histoire de Saint Louis* (ed. N. de Wailly. Paris, 1874), 65.
4 *Ibid.*, 59, 60.
5 Deprez, *Les Préliminaires*, 26.
6 Rymer I, iv, 80.
7 'Chronique de Primat, traduit par Jean de Vignay', *Recueil des historiens des Gaules et de la France* 23 (Paris, 1894), 16–17.
8 Renouard, *Études* II, 883–910; Chaplais, 'Traité'.
9 Trabut-Cussac, *L'Administration anglaise*, 30–32.
10 Trabut-Cussac, 'Le financement de la croisade anglaise de 1270', *RHB* 1961, 113–40.

CHAPTER IV EDWARD I: DUKE OF AQUITAINE

1 *CPR 1247–58*; 50, 41; *CChR 1226–57*, 345, 389.
2 Rymer I, i, 188.
3 Trabut-Cussac, 'Rôle', 599–615.
4 *Recogniciones Feodorum*, n. 399; Rymer I, i, 189.
5 Trabut-Cussac, 'Prince Edouard', 190–99; Gouron, *Chartes*, nos. 495, 496; *Recogniciones Feodorum*, n. 451.
6 *Livre des Hommages*, nos. 503, 504, 1, 2; *Recogniciones Feodorum*, nos. 394, 396, 411, 479.
7 *CPR 1258–66*, 126.
8 *Recogniciones Feodorum: Livre des Hommages*.
9 *RG* III, xix–xxiii.
10 *CCR 1272–79*, 493.
11 *Flores Historiarum* (ed. H. R. Luard. *RS*, 1890) III, 31.
12 Rymer I, ii, 179–80.
13 Langlois, *Le Règne de Philippe III*, 433–34.
14 S. Runciman, *The Sicilian Vespers* (Cambridge, 1958), 240–41.
15 The Gascons provided the most effective foot-soldiers in the Welsh war. At one time their total strength was 210 horses and 1,313 foot-soldiers armed with crossbows. Prestwich, *War Finance and Politics*, 109.
16 Trabut-Cussac, *L'Administration anglaise*, 79, n. 214.
17 Rymer I, iii, 8.
18 *Ibid.*, 14–15.

1 *CPR 1258-66*, 211, 216; Trabut-Cussac, *L'Administration anglaise*, 36.
2 *Lettres des rois* I, 223; *RG* II, nos. 199-200.
3 Rymer I, iv, 85; Langlois, *Philippe III*, 224-25.
4 Langlois, *op. cit.*, 435-38.
5 *Lettres des rois* I, 209.
6 The clearest account is in Powicke, *King Henry III*, 220-26; Trabut-Cussac, *L'Administration anglaise*, 72-77 adds further details.
7 *RG* III, no. 2049.
8 *RG* III, xxxiii-xlvii, Trabut-Cussac, *L'Administration anglaise*, passim.
9 *Gascon Register A*, 206-17; Trabut-Cussac, 'Actes dispersées', 122-33.
10 Maurice de Craon was the son of Isabelle de Lusignan, Henry III's stepsister, and lord of Craon and Sablé in the county of Maine, where he held the title of hereditary seneschal of Anjou, Maine and Poitou. From 1275 he played a growing part at the English court and was frequently used on diplomatic missions to the French, as he was well known and accepted on both sides of the Channel. He was very well informed on Gascon matters. Some of the letters between Edward and Maurice are pleasantly personal and suggest genuine affection. Maurice died at Paris in February 1292 and was buried at Angers. *RG* III, l-lii; *Lettres des rois* I, 274, 298-99.
11 *RG* II, nos. 1718, 1698.
12 *RG* II, no. 1840.
13 *RBP* IV, 478.
14 *RG* II, no. 1820.

CHAPTER VI CONFLICT BEGUN

1 C. Bemont in his introduction to *RG* III, cxxiv-cxlxxiii, provides a full and detailed study of the military campaigns of the war with complete references. M. Prestwich, *War, Politics and Finance* adds useful material from the English side while J. Strayer, 'Costs and Profits of War' summarizes the most recent work on war financing. The *Chronicle of Walter of Guisborough* is the most useful English source; the French chroniclers deal with the war only incidentally.
2 W. E. Rhodes, 'Edmund, earl of Lancaster', *EHR* 10 (1895), 213-216.
3 Rymer I, iii, 123-24.
4 *Ibid.*, 124-25.
5 Rhodes, 'Edmund', 227-30.
6 Guisborough, 242.
7 R. Fawtier, *L'Europe occidentale de 1270 à 1380; pt. I de 1270 à 1328* (G. Glotz, *Histoire Générale. Histoire du Moyen Age* 6, Paris, 1940), 317.
8 Guisborough, 242.

9 Among those who received pardons for service in Gascony and elsewhere was Robert de LaBarge who had been indicted for homicides, robberies, burning of ships and other trespasses against men of the Cinque Ports, *CPR 1301–07*, 436.

10 B. Cotton, *Historia Anglicana* (ed. H. R. Luard, RS, 1859), 306.

11 Rymer I, iii, 150.

12 J. G. Edwards, 'The Treason of Thomas Turberville, 1295', *Studies in Medieval History presented to F. M. Powicke*, ed. R. W. Hunt, W. A. Pantin, R. W. Southern (Oxford, 1948), 296–309.

13 Guisborough, 286–88.

14 *Ibid.*, 290; Knighton I, 331.

15 Knighton I, 327–28.

16 Rymer I, iii, 192–93.

17 H. Rothwell, 'Edward I's case against Philip the Fair over Gascony in 1298', *EHR* 42 (1927), 572–82.

18 J. G. Black, 'Edward I and Gascony in 1300', *EHR* 17 (1902), 518–27.

19 RG II, nos. 1234, 1235, 1237; *CPR 1281–92*, 129, 357; *CPR 1292–1301*, 169.

20 P. Chaplais, 'Le Duché-Pairie de Guyenne', 29–33; G. P. Cuttino, 'Another Memorandum Book of Elias Joneston', *EHR* 63 (1948), 95–7.

21 M. C. L. Salt, 'English Embassies to France, 1272–1307', *EHR* 44 (1929), 271–73.

22 P. Chaplais, 'Some Private Letters of Edward I', *EHR* 77 (1962), 84–5, 86. I am indebted to Dr. Chaplais for bringing these to my attention.

23 Black, 'Edward I and Gascony', 523.

24 Rymer I, iv, 124; *Treaty Rolls* I, n. 324.

25 Strayer, 'Costs and Profits', 269–91.

26 *CPR 1292–1301*, 418–19.

CHAPTER VII   THE YEARS OF PROSPERITY

1 *Bordeaux*, 224–25; Renouard, *Études* I, 167–70.

2 *Bordeaux*, 225–27.

3 P. Capra, 'Le séjour du Prince Noir, lieutenant du roi, à l'archévêché de Bordeaux', *RHB* 7 n.s. (1958), 251.

4 M. Gouron, 'Reconstitution', 212–15.

5 Capra, *L'Administration Anglo-Gasconne*, 359.

6 Quoted *Bordeaux*, 206.

7 *AMB V, Coutumes*, 407–13.

8 Bemont, 'Factions', 143.

9 *Ibid.*, 146–52.

10 Trabut-Cussac, 'Actes dispersées', 83–86; *RG* II, nos. 897, 921.

11 James, *Studies*, 32. The English tun was reckoned as two pipes, equivalent to 252 gallons or about 900 litres. Some French scholars have estimated that the Gascon tun may have been rather less, somewhere between 750 and 900 litres. See Renouard, *Études* I, 167–79.

12 *Red Book of the Exchequer* (ed. II. Hall. *RS*, 1896) III, 1060–64. *English Historical Documents* III (1189–1327) (London, 1975), 512–14 gives an English translation.

13 B. C. Keeney, 'Military Service and the Development of Nationalism in England, 1272–1327', *Speculum* 22 (1947), 536 n. 9.

14 James, *Studies*, 81.

15 *CCR 1279–88*, 60.

16 *RG* II, no. 1524

17 C. Higounet, 'Bastides et frontières', *MA* 54 (1524) (1948), 113–21; Trabut-Cussac, 'Bastides ou forteresses', *MA* 60 (1954), 81–135.

18 *RG* II, no. 1806.

19 Rymer I, ii ,226–27.

20 *RG* II, nos. 1056, 1053.

21 Higounet, 'Cisterciens et bastides', *MA* 56 (1960), 69–84.

22 Higounet, 'Le cas français: villeneuves et bastides désertées', *Villages désertées et histoire économique XIᵉ–XVIIIᵉ siècle*, (SEVPEN, 1965), 263.

23 *RG* II, no. 1042; Trabut-Cussac, 'Date, fondation et identification de la bastide de Baa', *RHB* 10 n.s. (1961), 133–44.

24 M. Beresford, *New Towns of the Middle Ages* (New York, 1967), 237.

25 Samaran, *Gascogne*, no. 497.

26 Trabut-Cussac, 'Bastides ou forteresses', 132.

Chapter VIII   Clement V: A Gascon Pope

1 Renouard, *Études* II, 911–24; J. H. Denton, 'Pope Clement V's early career as a royal clerk', *EHR* 83 (1968), 303–14.

2 Guillemain, *Cour pontificale*, 187, 189 n. 40, 192–95.

3 C. V. Langlois, 'Documents relatifs à Bertrand de Got', *Revue Historique* 40 (1889), 51–2.

4 *RG* III, cxxvii–cc; H. E. Sigerist, *The Earliest Printed Book on Wine* (New York, 1943), 40.

5 *CPR 1301–7*, 433.

6 *Papal Letters* II, 2, 14, 15, 22, 20, 25, 34, 60.

7 Guillemain, *Cour pontificale*, 114.

8 *CCR 1302–7*, 435.

9 Sauviac was given the castles of Lados (Gironde) and Toutoulon (near Bazas), a fishery at Saint-Macaire and a tithe in the parish of Maillas (Landes). Samaran, *Gascogne*, nos. 49–50.

10 Renouard, *Études* II, 935–57.

11 *The Life of Edward the Second by the so-called Monk of Malmesbury*, ed. and trans. by N. Denholm-Young (London, 1957), 46.

12 Samaran, *Gascogne*, nos. 62, 67, 83, 46, 47, 82.

13 *The Mongol Mission*, ed. C. Dawson (London, 1955), xxxi–xxxiii.

14 P. Courteault, 'Une ambassade mongole à Bordeaux en 1287', *RHB* 17 (1924), 103–6.

15 *Bordeaux*, 293–324, 461–85.

16 Caillet, *La Papauté d'Avignon*, 496, 500–1.

17 Lopès, *L'Église metropolitaine*, 417–43, 467–76; Lodge, *Estates*.

18 Lodge, *Estates*, 20–28.
19 *Cartulaire Saint-Seurin*, nos. 331–33, 394.
20 Trabut-Cussac, 'La Sauve-Majeure et le Prieuré de Burwell', *BPH* (1957), 137–83.
21 Richardson and Sayles, *Rotuli Parliementorum*, 220–21; Gouron, *Chartes*, nos. 526, 527.

Chapter IX   Conflict Continued

1 *CRP 1301–7*, 424.
2 Chaplais, 'Chancery', 61.
3 *Ibid.*, 70 n. 3.
4 R. W. Kaeuper, 'The Frescobaldi of Florence and the English Crown', *Studies in Medieval and Renaissance History* 10 (1973), 79–81.
5 *RG* IV, xxiv and passim.
6 *Ibid.*, xxiv–xxv.
7 *Ibid.*, no. 661.
8 *Gascon Register A*, 226.
9 *RG* IV, no. 660.
10 Rymer I, iv, 178–79; I am indebted to Dr. John Parsons for detailed information on both Guy Ferre and the Haustede family, derived from his study of the members of the court of Queen Eleanor of Castile.
11 *AMB* I, *Bouillons*, 169–71; V, *Coutumes*, 632–35.
12 Rymer II, ii, 61–2.
13 Cuttino, *English Diplomatic Administration*, 65.
14 Guerard, 'Documents pontificaux', II, no. 53.
15 *Ibid.*, II, nos. 134, 137.
16 *Ibid.*, II, nos. 70–73, 106–12; VI, nos. 213, 230–34, 237; Renouard, *Études* II, 932–33.
17 Chaplais, 'Règlement', *MA* 57 (1951), 269–94.
18 Samaran, *Gascogne*, nos. 55–58, 60, 247.
19 Langlois, 'Rouleaux' (50), 53–6.
20 Trabut-Cussac, *L'Administration anglaise*, 223–29, 235–47; Tout, *Chapters* II, 10–14.
21 Cuttino, *English Diplomatic Administration*, 25–8.
22 Chaplais, ed., *War of Saint-Sardos*, ix–xiii.
23 *Ibid.*, 3–4.
24 *Grandes Chroniques* V, 278–82.
25 Rymer II, ii, 137–38.
26 Geoffrey le Baker, 19.
27 Rymer II, ii, 142.
28 *CPR 1327–30*, 16.
29 Rymer II, ii, 185–86.

Chapter X   Henry, Earl of Lancaster and the Beginnings of The Hundred Years War in Gascony

1 *Grandes Chroniques* V, 324.
2 *CCR 1327–30*, 453.

3 Knighton I, 451.
4 G. P. Cuttino, 'The Process of Agen', *Speculum* 19 (1944), 161–70.
5 Rymer II, iii, 50–51.
6 M. Jusselin, 'Comment la France se préparait à la guerre de Cent Ans', *BEC* 73 (1912), 222–26.
7 Froissart xviii, 34–37.
8 E. Perroy, *The Hundred Years War* (London, 1965) is still the standard study. More modern work is summed up in *The Hundred Years War*, ed. K. Fowler (London, 1971). Fowler's *Age of Plantagenet and Valois* is beautifully illustrated and more general in its treatment.
9 Knighton II, 1.
10 Cazelles, ed., *Lettres close*, 64–65.
11 Marquette, ed., *Trésor des Chartes*, nos. 445–47.
12 *Ibid.*, nos. 454–57; *CPR 1338–40*, 382.
13 *CPR 1338–40*, 400.
14 N. de Pena, 'Vassaux gascons au service du roi d'Angleterre dans la première moitié du XIVᵉ siècle', *AM* 88 (1976), 5–21.
15 *CCR 1341–43*, 458.
16 K. Fowler, 'Les finances et la discipline dans les armées anglaises en France au XIVᵉ siècle', *Actes du Colloque International de Cocherel: Les Cahiers Vernonnais* 4 (1964), 59.
17 *CCR 1343–46*, 99.
18 Fowler, *The King's Lieutenant*, is an excellent study of Henry.
19 *Chronique des quatre premiers Valois*, 12.
20 Fowler, *King's Lieutenant*, app. IV, 230–32.
21 Carte, *Catalogue RG*, 117.
22 Fowler, *King's Lieutenant*, 53–54.
23 Froissart IV, 231.
24 *AHG* I, 302–3.
25 Fowler, *King's Lieutenant*, 63.
26 *CPR 1345–48*, 538.
27 E. Carpentier, 'Autour de la peste noire: famines et épidémies dans l'histoire du XIVᵉ siècle', *Annales* 17 (1962), 1062–92.
28 Boutruche, *Crise*, 200.
29 *Livre de Seyntz Medicines*, 239.
30 *Ibid.*, 10, 16, 67.
31 *Ibid.*, 77–8, 19, 76.
32 *Ibid.*, 85, 86, 92–3.
33 *Ibid.*, 104–16.
34 *Ibid.*, 117–23.
35 *Ibid.*, 135, 149–50, 194, 161.
36 Gaston Fébus, *Livre des Oraisons*, ed. G. Tilander, P. Tucoo-Chala (Pau, 1974).

CHAPTER XI THE BLACK PRINCE

1 Chandos Herald, lines 511–45.
2 Stendhal, *Travels in the South of France* (New York, 1970), trans. by

Elizabeth Abbott, 104–5; R. Lafont, *Lettre ouverte aux Français d'un Occitan* (Paris, 1973), 138.

3 There has been a recent flurry of books on the Black Prince, inspired by the sixth centenary of his death in 1976. The most informative are R. Barber, *Edward, Prince of Wales and Aquitaine*, (London, 1978) and B. Emerson, *The Black Prince* (London, 1976).

4 *Histoire Générale de Languedoc* X, 1103–5.

5 Carte, *Catalogue* RG, 133–34; *RBP* IV, 143–45.

6 Hewitt, *Expedition*, 21–3. This book is the most useful survey of the military campaigns of the Black Prince which culminated at Poitiers.

7 *Cartulaire Saint-Seurin*, 4–5.

8 *AHG*, 21, 231, 234.

9 Avesbury, 434–37, 439–43.

10 Geoffrey le Baker, 128–39.

11 *Bourgeois de Valenciennes*, 282.

12 Carte, *Catalogue* RG, 136–37; *RBP* III, 223–24.

13 The Black Prince's letter on the battle is translated in H. T. Riley, *Memorials of London and London Life in XIIIth, XIVth and XVth Centuries* (London, 1858), 285–88. Among the major discussions of the battle are J. M. Tourneur-Aumont, *La Bataille de Poitiers* (1356) *et la construction de la France* (Paris, 1940) which was written by a local man, but is extremely pro-French: V. H. Galbraith, 'The Battle of Poitiers', *EHR* 54 (1939): A. H. Burne, *The Crécy War* (London, 1955), 275–321 has been corrected by Hewitt, *op. cit.*

14 N. Zaccour, *Talleyrand, the Cardinal of Périgord* (1301–64), American Philosophical Society n.s. 50, pt. 7 (Philadelphia, 1960), 52–4.

15 Froissart V, 440–49.

16 *Ibid.*, 433–34.

17 *Chronique Normande*, 116.

18 Froissart (Jolliffe), 174.

19 Bibliothèque Municipale, Bordeaux: MS 769 (Stein 1910) Série H2 Abbaye de La Sauve, Reg. 16.

20 P. Capra, 'Le Prince Noir en Aquitaine: Compte Rendu', *AM* 1954, 244–46.

21 Riley, *op. cit.*, 285–88.

22 F. Bock, 'Some New Documents illustrating the early years of The Hundred Years War', *Bull. John Rylands Library* 15 (1931), 97–99.

23 Rymer III, i, 133–36.

24 Froissart VI, 16–17.

25 J. Quicherat, 'Récit des tribulations d'un religieux du diocèse de Sens pendant l'invasion anglaise de 1358', *BEC* 3 ser, 4 (1857), 359–60.

26 L. Thorndike, *A History of Magic and Experimental Science* II (New York, 1923), 801–2. I owe this reference to the kindness of Prof. C. C. Willard.

27 *RBP* III, 231, 254–61, 234.

28 *Ibid.*, 277.

29 *RBP* IV, 251–52, 253–54.

30 Cosneau, *Les grands traités*, 3–32.
31 Rymer III, i, 202–9.
32 D. M. Broome, 'The Ransom of John II, King of France, 1360–70', *Camden Miscellany* 14 (Camden Third Series 37, 1926), viii–x.
33 Rymer III, ii, 1–6.
34 *Ibid.*, 71–2; Chaplais, 'Some documents', 6–8.

CHAPTER XII THE PRINCIPALITY OF AQUITAINE

1 Rymer III, ii, 66–7.
2 Denifle, *Désolation* II, 532.
3 *RBP* IV, 467, 479.
4 Bardonnet, 'Procès-verbal', 2–116.
5 Rouquette, *Rouergue*, 77.
6 L. Babinet, 'Jeanne de Kent, princesse de Galles et d'Aquitaine', *Bull. de la Société des Antiquaires de l'Ouest* (1894), 3–17.
7 A. Grandsden, 'Propaganda in English Medieval Historiography', *Journal of Medieval History* 1 (1975), 363–81.
8 Capra, *L'Administration Anglo-Gasconne*, 916 n. 23.
9 *CPR 1361–64*, 302–3.
10 *Livre des Hommages*, nos. 108–15; Delpit, *Collection Générale*, 86–121.
11 *Chronique de Richard Lescot*, 161.
12 Tucoo-Chala, *Gaston Fébus*.
13 *Le Livre de la Chasse par Gaston Phébus*, traduction, introduction et notes par R. et A. Bossuat, Paris, 1931. The work was very popular among the nobility and Edward, duke of York, who died in 1415, translated it into English and added some comments of his own. This, known as *The Master of Game*, ed. by W. A. and F. Baillie-Grohman (London, 1904) had an introduction by that formidable hunter of the turn of the century, Theodore Roosevelt.
14 *AHG* 4, 111–12.
15 P. Wolff, 'The Armagnacs in Southern France', *BIHR* 20 (1945), 186–91.
16 Tucoo-Chala, *Gaston Fébus*, 88–92.
17 *Ibid*', 93–7.
18 Froissart VI, 368.
19 Froissart VII, 253–54.
20 P. Capra, 'Les deux missions de Jean Streatley à Paris en 1361 et en 1368', *AM* 78 (1966), 409–11; Chaplais, 'Chancery', 85–6.
21 Capra, *L'Administration Anglo-Gasconne*, 423–33.
22 Rouquette, *Rouergue*, 92, 95.
23 Chaplais, 'Chancery', 88–92. For a valuable account of the broader pattern of organization see Capra, 'Les bases sociales'.
24 The standard work on the prince's Spanish campaign is Russell, *The English Intervention*, 1–126.
25 Rymer III, ii, 103.
26 *Ibid.*, 116–22.
27 Chandos Herald, lines 2025–30.
28 Froissart VII, 123.

29 Chandos Herald, lines 2325, 2365–90.
30 Loirette, 'Arnaud Amanieu sire d'Albret', *Mélanges . . . Bemont*, 325.
31 Froissart VII, 122–23.
32 *AMB I, Bouillons*, 172–77.
33 *The Anonimalle Chronicle 1333 to 1381*, ed. V. H. Galbraith (Manchester, 1927), 56; Froissart VII, 254.
34 Loirette, 'Arnaud Amanieu d'Albret' *MA* (1931), 5–21: 'Arnaud Amanieu sire d'Albret', *Mélanges . . . Bemont*, 317–40.
35 Delachenal, *Charles V* V, 88–91.
36 Perroy, 'Edouard III', 91–6.
37 Delachenal IV, 132.
38 Froissart VII, 291–92.
39 Denifle, *Désolation* II, 340.
40 *Anglo-Norman Letters*, 198.
41 Delachenal IV, 171. The manifesto of the duke of Anjou in December 1368 is in *Histoire Générale de Languedoc* X, 1404–6.
42 Froissart VII, 459.
43 Chandos Herald, lines 4036–42.
44 Froissart VIII, 38.
45 *Ibid.*, 60–1.

CHAPTER XIII THE EBB OF ENGLISH POWER

1 Sherborne, 'Cost', 149.
2 *Ibid.*, 139. T. Runyan has edited the constable's accounts for 1372–75, giving a more general look at the duchy's finances, in 'The Constabulary of Bordeaux'.
3 Henneman, *Royal Taxation in Fourteenth Century France*, provides a detailed and clear account of this process.
4 Sherborne, 'Battle of La Rochelle', 17–21.
5 *Letters and Papers illustrative of the wars of the English in France during the reign of Henry the Sixth*, ed. J. Stevenson (*RS* 1861–64) II, 750–51.
6 Froissart VIII, 171; Babinet, 'Jean III de Grailly', xix–l.
7 *AHG* 6, 371–72.
8 Froissart VIII, 400–3.
9 Sherborne, 'English Navy', 171.
10 *Rot. Parl.* II, 309–10.
11 Prou, *Relations politiques*, 65–7.
12 Delachenal IV, 507–15.
13 Perroy, 'Anglo-French Negotiations', 1–85.
14 Chaplais, 'A Propos', 113–18.
15 *Ibid.*, 118.
16 *AMB I, Bouillons*, 291–92.
17 *AHG* 26, 149–63.
18 Delachenal V, 55.
19 Marquette, *Trésor des Chartes*, nos. 785, 784; Delachenal V, 49–59.
20 *AHG* 8, 197; *CPR 1377–81*, 543.
21 Froissart IX, 14.
22 *Ibid.*, 116–19.

23 James, *Studies*, 32–3.
24 Stratton's career can be pieced together from a number of sources, including an article by J. G. Escudey, 'La contau de Landiras', *RHB* 18 (1925), 217–24; the inventory of the Archives Départmentales I, 286; II, 222, material gathered by J. R. Robertson, *The English Administration of Gascony 1372–90* (unpublished Ph.D. thesis, Emory University, 1963), and the further references given below.
25 *AHG* 16, 172–73.
26 G. F. Beltz, *Memorials of the Most Noble Order of the Garter* (London, 1841), 265–67.
27 *CCR 1395–99*, 99; Escudey, *op. cit.*, 217–19.
28 Valios, *La France et le Grand Schisme* I, 248–50.
29 *CPR 1388–92*, 170; *CCR 1377–81*, 301, 386.
30 *AMB I, Bouillons*, 224–27.
31 Palmer, *England, France and Christendom*, 128–30, 142–65.
32 *AMB I, Bouillons*, 228–29; Rymer III, iv, 79.
33 *Anglo-Norman Letters*, 216–18.
34 *Ibid.*, 63.
35 *AMB I, Bouillons*, 264–67, 269–72.
36 Froissart XV, 160–67.
37 *Ibid.*, 151–53.
38 Rymer III, iv, 115–18.
39 Palmer, *op. cit.*, 166–78.

CHAPTER XIV LANCASTRIAN POLICY IN GUYENNE

1 *CPR 1377–81*, 120, 159, 609.
2 Froissart XVI, 213.
3 *Ibid.*, 217.
4 Vale, *English Gascony*, 38–40. This monograph with its extensive exploration of the MS sources is a prime source of information for the last years of the duchy.
5 *AMB I, Bouillons*, 321–46, xxxvii–xliii.
6 Flourac, *Jean Iᵉʳ*, 16–28; Samaran, *Gascogne*, 1042.
7 Vale, 45.
8 *Royal and historical Letters during the reign of Henry the Fourth*, ed. F. C. Hingeston (RS, 1860), 45, 52–7.
9 *PPC* I, 181.
10 *Cartulaire de Saint-Seurin*, 419.
13 *AMB III, Jurade I*, 87–93.
14 *Ibid.*, 89.
15 *Ibid.*, 40–86, 93–149.
16 *Ibid.*, 109.
17 *Religieux de Saint-Denys* III, 453.
18 *St. Albans Chronicle*, 10.
19 *Religieux de Saint-Denys* III, 457–59.
20 *AMB III, Jurade I*, 155–56.
21 *PPC* II, 8–9.

252

22 CCR *1409–13*, 350–52; Rymer IV, ii, 12–15.
23 *Lettres des rois* II, 328–30.
24 *Ibid.*, 330–32.
25 Wolff, 'Armagnacs', 186–91.
26 Flourac, *Jean I⁽ʳ⁾*, 43–4.
27 Vale, 63–6.
28 Wylie, *Henry V* I, 116–20.
29 *Gesta Henrici Quinti*, 17–18.
30 *AHG* 16, 88–93, 110–16, 177–79.
31 *PPC* III, 62–4, 227.
32 *AMB IV, Jurade* II, 256, 264.
33 Delpit, *Collection générale*, 226.
34 *PPC* II, 263–66.
35 Wylie, *Henry V* III, 366–69.
36 Rymer IV, iii, 171–74.
37 Vale, 83–96.
38 *AHG* 16, 220–22.
39 CCR *1435–41*, 417.
40 *AHG* 16, 199.
41 *Ibid.*, 173–77, 264–65.
42 *Ibid.*, 189–90, 228–29.
43 *Ibid.*, 308–13.
44 Allmand, 'Documents', 116.

CHAPTER XV LOOMING DEFEAT

1 Froissart XI, 226–29. Boutruche, *Crise*: This book is fundamental
   for an understanding of Gascon society during the Hundred
   Years War.
2 E. Le Roy Ladurie, *Montaillou; The Promised Land of Error* trans.
   by Barbara Bray (New York, 1978).
3 Boutruche, 'Devastation', 25.
4 Vale, 10.
5 The most recent summary of Pey Berland is by Guillemain,
   'L'Archevêque Pey Berland et la fondation de l'Université' in
   Bordeaux, 523–40. Of the older lives, written to urge his canonization, J. H. Gaston de Laborie, *Biographie de Pierre II ou Pey Berland*
   (Bordeaux, 1885) includes a number of documents on his life.
6 *AHG* 3, 445–63; Gaston de Laborie, 76–126.
7 *AHG* 3, 463, 449; Gaston de Laborie, 117, 85.
8 Gaston de Laborie, 187–88.
9 Ribadieu, *Histoire de la conquête*, 128–24.
10 Vale, 115–17.
11 Bekynton, *Correspondence* II, 177–244; Bernard et Gîteau, 'Comptes',
   182–215.
12 Bekynton, 187.
13 *Ibid.*, 189.
14 *Ibid.*, 200–1.
15 Bernard et Gîteau, 'Comptes', 190–91.

16 Bekynton, 190–93.
17 *Ibid.*, 203–5.
18 *Ibid.*, 196.
19 *Ibid.*, 203.
20 *Ibid.*, 214.
21 *Ibid.*, 217–18.
22 *Ibid.*, 236.
23 Rymer V, i, 133–36.
24 For the controversy and the final arbitral sentence see *AHG* 16,
   281–83, 290–91, 293–94, 326, 332–33, 359–64.
25 Vale, 206–10; Samaran, 'Quelques Aspects', 21–34.
26 Samaran, *La Maison d'Armagnac*, 90–9.

CHAPTER XVI FINAL COLLAPSE

 1 Escouchy I, 322–29; Ribadieu, *Histoire de la conquête*, 185–94.
 2 *AHG* 3, 462; Gaston de Laborie, 115.
 3 Basin II, 160.
 4 *Ibid.*, 162.
 5 *AHG* 12, 342.
 6 Escouchy I, 329–39.
 7 *AMB I, Bouillons*, 543–51.
 8 Gebelin, 'Un récit', 406–10.
 9 Escouchy I, 361–66.
10 *Ibid.*, 366–67; *Chronique du Mont-Saint Michel* I, 60.
11 Pérotin, 'Les chapitres Bordelais', 34–5.
12 Basin II, 176–82.
13 R. J. Virgoe, 'The Composition of the king's council, 1437–61',
   BIHR 43 (1970), 134–60; *CPR 1446–51*, 468–69, 511.
14 Escouchy I, 413–15.
15 Ribadieu, *Histoire de la conquête*, 323.
16 He was ultimately freed from his obligation to pay the ransom
   when he married a daughter of King Charles' favourite mistress,
   Agnes Sorel. (Basin II, 187 n. 2.)
17 *Ibid.*, 190.
18 *Ibid.*, 186–98; Escouchy II, 34–41.
19 Escouchy II, 42–3.
20 Ribadieu, *Histoire de la conquête*, 313.
21 Escouchy II, 64–9.
22 *Ibid.*, 70–5, 79.
23 *AMB II, Privilèges*, 243–46.
24 Escouchy II, 77–8.
25 Rymer V, iii, 65–7.
26 Peyrègne, 'Les emigrés gascons', 122.
27 Basin II, 200.
28 *AMB II, Privilèges*, 246–52.
29 Pérotin, 'Les chapitres Bordelais', 37.
30 *AMB II, Privilèges*, 3–11.
31 Ribadieu, *Histoire de la conquête*, 495.

CHAPTER XVII   THE BALANCE SHEET

1 Peyrégne, 'Les emigrés gascons', 127.
2 *Ibid.*, 115 28.
3 *Supra*, p. 69.
4 Cuttino, 'King's Clerks', 396.
5 Renouard *Études* II, 864–74.
6 G. Mattingly, *Renaissance Diplomacy* (London, 1962), 129.

Select Bibliography

A. SOURCES

Allmand, C. T., 'Documents relating to the Anglo-French Negotiations of 1439', *Camden Miscellany* 24, Camden Fourth Series 9, 1972.

Anglo-Norman Letters and Petitions, ed. M. D. Legge. (Anglo-Norman Text Society n. 3) Oxford, 1941, reprint 1967.

Archives Historiques de la Gironde 58, Bordeaux, 1858–1932.

Archives Municipales de Bordeaux: I, Livre des Bouillons; II, Livre des Privilèges; III, Registres de la Jurade de 1406 à 1409, I; IV, Registres de la Jurade 1416 à 1419 et 1420 à 1422, II; V, Livre des Coutumes. Bordeaux, 1867–90.

Avesbury, R. *De gestis mirabilibus regis Edwardi tertii.* A. Murimuth, *Continuatio chronicarum*, ed. E. M. Thompson, *RS*, 1889.

Bardonnet, A. 'Procès-verbal de déliverance à Jean Chandos des places françaises abandonnées par le traité de Brétigny', *Mémoires de la Société de Statistique, Sciences, et Arts du département des Deux-Sèvres.* Niort, 1867.

Basin, T. *Histoire de Charles VII*, ed. et trad. par C. Samaran. 2 v. Paris, 1933–44.

Bekynton, T. *Official Correspondence*, ed. G. Williams. 2 v. *RS*, 1872.

Bernard, J. et Gîteau, F. 'Comptes du trésorier de la ville de Bordeaux pour 1442 (février-août)', *BPH*, 1961.

Bourgeois de Valenciennes, Récits d'un, ed. Kervyn de Lettenhove. Louvain, 1879.

Calendar of Charter Rolls.

Calendar of Close Rolls.

Calendar of Liberate Rolls.

Calendar of Patent Rolls.

Carte, T. *Catalogue des Rôles Gascons, Normans et Français dans les archives de la Tour de Londres.* London and Paris, 1746.

Cartulaire de l'Eglise Collégiale Saint-Seurin de Bordeaux, ed. J. A. Brutalls. Bordeaux, 1897.

Cazelles, R., ed. *Lettres close de Philippe de Valois.* SHF Paris, 1958.

Chandos Herald. *Life of the Black Prince by the Herald of Sir John Chandos.* ed. M. K. Pope and E. C. Lodge. Oxford, 1910, reprint 1974.

Chaplais, P., ed. *The War of Saint-Sardos.* Camden Third Series 87, 1954.
'Some documents regarding the fulfilment and interpretation of the

Treaty of Brétigny 1361–69' *Camden Miscellany* 19. Camden Third Series 80, 1942.

'Chronique de Guyenne', *AMB V, Coutumes.* Bordeaux, 1890.

Chronique de Richard Lescot, ed. J. Lemoine. Paris, 1896.

Chronique des règnes de Jean II et de Charles V, ed. R. Delachenal. 2 v. SHF Paris, 1910–16.

Chronique des quatre premiers Valois (1327–1393), ed. S. Luce. SHF Paris, 1862, reprint 1965.

Chronique du Mont-Saint-Michel, ed. S. Luce. 2 v. Paris, 1879, reprint 1966.

Chronique normande du XIVᵉ siècle, ed. E. and A. Molinier. SHF Paris, 1882.

Close Rolls Henry III.

Cosneau, E. *Les grands traités de la guerre de Cent Ans.* Paris, 1889.

Delpit, J. *Collection générale des documents français qui se trouvent en Angleterre.* Paris, 1847, reprint 1971.

Escouchy. *Chronique de Matthieu d'Escouchy.* ed. G. Du Fresne de Beaucourt. 2 v. SHF Paris, 1863–64.

Froissart. *Chroniques,* ed. Kervyn de Lettenhove. 25 v. Brussels, 1870–1877. *Chronicles,* ed and trans. by John Jolliffe. London, 1967.

The Gascon Calendar of 1322, ed. G. P. Cuttino. Camden Third Series 70, 1949.

Gascon Register A (1318–19), ed. G. P. Cuttino. 3 v. Oxford, 1975–77.

Gebelin, F. 'Un récit de l'entrée de Dunois à Bordeaux en 1451', *Mélanges d'histoire offerts à M. Charles Bemont.* Paris, 1913.

Geoffrey le Baker. *Chronicon Galfridi le Baker de Swynebroke,* ed. E. M. Thompson. Oxford, 1889.

Gesta Henrici Quinti, trans. from the Latin with intro. and notes by F. Taylor and J. S. Roskell. Oxford, 1975.

Gouron, M., ed. *Les chartes des franchises de Guienne et Gascogne.* Paris, 1935.

Les Grandes Chroniques de France, V, ed. P. Paris. SHF Paris, 1837.

Guerard, L. 'Documents Pontificaux sur la Gascogne', *Archives Historiques de la Gascogne.* Second Series, v. 2 and 6, 1896, 1903.

Guisborough. *Chronicle of Walter of Guisborough,* ed. H. Rothwell. Camden Third Series 89, 1957.

Histoire générale de Languedoc. C. Devic et J. Vaissete. v. 9 and 10, new edition. Toulouse, 1885.

Knighton. *Chronicon Henrici Knighton,* ed. J. R. Lumby. *RS,* 1889–93.

Langlois, C. V. 'Rouleaux d'arrêts de la cour du roi au XIIIᵉ siècle', *BEC* v. 48 (1887), 50 (1889).

Lettres des rois, reines, et autres personages des cours de France et d'Angleterre, ed. J. Champollion-Figeac. 2 v. (Coll. des documents inédits pour l'hist. de France) Paris, 1839, 1847.

Le Livre de Seyntz Medicines, ed. E. J. Arnould. (Anglo-Norman Text Society, n. 2). Oxford, 1940.

Le Livre des hommages d'Aquitaine, ed. J. P. Trabut-Cussac. Bordeaux, 1959.

Marquette, J. B., ed. *Le Trésor des chartes d'Albret*. (Coll. des documents inédits) Paris, 1973.

Papal Letters. Entries in the Papal Registers relating to Great Britain and Ireland. Papal Letters II, 1305–1342.

Perroy, E. 'The Anglo-French Negotiations at Bruges 1374–77'. *Camden Miscellany* 19, Camden Third Series 80, 1952.

'Petite chronique de Guyenne jusqu'à l'an 1442', ed. G. Lefèvre-Pontalis, *BEC* 47 (1886).

Proceedings and Ordinances of the Privy Council of England, ed. H. Nicolas. 6 v. London, 1834–37.

Recogniciones Feodorum. Recueil d'Actes relatifs à l'administration des rois d'Angleterre en Guyenne au XIIIe siècle (Recogniciones Feodorum in Aquitania), ed. C. Bemont. Paris, 1914.

Register of the Black Prince preserved in the Public Record Office. 4 v. 1930–33.

Religieux de Saint-Denys. *Chronique du Religieux de Saint-Denys, 1380–1422*, ed. L. Bellaguet. 6 v. (Coll. des documents inédits) Paris, 1839–52.

Richardson, H. G. and Sayles, G., ed. *Rotuli Parliamentorum Anglie hactenus inediti, 1289–1373*. Camden Third Series 51, 1935.

Rôles Gascons: I, 1242–54. ed. F. Michel. Paris, 1885.

        I suppl., 1254–55. ed. C. Bemont. Paris, 1896.

        II, 1273–90. ed. C. Bemont. Paris, 1900.

        III, 1290–1307. ed, C. Bemont. Paris, 1906.

        IV, 1307–17. ed. Y. Renouard. London, 1964.

Rotuli parliamentorum. 5 v. London, 1783. Index v., 1832.

Royal Letters. Royal and other historical letters illustrative of the reign of Henry III, ed. W. W. Shirley. 2 v. *RS*, 1862, 1868.

Runyan, T. 'The Constabulary of Bordeaux', *Mediaeval Studies* 36 and 37 (1974, 1975).

Rymer, T. *Foedera conventiones literas*. v. I–V. third ed., The Hague 1739–41, reprint 1967.

The St. Albans Chronicle 1406–20. ed. V. S. Galbraith. Oxford, 1937.

Samaran, C., ed. *La Gascogne dans les registres du Trésor des Chartes*. (Coll. des documents inédits) Paris, 1966.

Trabut-Cussac, J. P. 'Actes gascons dispersés d'Edouard I (1286–89)', *BPH*, 1962.

                'Un rôle de lettres patentes émanées du Prince Edouard pendant son premier séjour en Gascogne', *Recueil de travaux offerts à M. Clovis Brunel* II. Paris, 1955.

Treaty Rolls; I, 1234–1325; II, 1337–1339.

Vielliard, J. *Le Guide du Pèlerin de Saint-Jacques de Compostelle*, third ed. Macon, 1963.

B. Secondary Works

Albe, E. 'Les suites du traité de Paris de 1259 pour le Quercy', *AM* 23 and 24 (1911, 1912).

Allmand, C. T. 'The Anglo-French Negotiations, 1439', *BIHR* 40 (1967).
    'Historians Reconsidered: Froissart', *History Today* 16 (1966).
Allmand, C. T., ed. *War, Literature and Politics in the Late Middle Ages.* Essays in honour of G. W. Coopland. Liverpool, 1976.
Armitage-Smith, J. *John of Gaunt.* London, 1904, reprint 1964.
Babinet, L. 'Jean III de Grailly, captal de Buch', *Mémoires de la Société des Antiquaires de l'Ouest*, Second Series 18 (Poitiers, 1896).
Barber, R. *Edward, Prince of Wales and Aquitaine: A Biography of the Black Prince.* London, 1978.
Barnie, J. *War in Medieval Society.* London, 1974.
Beltz, G. F. *Memorials of the Most Noble Order of the Garter.* London, 1841.
Bemont, C. *La Guyenne pendant la domination anglaise 1152–1453.* (Helps for Students of History 9, no. 27.) London, 1920.
    Simon de Montfort, comte de Leicester. Paris, 1884.
    'Les factions et les troubles à Bordeaux de 1300 à 1330 environ', *BPH*, 1916.
Bois, G. 'Noblesse et crise de revenus seigneuriaux en France aux XIVe e XVe siècles', *La Noblesse au Moyen Age XIe–XVe siècles*, ed. P. Contamine, Paris, 1976.
Bordeaux sous les Rois d'Angleterre, Histoire de Bordeaux III. Y. Renouard avec J. Bernard, P. Capra, J. Gardelles, B. Guillemain et J. P. Trabut-Cussac. Bordeaux, 1965.
Boutruche, R. *La Crise d'une Société: seigneurs et paysans du Bordelais pendant la guerre de Cent Ans.* Paris, 1947.
    Une société provinciale en lutte contre le régime féodal. Rodez, 1947.
    'Anglais et gascons en Aquitaine du XIIe au XIVe siècle', *Mélanges d'histoire du Moyen Age à la mémoire de Louis Halphen.* Paris, 1951.
    'The Devastation of Rural Areas during the Hundred Years War and the Agricultural Recovery of France.' *The Recovery of France in the Fifteenth Century*, ed. P. S. Lewis. London, 1971.
Breuils, A. 'Jean I, comte d'Armagnac, et le mouvement national dans le Midi au temps du Prince Noir', *Revue des Questions Historiques* 49 (1896).
Brissaud, L. D. *Les Anglais en Guyenne.* Paris, 1875.
Brown, E. A. R. 'Gascon Subsidies and the Finances of the English Dominions, 1315–24', *Studies in Medieval and Renaissance History* 8 (1971).
Caillet, L. *La Papauté d'Avignon et l'église de France.* Paris, 1975.
Capra, P. *L'Administration Anglo-Gasconne au temps de la lieute-nance du Prince Noir 1354–62: Essai sur une mentalité politique.* Unpublished thesis. Paris, 1972.
    'Les bases sociales du pouvoir anglo-gascon au milieu du XIVe siècle', *MA* 1975.

Capra, P. 'L'évolution de l'administration anglo-gasconne au milieu du XIVe siècle', *Bordeaux et les îles britanniques de XIIe au XXe siècle*. University of York symposium, 1973.

'L'histoire monétaire de l'Aquitaine anglo-gasconne au temps du Prince Noir (1354–72)', *Bull. et Mémoires de la Société Archeologique de Bordeaux* 64 (1968).

'Le Léopard et le Guyennois d'or, monnaies d'Aquitaine', *AM*, 72 (1960).

'Recherches sur la valeur des monnaies dans le Bordelais au temps de la lieutenance du Prince Noir (1354–1357)', *BPH* 1957.

Carus-Wilson, E. *Medieval Merchant Venturers: Collected Studies.* London, 1954.

Chaplais, P. 'A propos de l'ordonnance de 1375 sur la bourgeoisie et la jurade de Bordeaux', *AM* 65 (1953).

'The Chancery of Guyenne, 1289–1453', *Studies presented to Sir Hilary Jenkinson*, ed. J. Conway Davies. London, 1957.

'Le Duché-Pairie de Guyenne: l'hommage et les services féodaux de 1259–1307', *AM* 69, 70 (1957, 1958).

'English Arguments concerning the feudal status of Aquitaine in the 14th century', *BIHR* 21 (1946–48).

'Règlement des conflits internationaux franco-anglais au XIVe siècle (1293–1377)', *MA* 57 (1951).

'Le Sceau de la Cour de Gascogne', *AM* 57 (1955).

'La souveraineté du roi de France et le pouvoir législatif en Guyenne au début du XIVe siècle', *MA* 69 (1963).

'Le Traité de Paris de 1259 et l'inféodation de la Gascogne allodiale', *MA* 61 (1955).

Contamine, P. *Guerre, état et société à la fin du Moyen Age.* Paris, 1972.

La Vie quotidienne pendant la guerre de Cent Ans France et Angleterre (XIVe siècle). Paris, 1976.

Cuttino, G. P. *English Diplomatic Administration 1259–1339.* Oxford, 1940.

'The Archives of Gascony under English Rule', *American Archivist* 26 (1962).

'The Causes of the Hundred Years War', *Speculum* 31 (1956).

'King's Clerks and the Community of the Realm', *Speculum* 29 (1954).

Daumet, G. *Etude sur l'alliance de la France et de la Castille au XIVe et au XVe siècles.* Paris, 1898.

Delachenal, R. *Histoire de Charles V.* 5 v. Paris, 1909–31.

'Journal des Etats Généraux réunis à Paris au mois d'octobre 1356', *Nouvelle revue historique de droit français et étranger* 24 (1900).

Denifle, H. *La Désolation des églises, monastères, et hôpitaux en France pendant la guerre de Cent Ans.* 2 v. Paris, 1899.

Deprez, E. *Les Préliminaires de la guerre de Cent Ans.* Paris, 1902, reprint, 1975.

Drouyn, L. *Bordeaux vers 1450*. Bordeaux, 1874.
    La Guienne Militaire. 2 v. Bordeaux, 1865.
Du Fresne de Beaucourt, G. *Histoire de Charles VII*. 6 v. Paris, 1881–91.
Dupont-Ferrier, G. *Les officiers royaux des bailliages et sénéchaussées et les institutions monarchiques locales en France à la fin du Moyen Age*. Paris, 1902, reprint, 1974.
Emerson, B. *The Black Prince*. London, 1976.
Faucon, M. 'Prêts faits aux rois de France par Clement VI, Innocent VI et le comte de Beauport (1345–60)', *BEC* 40 (1879).
Flourac, J. *Jean Ier, comte de Foix, vicomte souverain de Béarn*. Paris, 1884.
Fowler, K. *The King's Lieutenant: Henry of Grosmont, first duke of Lancaster*. London, 1969.
Fowler, K., ed. *The Hundred Years War*. London, 1971.
Gardelles, J. *Les châteaux du Moyen Age dans la France du sud-ouest: la Gascogne anglaise de 1216–1327*. Paris, 1972.
Gouron, M. 'Reconstitution du trésor des chartes du château de Bordeaux au Moyen-Age', *RHB* 26 (1933).
Guillemain, B. *La Cour pontificale d'Avignon* (1309–76). Paris, 1966.
    'Les tentatives pontificales de médiation dans le litige Franco-Anglais de Guyenne au XIVe siècle', *BPH* 1957.
Guinodie, R. *Histoire de Libourne*. 3 v. 2nd ed. Libourne, 1876.
Henneman, J. B. *Royal Taxation in Fourteenth Century France: The Development of War Financing, 1322–1356*. Princeton, 1971.
    Royal Taxation in Fourteenth Century France: The Captivity and Ransom of John II, 1356–1370. Philadelphia, 1976.
Hewitt, H. J. *The Black Prince's Expedition of 1355–1357*. Manchester, 1958.
    The Organisation of War under Edward III. Manchester, 1966.
James, M. K. *Studies in the Medieval Wine Trade*, ed. E. M. Veale. Oxford, 1971.
Langlois, C. V. *Le Règne de Philippe III le Hardi*. Paris, 1887.
LePatourel, J. 'Edward III and the Kingdom of France', *History* 43 (1958).
    'The King and the Princes in Fourteenth Century France', *Europe in the Late Middle Ages*, ed. J. R. Hale, J. R. L. Highfield and B. Smalley. London, 1965.
    'The Treaty of Brétigny 1360', *TRHS* Fifth Series 10 (1960).
Lewis, P. S. 'Decayed and Non-Feudalism in Later Medieval France', *BIHR* 37 (1964).
Lodge, E. C. *The Estates of the Archbishop and Chapter of Saint-André of Bordeaux under English Rule*. (Oxford Studies in Social and Legal History 3) Oxford, 1912, reprint 1974.
    Gascony under English Rule. London, 1926.
    'The Constables of Bordeaux in the Reign of Edward III', *EHR* 50 (1935).

Lodge, E. C. 'The Relations between England and Gascony 1152–1453' *History* 19 (1934).

Loirette, G. 'Arnaud Amanieu d'Albret et ses rapports avec la monarchie française pendant le règne de Charles V 1364–80)', *AM* 43 (1931).

    'Arnaud Amanieu sire d'Albret et l'appel des seigneurs gascons en 1368', *Mélanges d'histoire offerts à M. Charles Bemont*. Paris, 1913.

Lopès, H. *L'Eglise metropolitaine et primatiale Sainct André de Bourdeaux*. 2nd ed., revised by Abbé Callen. 2 v. Bordeaux, 1884.

Lubimenko, I. *Jean de Bertagne, comte du Richmond*. Lille, 1908.

Luce, S. *Histoire de Bertrand du Guesclin et son époque*. Paris, 1882.

McFarlane, K. B. *The Nobility of Later Medieval England*. Oxford, 1973.

Mirot, L and Deprez, E. 'Les ambassades anglaises pendant la guerre de Cent Ans', *BEC* 59, 60, 61 (1898, 1899, 1900).

Moisant, J. *Le Prince Noir en Aquitaine 1355–56, 1362–70*. Paris, 1894.

Mollat, G. *The Popes at Avignon 1305–1378*. New York, 1963.

    'Innocent VI et les tentatives de paix entre la France et l'Angleterre (1353–55)', *Revue d'histoire ecclésiastique* 10 (1909).

    'Le Saint-Siège et la France sous le pontificat de Clement VI (1343–52)', *Revue d'histoire ecclésiastique* 55 (1960).

Palmer, J. J. N. *England, France and Christendom 1377–99*. London, 1972.

Pérotin, Y. 'Les chapitres Bordelais contre Charles VII', *AM* 63 (1951).

Perroy, E. *The Hundred Years War*. London, 1965.

    'Edouard III d'Angleterre et les seigneurs gascons en 1368', *AM* 61 (1948–49).

Petit, J. *Charles de Valois (1270–1325)*. Paris, 1900.

Peyrègne, A. 'Les emigrés gascons en Angleterre (1453–1485)', *AM* 66 (1954).

Powicke, F. M. *King Henry III and the Lord Edward*. Oxford, 1947.

    The Thirteenth Century 1216–1307. (Oxford History of England) Oxford, 1953.

Prestwich, M. *War, Politics and Finance under Edward I*. London, 1972.

Prou, M. *Relations politiques du pape Urbain V avec les rois de France Jean II et Charles V*. (Bibliothèque de l'école des Hautes Etudes, 76) Paris, 1888.

Renouard, Y. *Etudes d'histoire médiévale*. 2 v. Paris, 1968.

Ribadieu, H. *Histoire de la conquête de la Guyenne par les Français*. Bordeaux, 1866.

Rouquette, J. *Le Rouergue sous les Anglais*. Millau, 1887.

Royer, J. P. *L'Eglise et le Royaume de France au XIVe siècle*. Paris, 1969.

Russell, P. E. *The English Intervention in Spain and Portugal in the time of Edward III and Richard II*. Oxford, 1955.

Samaran, C. *La Maison d'Armagnac au XVe siècle*. Paris, 1907, reprint 1975.

    'Quelques aspects des rapports Franco-Anglais en Guyenne et Gascogne à la fin de la guerre de Cent Ans', *AM* 65 (1953).

Sherborne, J. W. 'The Battle of La Rochelle and the War at Sea 1372–5', *BIHR* 42 (1969).
'The Cost of English Warfare with France in the later Fourteenth Century', *BIHR* 50 (1977)
'The English Navy: Shipping and Manpower 1369–1389', *Past and Present*, n. 37 (1967).
'Indentured Retinues and English Expeditions to France, 1369–80', *EHR* 79 (1964).
Strayer, J. R. 'The Costs and Profits of War', *The Medieval City*, ed. H. Miskimin. New Haven, Conn., 1976.
Tout, T. F. *Chapters in Medieval Administrative History*. 6 v. Manchester, 1920–33.
Trabut-Cussac, J. P. *L'Administration anglaise en Gascogne*. Geneva, 1972.
'Bordeaux dans les Rôles Gascons d'Edouard II (1307–17)', *AM* 77 (1965).
'Les cartulaires gascons d'Edouard II, d'Edouard III et de Charles VII', *BEC* 111 (1953).
'Itinéraire d'Edouard Ier en France 1286–89', *BIHR* 25 (1952).
'Le Prince Edouard et les rivalités municipaux à Bordeaux (1248–61)', *RHB* 11 n.s. (1952).
Troplong, E. 'De la fidélité des Gascons aux Anglais pendant le moyen age (1152–1453)', *Revue d'histoire diplomatique* 16 (1902).
Tuck, A. *Richard II and the English Nobility*. London, 1973.
Tucoo-Chala, P. *Gaston Fébus et la vicomté de Béarn (1343–91)*. Bordeaux, 1954.
La vicomté de Béarn et le problème de sa souveraineté. Bordeaux, 1961.
'Contribution à l'étude des péages de la Moyenne Garonne aux XIVe–XVe siècles', *RHB* 19 n.s. (1960).
Vale, M. G. A. *English Gascony 1399–1453*. Oxford, 1970.
Valois, N. *La France et le Grand Schisme d'Occident*. 4 v. Paris, 1896.
Wolff, P. 'The Armagnacs of Southern France', *BIHR* 20 (1945).
'Bordeaux et Toulouse au Moyen Age', *RHB* 14 n.s. (1955).
Wylie, J. H. *History of England under Henry the Fourth*. 4 v. London, 1884–98, reprint, 1969.
Wylie, J. H. *The Reign of Henry the Fifth*. v. I and II (1914, 1918); v. III, with W. T. Waugh (1929) London, reprint, 1968.
Zacour, N. *Talleyrand, the Cardinal of Périgord (1301–1364)*. (American Philosophical Society n.s. 50, pt. 7) Philadelphia, 1960.

Index

Blanche of Castile, q. of France (d. 1252), 6, 19
Blanche, countess of Champagne and q. of Navarre (d. 1302), 64–5
Blanquefort (Gironde), castle of, 97, 217, 227, 228
Blaye (Gironde), 8, 9, 66, 67, 77, 121, 122, 127, 189, 190, 218, 219, 220, 224
Blois (Loir-et-Cher), 194
Bochard, Master Itier, of Angoulême, constable of Bordeaux (1289–93), 58
Boniface VIII, Pope (Benedict Caetani) (1294–1303), 68, 70, 72, 73, 74, 92, 93, 107, 109
Bonnegarde (Landes), 71
Bordeaux (Gironde), 1, 7, 10, 14, 20, 25, 64, 65, 67, 69, 95, 104, 116, 121, 124, 126, 130, 131, 137, 155, 175, 176, 185, 199, 207, 209, 210, 223, 233
   Bekynton and Roos in, 212–15; Black Prince in, 137–39, 142–144, 151, 154, 162, 163
   campaign of, 1406, 188–92; campaign by, 1420, 199–201; citizens of, 11, 84, 100, 215; Clarence in, 194–96; custom of, 40, 60, 84, 128, 198; description of, 78–80; 'duel' of, 47; duke of Lancaster in, 170, 171, 181
   factional struggles in, 20–21, 42
   inhabitants of (Bordelais), 20, 82, 222, 230
   jurats of, 172, 180, 181, 189–92, 220, 231
   La Male Journade of, 217–18
   markets of, 198; mayors of, see Cailhau, Shorthose, Swynbourne, Trailly
   Pope Clement's visit to, 93–5; population of, 78, 206
   revolt in (1303), 81–3
   salt-works of, 52; surrender of (1451), 219–20, 222
   Talbot and surrender of 1453, 223–25, 227–28, 232

   under French rule, 81, 221–22, 229–31
   wine trade in, 84–6, 177, 222, 232–33
Bordeaux, diocese of, 10, 96, 179
   archbishop of, 96, 98; see also Berland, Canteloup, Clement V, Greelle, Lamothe, Malemort, Montferrand, Salignac, Uguccione; palace of abp, 25–26, 79, 95, 194
   cathedral of Saint-André, 79, 92, 99, 137, 151, 207, 220, 222
   chapter of, 96, 99, 137, 202, 208, 222; dean of, 214
   Saint-Pierre, hospital of, 209
   Saint-Seurin, 19, 137, 181, 210, 214
   chapter of, 96, 99, 222; canons of, 131, see also Gerard; dean of, 100, see also Ferrières, Tasta; cartulary of, 137, 188
   Sainte-Croix, abbey of, 79, 100
Bordelais, district of, 8, 13, 84, 93, 98, 121, 127, 205, 210, 218, 234
Boucicaut, Marshal, 140, 153, 182
Bouliac (Gironde), 208
Bourbon, duke of, 171, 184, 193
   Blanche of, 157; Marguerite of, 162
Bourg (Gironde), 23, 66, 67, 77, 121, 122, 189, 190, 191, 205, 218, 219, 223, 224
Bourges (Cher), 1, 96, 140, 193, 222
Bouteville (Charente), 181, 187
Bouvines, battle of (1214), 15
Bowet, Henry, constable of Bordeaux, bp. of Bath, abp. of York (d. 1423), 185, 186, 192
Bréquit, Augen de, 219
Brest (Finisterre), 176, 236
Brétigny (Eure-et-Loire), 146
   treaty of (1360), 146, 147, 148, 149, 161, 176, 193, 203
Bristol, 85, 236
Brittany, 4, 6, 13, 17, 124, 136, 181
   Arthur of, 6
   John II, duke of, 38; John (2nd son of John II), earl of Rich-

mond, lieutenant of Gascony 1294–95 (d. 1334), 66, 67, 76, 104, 105; John III, duke of (d. 1341), 124

Pierre Mauclerc, count of, 17

Bromfield, Edmund, abbot of La Sauve, bp. of Llandaff (d. 1393), 179

Bruges, truce of (1375), 171–72

Brutails, Louis de, 223, 229

Budos (Gironde), 201

Bureau, Jean, master of artillery, mayor of Bordeaux (1451), 217, 218, 219, 220, 222, 224, 228

Burg, Guitard de, 54

Burgos (Castile), 26, 158, 160

Burgundy, 53
duke of, 184, 192, 194; Charles the Bold (d. 1477), 229; John the Fearless (d. 1419), 194; Philip the Bold (d. 1409), 142, 170; Philip the Good (d. 1467), 229

Burnell, Robert, bp. of Bath and Wells (d. 1292), 43, 44, 48, 51, 54, 55, 88, 89

Burwell (Lincs) priory of, 100

Cadillac (Gironde), 89, 169, 175, 176, 227, 228

Cahors (Lot), 1, 205
diocese of, 31, 46, 49, 73

Cailhau, Arnaud, mayor of Bordeaux, 81, 82, 83
Pierre, mayor of Bordeaux, 82
Bernard, 104

Calais (Pas-de-Calais), 146, 147, 166, 169, 176, 193, 197, 235, 236
treaty of (1360), 147–48, 162, 176
truce of (1347), 131, 136

Calveley, Sir Hugh, 144, 156, 171

Camoys, Roger, Lord, seneschal of Guyenne (1453), 224, 227, 228

Canteloup, Arnaud de, abp. of Bordeaux (1306–32), 96

Canterbury, 74
archbishop of, 70, 229; see also Arundel, Pecham

Capbreton (Landes), 158

Captal de Buch, see Grailly

Carcassonne (Aude), 81, 138

Castelbon, Matthieu de, see Foix
viscounty of, 196

Castelsagrat (Tarn-et-Garonne), 129

Castillon (Ariège), 152

Castillon-de-Médoc (Gironde), 127, 196, 212

Castillon-la-Bataille (Gironde), 127, 174, 227
battle of (1453), 224–27

Cavreroche, Arnauld de, abbot of La Sauve, 179

Cauma, Rabban, 98

Caumont, Alexandre de, 108
Nompar de, seneschal of the Agenais, 185

Castile, king of, 18, 180
Alfonso VIII (d. 1214), 14, 18; Alfonso X (d. 1284), 24, 25, 26, 27, 41, 53
Enrique of Trastamara (d. 1379), 157, 158, 159, 160, 170, 171
Pedro the Cruel (d. 1369), 131, 157, 158, 160, 169
Constance, daughter of, 169

Castile, kingdom of, 10, 15, 25, 26, 27, 90, 131, 157, 158, 167, 169, 236

Cazes, Master Guilhem de, 105, 110

Chaceporc, Peter, 27

Chalais (Charente), 187, 224

Chandos, Sir John, 136, 141, 144, 145, 150, 152, 154, 155, 158, 159, 163, 164, 165, 168, 226

Chandos Herald, 158, 159, 164

Channel, English, 12, 48, 124, 167, 176, 236

Charente river, 8, 32, 46, 49, 116, 205

Charlemagne, 2, 3, 9, 20

Charles IV, k. of France (1322–28), 113, 114, 115, 117

Charles V the Wise, k. of France (1364–80), 145, 147, 157, 158, 161, 162, 163, 167, 168, 169, 173, 176; as dauphin, 141, 144, 146

Charles VI, k. of France (1380–1422), 177, 187, 192, 194, 200

Charles VII, k. of France (1422–61), 202, 210, 212, 215, 216, 217, 219, 220, 222, 224, 227, 228, 229

Cherbourg (Manche), 176, 194, 236

Chester, 139, 145

Chiverston, Sir John, seneschal of Gascony, 155

Clarence, Thomas, duke of (d. 1421), 194, 196, 226

Clement V, Pope (Bertrand de Got) (1305–14), 92–7, 98, 101, 107

Clement VI, Pope (Pierre Roger) (1342–52), 118, 171

Clement VII, Avignon Pope (Robert of Geneva) (1378–94), 179

Clermont, count of, 187, 223
Beatrice de, 153
Jean de, Marshal of France, 141

Clifford, William, constable of Bordeaux (1413–18), 196

Clifton, Sir Robert, constable of Bordeaux (1439–42), 210, 214

Cobham, Sir Reginald, 136, 142, 144
Master Thomas, 112

Cocherel, battle of (1364), 168

Coetivy, Olivier de, French seneschal in Bordeaux (1451–53), 222, 223

Cognac (Charente), 139

Colom family, 20, 42, 82
Jean (d. 1377), 172, 173
Jean (early 14th c.), 83

Compostella, 3, 9
route to, 8, 89, 100

Condom (Gers), 55, 56

Constance, Council of (1414–17), 197

Corbeil, treaty of (1258), 32–3

Cornere, Guillaume de la, bp. of Salisbury (d. 1291), 54

Court of Sovereignty, 156–57, 201, 208, 220

Courtrai, battle of (1302), 75, 81

Craon, Amaury de, seneschal of Gascony (1313–16, 1320–22), 103, 106, 110

Maurice de, lieutenant of Gascony (1289–92), 57, 58, 103, 244

Crécy, battle of (1346), 129, 136, 141, 226

Créon (Gironde), 10, 100, 174

Cubzac (Gironde), 23, 127

Dax (Landes), 11, 13, 20, 21, 26, 59, 69, 116, 159, 181, 185, 199, 212
bishop of, 44, 179; bishopric of, 44, 179

Despenser, Hugh the Elder and Younger (d. 1326), 113, 114, 115, 116, 213
Hugh (d. 1402), 185

Dordogne river, 9, 13, 20, 84, 89, 121, 122, 127, 128, 142, 173, 174, 224

Dorset, Thomas Beaufort, earl of (d. 1426), 194, 196

Dover, 12, 115, 147

Dropt river, 174

Du Guesclin, Bertrand, Constable of France (d. 1380), 158, 159, 160, 167, 170, 171, 174

Dunois, Jean de, bastard of Orléans, 218, 219, 220, 221

Duras (Lot-et-Garonne), 175
lords of, 174, 175, 220

Durfort family, 123, 127
Arnaud, 127
Gaillard, lord of Duras and Blanquefort, seneschal of Guyenne (1399–1415), 129, 185, 186, 187, 192, 228

Edward I, k. of England (1272–1307), 41, 45, 46, 51, 53, 57, 70, 76, 77, 87, 88, 102, 111, 117, 234, 235
as duke of Aquitaine, 43, 44, 47–9, 54, 55, 61, 62
Gascon ordinances of, 51, 55–61, 80
marriage to Eleanor of Castile, 25–6; to Margaret of France, 74, 75
prince, in Gascony, 23, 31, 33, 36, 39, 40, 41, 42, 43, 51, 81

Roquetaillade, lord of, 137; *see also*
     Lamothe
Rotour, Richard, constable of
     Bordeaux (1375–79), 175
Rouen, archbishop of, 29, 31
Rouergue, 149, 150, 155, 161, 163,
     174
Roussillon (Pyr.-Orientales), 152
Rudel, Elie II, lord of Bergerac and
     Gensac, 39
   Elie III, 39
   Marguerite, 39
Rutland, Edward, earl of, later
     duke of York, lieutenant in
     Guyenne (d. 1415), 187, 194,
     250

Saint-Antoine-d'Agen, priory of,
     179
Saint-Astier (Dordogne), 64
Saint-Denis (Seine), 38
Saint-Emilion (Gironde), 55, 64,
     122, 174, 189, 219, 227
Saint-Bertrand-de-Comminges
     (Hte.-Garonne), 93
Saint-Jean-d'Angely (Charente-
     Marit.), 12, 129, 134, 151, 219
Saint John, John of, seneschal of
     Gascony (1294–96), 66, 67, 71
   John of, mayor of Bordeaux
     (1413–22), 196, 199
Saint-Lizier (Ariège), 1
Saint-Loubès (Gironde), 215
Saint-Macaire (Gironde), 55, 59, 80,
     89, 122, 127, 174, 175, 199,
     213, 227, 233
Saint-Raphael (Gironde), parish of,
     207
   college of, 209–10, 230
Saint-Romains, abbey of, 190, 192
   abbot of, 190
Saint-Sardos (Lot-et-Garonne), 113
   priory of, 112
   war of, 112, 114
Saint-Sever (Landes), 13, 67, 114,
     212, 224
Saint-Symphorien, Isabel de, 178
Sainte-Bazeille (Lot-et-Garonne),
     214

Sainte-Foy-la-Grande (Gironde),
     174, 217
Saintes (Charente-Marit.), 11, 17,
     18, 96, 116, 151, 157
Saintonge, 7, 8, 12, 13, 17, 32, 46,
     48, 58, 59, 65, 114, 129, 149,
     155, 168, 169
Salignac, Boson de, abp. of Bor-
     deaux (1296–99), 94
Salisbury, earl of, 136, 150
Sandwich, 85, 169
Sarlat, abbey of, 112
Sauciprède, Elie, 81–2
Sault-de-Navailles (Pyr.-Atlan.), 43,
     120
Sauveterre-de-Guyenne (Gironde),
     174, 201
Sauviac, Bertrand de, 97
Savoy, 53, 65
   Peter, count of, 31, 51
Scrope, William Le, seneschal of
     Gascony (1385–92), 178, 180
Sens, archbishop of, 4
   diocese of, 144
Shorthose, Gadifer, mayor of Bor-
     deaux (1434–51), 210, 214, 217,
     218
Sicily, kingdom of, 29, 30, 46, 236
   kings of, *see* Anjou
Sluys, battle of (1340), 124, 167
Soler family, 20, 42, 82
   Gaillard, 42
Somerset, John Beaufort, earl of,
     (d. 1444), 215
Sorde (Landes), 67
Soubise, battle of (1372), 168, 169
Soudan de La Trau, *see* Preissac
Soulac (Gironde), 8
   prior of, *see* La Planche
Soule, viscount of, 19
Stafford, Ralph, baron of, seneschal
     of Gascony (1345–46), 126,
     127, 128
Stamford (Lincs), 150
Stapleton, Walter, bp. of Exeter
     (d. 1326), 115
Stratton, John, constable of Bor-
     deaux (1381–87), 178, 197,
     198